Medical Marijuana in America:
Memoir of a Pioneer

Alice O'Leary-Randall

This book chronicles the beginning of the medical marijuana movement in the United States. It is an issue that is constantly evolving. For further information please visit
www.medicalmarijuanapioneer.com

Copyright © 2014 Alice O'Leary-Randall

All rights reserved.

ISBN-13: 978-1496170606

DEDICATION

To the brave men and women whose stories
are contained in this book.
And to the thousands of others who
have helped to right this wrong.

TABLE OF CONTENTS

PREFACE I

SECTION I: FATE PAYS A CALL 1
   1. ONE IN 213 MILLION 3
   2. A GENTLE BUST 5
   3. FIRST STEPS 12
   4. MEMORY HOLE 20
   5. PROVING IT 27
   6. BUILDING THE CASE 37
   7. LOOSE ENDS 45
   8. TRIALS AND NEGOTIATIONS 49
   9. DEUS EX MACHINA 62
   10. GIVING THANKS 71

SECTION II: CHANGING LAWS 77
   11. ALONE IN THE LIFEBOAT 79
   12. SQUARE ONE…AGAIN 92
   13. STEPTOE STEPS IN 101
   14. NEW MEXICO 104
   15. BACK IN THE LIFEBOAT 111
   16. SUFFER TO THEIR DEATHS 125
   17. THE RIPPLES OF CHANGE 131
   18. CRITICAL MASS 136
   19. SOMEONE IS TELLING AN UNTRUTH 142

SECTION III: SYNTHETIC SOLUTIONS 149
   20. LET 'EM EAT THC 151
   21. GOVERNMENT IS THE PROBLEM 161
   22. PROFILES IN PATHETIC 169
   23. CHANGING GEARS 173
   24. IN THE MATTER OF 177

SECTION IV: NEW ALLIES **185**
   25. THE NECESSITY OF NECESSITY 187
   26. PRIZES, PAWNS AND PATRONS 193
   27. MESSAGE IN A BOTTLE 207
   28. HEARTS AND MINDS 218
   29. MARS 229
   30. THE COLLAPSE OF COMPASSION 239
   31. BITTER BLOWS 249
   32. MARS ON THE MALL 256
   33. FALSE HOPE 264

SECTION V: END OF THE BEGINNING **271**
   34. BEYOND MARS 273
   35. GOING GLOBAL 277
   36. A PASSING SHADOW 287
   37. THE END 294
   38. THE BEGINNING AGAIN 298

GLOSSARY **302**

PREFACE

Much of this book was first published in 1998 as a memoir entitled *Marijuana Rx: The Patients' Fight for Medicinal Pot*. It was co-written by Robert C. Randall and me, his wife Alice O'Leary-Randall. More than fifteen years have passed and there have been many changes. Robert died in 2001, agents have retired, publishers have gone defunct, and e-pub books are the norm. Our original book is technically "out of print" although copies can still be obtained on Amazon.com.

At the time of Robert's death in 2001 I felt that my days in the medical marijuana movement were complete. I had no burning desire to "keep up the good fight" and, thankfully, Robert did not extract a promise from me that I would do so. Instead I pursued my dream of becoming a hospice worker and spent six years as a hospice nurse before retiring.

Now it is 2014 and the fight for medical access to marijuana continues. Twenty states and the District of Columbia currently recognize marijuana's medical use and provide a means of legal access to the drug, usually through a "grow your own" method. But the federal government remains unyielding, still classifying marijuana as a drug "with no currently accepted medical use."

The familiar adage that those who do not read history are condemned to repeat it certainly applies to the medical marijuana issue. On a certain level it saddens me to read press reports about the passage of state laws in the 21st century when I know that many of these same states—some thirty-four states in all—passed laws more than three decades ago which attempted to provide the citizens of their states with legal, medical access to marijuana. If those laws had been honored by the federal government years of suffering by countless seriously ill individuals would have been avoided.

It is wrong that medical care should be based on politics and geography rather than medical need. For the issue to be resolved citizen activists must turn their attention to removing the federal roadblocks against marijuana's medical use.

In preparing this edition I have sought to retain as much of the original work as possible while also acknowledging that in our first book there was, perhaps, too much detail. Thus excessive details have been removed as well as dated references to the late nineties. For those seeking detailed documents please contact the Wisconsin Historical Society where our archives now reside. www.wisconsinhistory.org

What remains in tact in this current book are the stories of the brave men and women who with honesty and great concern for their fellow human beings approached the federal government for help and were repeatedly denied and ridiculed for their efforts. It is a shameful legacy of our federal government that those who are seriously ill are denied access to this venerable plant with a 5,000 year history of medical application.

Section I:

Fate Pays A Call

1. ONE IN 213 MILLION

Robert Carl Randall, glaucoma patient and founder of the medical marijuana movement in America died on June 2, 2001. He was 53 years old. At the time of his death he was one of a dozen recipients of medical marijuana supplies from the federal government. Several states, notably California and Arizona, had enacted state laws allowing seriously ill patients or caregivers to grow marijuana legally for medical use.

But there was a time when Robert was the ONLY individual in the country allowed to legally use marijuana for medical purposes. As one headline put it "One in 213 million!"

Through a series of criminal and civil proceedings in 1976, Robert convinced the judiciary and the federal government that marijuana was THE drug that was saving his sight. This was a remarkable feat since the federal prohibition against any use of marijuana was viewed as impenetrable. The retired director of the Bureau of Narcotics once boasted, "We've got [marijuana] locked up so tightly now they'll never change the law."

But the system was flawed—first in its premise that marijuana has no medical value and secondly in the myopic focusing of bureaucracies which view threats in large terms such as organizations, governments, or armies. No one in the federal drug bureaucracies ever considered the power of a lone individual, afflicted with a serious illness. Robert's brilliant mind and his masterful talent for rhetoric prevailed, revealing the sham of the federal prohibition and setting the stage for the battle that continues to this day.

As Robert wrote in 1998:

This is our story of medical marijuana in America. The gods have granted me a reprieve to bring you this story but I am not so prideful as to think this is a one-man show. The medical marijuana story encompasses many people in many places. You will learn about a White House aide and a British Lord, a ten-year-old with cancer and an 80-year-old with glaucoma, an Arizona cowboy and a Pennsylvania doll shop owner, and more. This story is about the kindness of strangers and betrayal by friends. It is about the brutality of the system and banality of bureaucrats who are charged with managing it. Medical marijuana reveals the failure of elites and the success of common citizens intent on righting a wrong.

And, in the final analysis, it is about much more than marijuana. It is a story of a remarkable public consensus that was ignored, denigrated, and trampled on in order to maintain a deeply entrenched policy. It is about the failure of government to trust its citizens and the casualties of that failure.

This is a modern accounting of David and Goliath. Like the Biblical hero, Robert Randall's actions would bring down a giant and rally an army, an unlikely army of individuals with life- and sense-threatening ailments. Their campaign changed the way America views marijuana.

2. A GENTLE BUST

Drug Bust! The words conjure images of SWAT teams, battering rams, yelling, total confusion, and handcuffs. But our drug bust, the event that began our odyssey, was different. In fact, we weren't even present. It was August 26, 1975 and we were driving through Cincinnati, on our way home to Washington, D.C. from a vacation in Indiana.

We returned to find a ransacked house, a search warrant on the kitchen table, and a note requesting that we turn ourselves in to the police. It was, by any measurable standard, a gentle bust.

It also seemed to be Fateful. It would not be the last time that Fate seemed to be a principle player in this story but the bust itself was truly a twist of fate.

We had been carefully growing four marijuana plants on our second-story sundeck in Washington, D.C. The area was quite secluded, especially considering it was just eight blocks from the U.S. Capitol. The marijuana plants were mixed in among tomato vines, coleus, and philodendron. I constantly went down to the alley and checked to see if they were visible from below. They were not.

Little did we know, however, that our neighbor was also growing marijuana and on the day we left for our Indiana vacation he placed them on his fire-escape stairs. His plants drew the attention of police during a routine patrol of the alleyway and the patrolman summoned the vice squad, which climbed onto the fire escape to investigate. From there it was easy to look down onto our deck where our four marijuana plants were discreetly hidden.

The neighbor saw the Friday afternoon visit from the vice squad and immediately disposed of his contraband plants. Then he tried to reach us by knocking on our door and calling. But there were no cell phones in 1975 and we were blissfully enjoying the American wonders of U.S. Route 50. When the police returned on Saturday with formal search warrants the neighbor would escape arrest.

Fate, it seems, had come to call.

Of course the roots of this adventure predate the "bust" of August 1975. As with any good story, the seeds are sown early and allowed to grow. In Robert's case the story began at conception, when heredity determined his vision would be marred by a condition called glaucoma.

There are two kinds of glaucoma: narrow-angle and open-angle. Narrow-angle glaucoma often comes on quickly, in an acute situation, which sends most people scurrying to an ophthalmologist.

In open-angle glaucoma, the process is more sinister. The inner pressure of the eye is elevated, pinching the optic nerve and starving the eye for nourishment. As a result, sections of the eye begin to die leading to progressive blindness. But the progress of the disease is slow and there is rarely any pain so the afflicted individual has time to compensate for the growing blindness without realizing that he or she is going blind. Over time the individual develops more and more blind spots until the brain can no longer compensate.

Further complicating the situation was the limited knowledge of open-angle glaucoma. For decades it was thought only the elderly developed the disease. Now we know glaucoma can strike at any age. Juvenile glaucoma is uncommon but not unusual. Often the disease is hereditary, manifesting itself younger in each generation.

So it was with Robert. Throughout his family there were cases of visual problems and some blindness but growing up in the 1950s and '60s there was little understanding of how these problems may have been passed on. Thus his early complaints of eyestrain in high school and college were never taken seriously.

At the age of 19 he was waiting for an eye exam and read a pamphlet called "Glaucoma: The Sneak Thief of Sight." The symptoms seemed so familiar he asked the doctor if he might have glaucoma. The doctor seemed amused. "You're studying too hard, young man," said the friendly optometrist. "You need to give those eyes a rest. That will clear up the eyestrain in no time."

But it didn't.

In September 1972 Robert's ocular problems became so severe that he sought out an ophthalmologist. He was 24 years old and living in Washington, D.C.

The ophthalmologist quickly diagnosed advanced open-angle glaucoma. There was already severe damage. When Robert asked "How long?" before the disease would render him blind, the reply was shocking.

"Two to five years," the doctor replied. "Perhaps a bit longer if the medications work well. And they are always working on new drugs. You may get lucky."

The ophthalmologist was right. Robert did get lucky.

Dr. Ben Fine gave Robert a handful of prescriptions and sent him on his way. Dr. Fine was a competent doctor, one of Washington's most respected ophthalmologists. In the following months he tried varying combinations of eyedrops and other medications in an effort to stabilize Robert's disease, which was stubborn and aggressive. Fine had to resort to the maximum strengths of available medications but the drugs didn't always work. At the time of his diagnosis, Robert had already lost a significant amount of eyesight and soon learned the telltale signs of elevated pressure: milky vision, tricolored haloes around lights, or complete "white-outs" which were virtually blinding.

For more than a year the doctor struggled to control Robert's disease and then, remarkably, things began to stabilize. His intraocular eye pressure (IOP) was regularly in the "safe range" and the loss of vision stopped. Fine couldn't understand what had happened but he was disinclined to look a gift horse in the mouth. He was pleased that the medications had finally begun to work. He didn't know Robert had added another medication to the regimen, albeit an illegal one— marijuana.

Robert had first smoked marijuana in 1968 while a student at the University of South Florida (USF) but he had little contact with the illegal substance after moving to Washington in 1971.

In late 1973, after a new friend gave him a marijuana cigarette, he discovered, quite by accident, that marijuana helped his glaucoma. He described it this way:

It was evening and looking out the window of my Virginia apartment I saw the now-familiar tricolored haloes around a nearby streetlight. My pressures were elevated despite the eyedrops and other medications from Dr. Fine. This had become "something to live with" and I didn't think much of it. I turned on the stereo, lit the joint, and settled back to listen to the music.

A few minutes later I rose from the chair and headed to the kitchen. On the way I glanced out the window again. What I saw stopped me in my tracks. Actually it was what I didn't see that stopped me. The haloes around the nearby streetlight were gone.

It was a singular moment. I immediately drew the connection between the use of marijuana and the now-absent haloes. Indeed, parts of my brain absorbed the connection so quickly and so assuredly that I was certain I must be stoned, which of course I was. I tried to follow the exploding synaptic spasm but was quickly left behind. The thought was too fast, too large and complex to pursue and understand, to place into words. Stuporific, I could do little more than smile at the building delusion. Marijuana beneficial? A delicious thought perhaps, but nothing to hang your sight on.

But the thought would not go away and over a period of months, through nothing more than cause and effect, the prospect became more believable. My observations were confirmed by Fine's regular ocular readings. My eye pressures were well controlled for the first time since his diagnosis.

Whatever confusion and reluctance Robert might have had in accepting marijuana's therapeutic promise ended with the droughts—long, barren periods when marijuana could not be bought for blood or money. Days would pass without so much as a twig of the substance and each of those days would be followed by an evening filled with brittle dancing lights. On random evenings he would visit friends lucky enough to have some of the weed. On those nights the rings would not appear. Or, more impressively, they would dissolve, vanishing before his eyes. By the summer of 1974 there were no more doubts and he began a program of self-medication. Marijuana had suddenly become more than a recreational drug, it had become a critical medication. He considered telling Dr. Fine about this discovery but worried about the impact of such a revelation. Fine might drop him as a patient and his knowledge of Robert's marijuana use could place the doctor at some legal liability. It was too risky. Best to keep the information to himself and let Fine believe the prescribed medications or some quirky element was the reason Robert's eye pressures were doing so well.

Actually in 1974 many things were going well. The immediate aftermath of Robert's glaucoma diagnosis had been difficult. He was forced into temporary disability but in 1974 he was writing drama reviews for a weekly newspaper chain and would soon find work as a part-time college professor.

In that year we began living together in a two-story apartment on Capitol Hill. Ours had been a long courtship. We had first met in 1965 at a junior college in Bradenton, Florida and went on to the University of South Florida in Tampa. Robert described our courtship this way:

We associated rather than dated. But in my final year of school I thought it was too soon to be entrapped by stability, to decide the future. First I wished to find out what was beyond college, so Alice and I separated for two years. She went off to graduate school to study theatrical design; I ventured to Washington... .

By the time Alice arrived in Washington she knew herself and had worked in various theaters as a lighting designer and technical director. Rounding the age of 25, we found the hormonal surges of youth were giving way to fuller emotions. We had played through an elaborate dance and finally we mated but did not wed, that would come later. We had long been friends and settled slowly into lovers. The arrangement worked well.

Alice came to live with me accepting the likelihood I would go blind. I told her of my marijuana discovery soon after she moved in. At first she thought it was a convenient way for me to rationalize an ever-increasing marijuana habit. But soon she became convinced of my increasingly critical need for the drug and she often helped in locating my illegal and expensive medication.

Procuring marijuana became a regular part of our life and trying to cover the dry spells became particularly important. In the spring of 1975, in an abandoned flower pot on the sundeck, a lone marijuana seed sprouted and began to grow, literally, like a weed. This uninvited, "volunteer" plant was the obvious solution to our problem—grow enough marijuana to cover the dry spells. We planted three more seeds and soon there were four healthy marijuana plants growing in the lengthening days of Washington's springtime.

Marijuana was illegal and it was a risk to grow the plants outdoors but we felt safe and content. Things were going well enough to think about a vacation. So, in August 1975, we entrusted the cats and plants to a friend's care and prepared to head out of town. As we loaded the car I considered the plants on the deck and asked, "Should the plants come in?" Robert argued the sun was good for them, they were well obscured. And so they stayed, sunning in seclusion until the vice squad arrived and took them away.

Less than 72 hours after our return home we stood on the steps of the D.C. Superior Court with our attorney, Paul Smollar. We had been arraigned, booked, and released on our own recognizance. We were criminals.

On Monday morning I had called the only lawyer I knew, John Karr. He had done some legal work for the American Theater where I worked as technical director and lighting designer. Karr was on vacation in Spain but his junior partner, Paul Smollar, listened to the story of our bust and agreed to represent us.

Paul had patiently accompanied us through the mechanics of our arrest and arraignment. He seemed certain the entire situation could be resolved easily. There would, however, be numerous legal procedures to endure. He advised us to relax and enjoy the upcoming Labor Day holiday. He was flying off to Maine for a week. Karr would be back after Labor Day. "Relax," he told us, "It's a simple enough case. Some of these drug cases can be tough but this one shouldn't change your life too much."

In our first meeting with Paul on Monday afternoon Robert hesitantly raised the issue of his marijuana use. "Paul, there's one thing you need to know."

"What's that, Bobby?"

Robert was unsure if the nickname conveyed affection or an impression of immaturity but he plunged forward.

"I smoke marijuana for medical reasons."

Paul's lips unconsciously moved into a friendly smirk. "I have glaucoma and," Robert plunged on even as we could see the lawyer was trying hard not to chuckle, "and marijuana has helped control it. Marijuana is helping me save my eyesight."

The final words came out strong and sure, startling the lawyer just as much as the entire premise had. Paul collected himself and said the only logical thing.

"Prove it, Bobby. Just prove it."

3. FIRST STEPS

There were certain advantages to getting busted in Washington, D.C. There was a wealth of information available and all at the cost of a local phone call or a short car ride. We quickly contacted the National Organization for the Reform of Marijuana Laws (NORML) and received a fat packet of information by mail, which included a brief mention of a NORML lawsuit brought against the federal drug agency, the Bureau of Narcotics and Dangerous Drugs (BNDD).

The suit was challenging marijuana's classification as a prohibited drug and it was doing so specifically on the basis of marijuana's medical utility! This little glimmer of hope was intriguing to us and Robert decided to visit NORML's office.

In the fall of 1975, NORML was well established in a three-story office building on M St. N.W., just on the fringe of Georgetown. The group received funding from The Playboy Foundation, wealthy individuals with liberal leanings, membership fees, and the sales of T-shirts and buttons. Robert made his way up the handsome slate stairs that led to the receptionist's desk. He explained that he had been arrested for marijuana possession and asked if there was anyone he could talk to about the situation. Much to his surprise, he was ushered into an office where the founder of NORML sat behind a huge desk piled high with manila folders and other papers.

R. Keith Stroup was a young, activist lawyer who had cut his teeth working on the National Commission on Product Safety. He had founded NORML in 1970, fashioning the group as a public-interest lobby which would use all legal means available to reform the nation's harsh and unjust marijuana laws and protect the marijuana "consumer."

Stroup listened to Robert's story of marijuana's beneficial effects in treating glaucoma and, unlike Paul Smollar, Stroup did not look bemused. He merely nodded and began thumbing through the stack of files, finally pulling out a bulky folder labeled "Medical Use" which he opened and quickly glanced through before handing it to a surprised Robert.

"Yeah, there are some reports," he said, "and there are some people you can contact." He quickly jotted down some names and phone numbers from a bulging rolodex on the corner of his desk.

Robert gratefully accepted the information and thanked Stroup as he prepared to leave. But Stroup felt compelled to add one further thought.

"I think what you're considering, this marijuana/glaucoma thing, might make for an interesting intellectual exercise. But we've been at it for years without any luck. Just don't count on anything working out. Don't," he searched for the right words, "...don't end up hurting yourself trying to prove something."

We greeted the folder from Stroup like beggars at a banquet. It contained numerous old newspaper clippings in which marijuana was variously described as a general, all-purpose tonic, a wonder drug, an elixir of youth, a painkiller, even as a tooth decay preventative. It seemed the drug could do a hundred helpful things.

Amidst these glowing articles, some plain silly, others approaching serious comment, was one from the *Medical World News* dated September 1973. The article reported the story of Dr. Fred Blanton, a south Florida ophthalmologist who had conducted "unauthorized" experiments on several willing glaucoma patients using marijuana brownies. Blanton reported his findings, which were impressive, in 1972. His fellow physicians, however, were not impressed. They promptly convened a medical ethics investigation and Blanton's license to practice medicine was suspended for several months. Strict limitations were imposed on him for several years after that.

The article went on to note that marijuana's ability to reduce inner eye pressure had first been discovered by researchers at UCLA in 1970.

The article had a curious effect on Robert. Initially he felt a stab of sorrow when he realized he was not the first to discover marijuana's unique property as a glaucoma control agent. But it was a micro-moment followed by a rapidly expanding sense of elation. A trail existed, a trail worth investigating. A trail that could lead to challenging The System.

Before acquiring that manila folder from Keith Stroup we were in a very shallow orbit of personal experience. As sure as we were about marijuana's medical benefits we were disinclined to challenge The System. Why make waves? Our only goal was to save Robert's sight.

But the arrest had infuriated both of us. We had done nothing more than grow some plants to help prolong Robert's sight. We had not harmed anyone. Yet our home was violated, our property seized, and our reputations impugned. We were facing considerable legal expense. All of this made us very angry and anger can be a strong motivation to action.

Three days after visiting with Keith Stroup, Robert began to dial his way through the list of contacts that Keith had provided.

"Phyllis Lessin speaking."

Keith had appended a short, written biography to each name. Phyllis was listed as a member of the President's Commission on Biomedical Research but the information was old. Robert had finally tracked her down in her new post at the National Institute on Drug Abuse (NIDA).

"Glaucoma? Oh yes, NIDA has done lots of research on that. In fact, I was working at UCLA when the discovery was made. Marijuana affects glaucoma positively, you know?"

Robert was totally surprised at her frankness and ability to answer his questions so quickly.

"Would you like a copy of the *Marijuana and Health Report for 1974?* The 1975 book won't be out until 1976, but the current book has some information on marijuana/glaucoma research that might help you."

The book arrived a few days later with Phyllis' business card attached to the cover. The table of contents led to a small section in the back titled "Therapeutic Aspects."

After providing a brief historical account the report went on to list areas of medical treatment that might be benefited by the use of marijuana. The first entry was "Intraocular Pressure."

> In 1971, Hepler (et al.) reported that normal subjects sustained a drop in intraocular pressure following the smoking of

marijuana...This finding has been confirmed by other investigators. Hepler has started a program for treating patients with ocular hypertension or glaucoma, particularly those whose intraocular pressure is not reduced with conventional medication for this purpose.

It was a stunning moment. There it was, in hard, unyielding black and white, printed under the stamp of the Department of Health, Education and Welfare. Delivered, by law, to Congress!

The report went on to list the other research work that supported the UCLA Hepler studies. All of the conclusions had been the same—promising. The report to Congress went on to suggest an aggressive program was under way to develop an eye drop based on one of marijuana's ingredients, something called THC. It had already been made into an eyedrop by a University of Georgia researcher named Keith Greene. The report noted research rabbits in Athens, Georgia were being tested with these eye drops and added, rather sadly, that the bunnies still got high.

We wondered how the researchers knew the bunnies were "high."

It was the *Marijuana and Health Report for 1974* that set our course. It was one thing for Robert and me to know marijuana worked as a glaucoma control drug. It was understandable that a pro-pot lobby would make whatever claims possible. But to find that federal agencies knew, had known for five years, was staggering. For the next couple of weeks Robert dialed himself through the bureaucracies. Everyone he called who knew anything at all about marijuana knew that it had a favorable impact on glaucoma.

"It works," they all said, "No question, really."

We wondered why this relationship—so obvious to those inside the government—was being concealed from Robert and his doctor? Some of the voices said not enough research had been done to release the drug to the public. After all, the bunnies still got high. Robert was endlessly reminded that most people with glaucoma were elderly. The rationale was hard to fathom. The concept that older Americans were somehow less able to endure euphoria struck us as suspect. Euphoria did not seem such a dreadful side effect for a drug that might prolong or secure an individual's sight. Would euphoria complicate an ailing soul's life as much as blindness? As for releasing the drug to the public, the report repeatedly noted marijuana was regularly used by more than ten million Americans for pleasure. It seemed marijuana was already "released."

Other federal officials appreciated Robert's situation, but thought it best to plead guilty and quietly continue his own program of self-therapy. One author of the NIDA Report, Dr. Robert Peterson, counseled that working through the bureaucratic structure could be "sheer hell." Both sides of the marijuana control argument—pro-pot and federal government—were saying the same thing. "Don't count on anything working out," Keith had said. "You'll never make it," added Bob Peterson. Neither understood that there was little choice. Without marijuana Robert would go blind.

Before the bust we were moving in our own orbit of personal knowledge of marijuana's medical use and the prospect of quietly going our own way was fine and dandy. But things had changed. No one in the federal government denied or even appeared to doubt marijuana's beneficial impact on glaucoma. Many of the scientists working at NIDA, the agency charged with marijuana research, would confess, without prodding, over the phone, what they would not venture to say in public: that after a decade of research devoted to finding marijuana's harm, none had been found. Years of research, millions of dollars and not one demonstrable harm. Indeed, it seemed, just the opposite was true. The most demonstrable effects of marijuana were beneficial, such as its ability to reduce intra-ocular pressures.

All of this made us very angry and we began to chart our course through the maze of The System.

After several weeks of reading research papers and talking with bureaucrats it was time to contact the principal researchers—the individuals who might actually help us prove Robert's case.

Dr. Robert Hepler was the UCLA ophthalmologist who first reported marijuana's ability to lower intra-ocular eye pressure. He had serendipitously discovered this while investigating the long held belief smoking marijuana caused the pupils to dilate. It was reasoned such a physical phenomenon could be useful to police officers in identifying suspected marijuana users. Hepler disproved the myth.

Phyllis Lessin was the first to mention Dr. Hepler and she had repeatedly encouraged Robert to call the UCLA physician. But Robert was nervous about striking out on his first call and having no where else to go.

So he began with Keith Greene, the Athens, Georgia researcher whose marijuana eye drop was getting the bunnies "high." Greene was unavailable but Robert spoke with his colleague, John Bigger. Like everyone else, Bigger was sympathetic but there was little he could do. The Georgia researchers were restricted to rabbit research. No human testing was allowed. He did provide enlightened information about the efforts to create marijuana eye drops but made it clear such medications were a long way from possible human use.

With Athens out of the running, Robert placed a call to Dr. Mario Perez-Reyes at the University of North Carolina-Chapel Hill. Mario Perez-Reyes had a thick accent and a quick interest. After listening to Robert's story, Perez-Reyes explained he had never experimented on a person with glaucoma, "only normals." He wasn't sure his license allowed for experiments on persons with glaucoma.

"Besides, I only work with pure THC, not with smoked marijuana. If you were to come here to Chapel Hill I would only be able to give you an injection." This qualification did little to diminish Robert's interest. The doctor stressed he would need a complete medical history before making any final decision and Robert promised to comply.

Perez-Reyes made it seem so simple and Robert was buoyed with the ease of it all. He mustered his courage and placed a call to Robert Hepler.

After briefly explaining to the receptionist that he was calling about the glaucoma study he was placed on hold for a short period of time and then he was connected directly to Dr. Hepler:

"Dr. Hepler, I was recently arrested for possession of marijuana and I have glaucoma ..." Static rumbled through the line and I faltered. Hepler was distant in more than miles. Coolly, without any tone of intent, he responded, "How exactly did you use this marijuana, Mr. Randall?"

"Yes, well I was using about five joints a day when I could get it. The effect seems to last four, maybe five hours. I noticed it a couple of years ago because if I don't smoke I get these rings, these tricolored haloes. Smoking causes the rings, the haloes to go away, and ..." I began to grab for words.

"What kind of glaucoma do you have?" Hepler asked, still cool but with a bit more interest.

"Open-angle. The pressure has been recorded as high as 35. Normal pressure is 20 or less, isn't that right?" I knew that was right but I was desperately trying to engage the physician in conversation. The curt "yes" from Hepler did nothing to dispel my growing nervousness.

"What medications are you on, Mr. Randall?" I listed the medications I was taking, drugs that had failed, and whatever else I could recall about my medical history. "It sounds like a very serious case of glaucoma. And you sound young. How old are you, Mr. Randall?"

"Twenty-seven, sir." There was that silence again but somehow it seemed warmer.

"Hmm ... Well, Mr. Randall, I'm not certain we can do anything for you here. Why don't you give me your address, though, and I'll send you some of our research findings. It will interest you." Hepler's tone had clearly changed and he had slipped into a practiced bedside manner with fatherly tones. He asked for my medical history and we exchanged mailing addresses. Upon saying good-bye Hepler added, "Keep those pressures under control."

Both marijuana researchers had requested a medical history so Robert realized it was time to inform Dr. Fine about his situation.

It was less than one month since our arrest when Robert went to a scheduled visit with his ophthalmologist. Not surprisingly the doctor was initially skeptical when Robert explained his use of marijuana as a medicine but Dr. Fine quickly softened as Robert rushed ahead with his narrative about researchers in North Carolina and at UCLA.

> "I've already contacted a couple of researchers, one in North Carolina and another at UCLA's Jules Stein Eye Institute." Fine's brow arched and he took the sheet of paper from me that had the addresses for both Perez-Reyes and Hepler.
>
> "This place is very well-considered in the field," he noted, pointing to Hepler's UCLA address. "I take it you want me to write up something for these doctors?" I nodded. "Okay, I'll do that, but I'm just not sure you should get wrapped up in something like this. You don't have a lot of eyesight to waste chasing after ..."
>
> "Would you be willing to testify in court if these researchers demonstrate that marijuana helps me?" I knew I was pressing.
>
> "Ah, well... sure. Sure! If you can prove to me that this stuff really works. Facts are facts. Show me facts and I'll testify, be glad to help you. But you've got to show me the facts."

Fine, true to his word, prepared a letter outlining Robert's medical history, noting the broad fluctuations in eye pressure and aggressive use of conventional medication. The same letter was sent to both researchers and concluded, "If with your medications you can hold his pressure at a lower level and more uniformly over a longer period of time, we feel that this would be most helpful."

Robert, filled with hope, mailed the medical history to each researcher. Things seemed promising, he had accomplished a great deal in a relatively short period of time. But we were neophytes in the world of marijuana politics. We had a lot to learn.

4. MEMORY HOLE

While Robert dialed his way through bureaucracies in Washington and researchers throughout the country, I was collecting historical information and contemporary news articles from the Library of Congress. The ornate and elegant depository of the written word was a calming retreat in the first few weeks following our arrest. It was also a treasure trove of information.

Clearly there was scientific evidence, both historic and current, to support claims of marijuana's medical utility. Moreover, there was ample scientific data to show that marijuana was no more harmful than currently approved medications. Indeed, there was evidence to show it was a great deal less harmful than some of the drugs Robert was using at Dr. Fine's direction.

In a sane society the discovery of such a medication would be cause for celebration. Yet the federal officials who spoke to Robert were not happy that he had found a means of preserving his sight. They were very sympathetic to his plight but none gave him any chance of succeeding. "Pay the fine," they said. "Don't rock the boat," they advised.

Robert began comparing it to The Memory Hole in George Orwell's chilling view of a totalitarian future, *1984*. In Orwell's classic book The Memory Hole was used to destroy all evidence of the past not in step with government policies. In many respects this was the status of marijuana's medical utility in 1975.

"There was a time in the United States when extracts of cannabis were almost as commonly used for medicinal purposes as is aspirin today." So began a 1971 book entitled *Uses of Marijuana* by Solomon Snyder. In fact, the history of marijuana's medical use predates the written word.

Every civilization since the dawn of man has employed the unique therapeutic properties of this plant. The Chinese were medically using cannabis twenty-eight centuries before the birth of Christ, recommending it for a variety of disorders including rheumatic pain and constipation. In cultures widely separated by geography and time there are consistent reports of marijuana's medical benefits in easing digestive upsets, enhancing appetites, relieving muscle spasms, and reducing melancholia.

British physician William O'Shaughnessy is credited with reintroducing cannabis to Western medicine in 1839 with a forty-page article entitled "On the Preparation of the Indian Hemp or Gunja." O'Shaughnessy, a man of wide interests and varied occupations, was traveling in India and noted the use of cannabis there for treatment of convulsive disorders, as an analgesic, and as a muscle relaxant. It was this latter quality that led to one of the most famous therapeutic applications of cannabis: the use by Queen Victoria to treat menstrual cramps.

O'Shaughnessy's reports, and later articles by Victoria's physician J. R. Reynolds, promoted considerable interest in cannabis by European and American physicians. But the cannabis tinctures of the late 1800s and early 1900s were unstable and quirky. As the Industrial Age began to place its imprint on every aspect of the culture there was a demand for uniformity and repeatable expectations even in the medicines of the time. Powders, tinctures and elixirs gave way to pills and injectable solutions. Many of our most common medications were synthesized during this time from natural products—morphine from poppies, digitalis from foxglove, and aspirin from birch bark. But, try as they might, doctors, scientists, and pharmacists could not synthesize cannabis.

It was during the turbulent 1920s and 1930s that the low hiss of The Memory Hole began. The Great Depression was ravaging the country and the broad cultural effects of alcohol prohibition were manifesting themselves in crime sprees and violence. As the "Noble Experiment" of alcohol prohibition began to collapse, threatening the layoff of enforcement personnel, one enterprising agent, Harry Anslinger, noted with considerable alarm the growing menace of marijuana—a "drug" particularly favored by Negroes, Mexicans, and purveyors of the subversive new music, jazz.

Mr. Anslinger must be given credit for creating opportunity where none existed before. Cannabis, a plant with a 5,000-year history of benign medical use, was suddenly characterized as an evil and addictive menace. In an effort to foment social hysteria, lurid press stories were published and propaganda films like *Reefer Madness* flickered across America's movie screens. It was a fearful time and Anslinger played upon that fear with terrific success. In such a climate it was easy for a young Orson Welles to create a believable Martian invasion. It was even easier to create a "Devil's Weed."

Anslinger and the newly created Federal Bureau of Narcotics (FBN) convinced the U.S. Congress that marijuana needed tight controls. It was claimed the use of marijuana led to violent behavior and appealed to only the lowest echelon of society. It had to be outlawed.

The Marijuana Tax Act of 1937 was proposed and during congressional hearings there were only two dissenting voices. One was from the birdseed industry, which, in fact, won some concessions. The other was from the American Medical Association (AMA). The AMA lobbyist, Dr. William Woodward, made two points. First, that marijuana was not dangerous enough to warrant a legal prohibition and criminal sanctions. Second, and more specific to his professional interests, Woodward told Congress that marijuana had important medical properties and expressed concern that the proposed prohibition would restrict marijuana's therapeutic use while inhibiting research with the plant. "There is a possibility," he noted presciently, "that a restudy of the drug by modern means may show other advantages to be derived from its medicinal use."

Woodward's efforts succeeded in preventing an absolute prohibition of the drug. In theory, the Tax Act, which became law in October 1937, did allow the continuing medical use of cannabis. Anslinger and the FBN, however, quickly used their newly granted authority to promulgate sixty pages of regulations that severely hampered legal access to the drug. Doctors, therefore, turned their attention to other, more easily obtained medications. Pharmaceutical companies quickly lost interest in attempting to synthesize cannabis. By 1941, with the helpful prodding of Mr. Anslinger, cannabis was removed from the *United States Pharmacopeia and National Formulary*. The Memory Hole had opened.

The nation, understandably, was considerably distracted during the 1940s by wars, both hot and cold. In the 1950s the communist menace became the Number 1 public fixation and marijuana remained in the background. As the country struggled its way through the 1960s the need for reorganization of drug laws and, particularly, drug agencies became obvious. Legislation was drafted during the presidency of Lyndon Johnson and, with some minor modifications, was sent to the Hill by newly elected President Richard Nixon in 1969.

The Comprehensive Drug Abuse Prevention and Control Act of 1970 (CDAPCA), as originally drafted, divided drugs into four schedules of legal control based on a scientific assessment of each substance's "potential for abuse." The proposed scheduling scheme alarmed several well-connected Washington attorneys, including Joseph Califano, who worked for pharmaceutical interests. They strongly objected to the CDAPCA's classification scheme because—based on a purely scientific assessment—legal drugs like Valium might end up in the same schedule as an illegal drug like marijuana. And that, they said, would confuse the public.

To remedy this problem they proposed segregating legal medicines from illegal drugs by creating a fifth control level to be known as Schedule I. By law, Schedule I drugs had "no accepted medical use," and were "unsafe for use under medical supervision." The purpose, quite clearly, was to create a regulatory firewall between officially prohibited "street drugs" and legally prescribed, highly profitable medicines. Drug warriors insisted this approach eliminated any possible public confusion, and would be viewed as a hard line on drug abuse.

Nixon, who was planning the 1970-midterm Congressional elections as a national referendum on the liberal politics of "pot, pornography and permissiveness," jumped on the idea of a rigid scheduling scheme based not on scientific assessment, but on law enforcement perceptions of "abuseability."

The deal was all but done when Ted Kennedy and other Senators objected to the seemingly arbitrary conclusion that marijuana was as dangerous as LSD (lysergic acid diethylamide) or addictive as heroin. Echoing the concerns of Dr. Woodward more than three decades before, they simply asked, "Where is the scientific proof?"

The Senators were able to access 5,000 years of history, from the first medical writings through 1937, literature of vastly divergent cultures containing a detailed and consistent appraisal of cannabis. In nearly every mention, cannabis was described in benign terms; its multiple medicinal properties enumerated; its mildly intoxicating and possible adverse affects carefully indicated. Significantly, there was nothing in this immense historical record that would warrant marijuana's classification as a Schedule I drug.

"Folk medicine," responded the Prohibitionists. Whoosh goes The Memory Hole.

After 1937? A black hole. At least, that's what Senator Kennedy and Congress was told. It was an almost credible lie. After the 1937 Tax Act there was little opportunity for private sector marijuana-related research. So, the senators responded, maybe we should do some research and find out just how dangerous marijuana really is?

Eventually, a compromise was reached. Marijuana would be temporarily placed on Schedule I as a drug with "no accepted medical use," and "unsafe for use under medical supervision." But a presidential commission would investigate marijuana's proper classification and make appropriate recommendations after a consideration of the facts. To make this compromise workable Nixon agreed to authorize a government-financed research effort designed to scientifically evaluate marijuana. This would, it was guaranteed, fill in any gaps in our knowledge.

Behind this boring public dance over marijuana's proper classification lurked a far darker reality: a CIA project with the code name MKULTRA.

It is not possible to know much about MKULTRA. It was approved in April 1953 but even at that point it was already operational under the name MKDELTA. Beyond the reach of official CIA controls, MKULTRA had free rein and big budgets. The Army was looking at the big picture of large-scale chemical and biological warfare. MKULTRA was the CIA's attempt to individualize chemical conflict and to explore the possibility of pharmacologically altering minds, individually or collectively, to alter political outcomes. It was a matter of national security.

Marijuana—sliced, diced, pulverized, brewed, tinctured, suspended, irradiated, atomized and otherwise—was clearly part of the earlier MKDELTA effort. Like the pharmaceutical companies in the mid-1930s, the spies discovered that marijuana's unique chemistry defied easy synthesis. Eventually they concluded that the best way to administer the drug was via inhalation. Tobacco cigarettes were laced with liquid marijuana and given to unsuspecting subjects. The primary goal was a "truth drug." Ultimately, marijuana failed in this particular role.

MKDELTA, and its bastard son MKULTRA, provided the U.S. government with ample information on marijuana. But in 1970, when Congress asked for information on marijuana, nobody mentioned MKDELTA. Whoosh went The Memory Hole. By denying the existence of virtually any information on marijuana, however, the intelligence complex opened the door to a congressional insistence for research to explore the very information MKDELTA was designed to obscure.

After much debate Congress enacted the CDAPCA, a massive piece of legislation. Within it, Title II to be exact, is the Controlled Substances Act of 1970, establishing the five schedules of drugs. A Presidential Commission was appointed to review marijuana's classification as a Schedule I drug. Chaired by former Pennsylvania Governor Raymond P. Shafer, the Commission reported its findings in March of 1972, recommending that marijuana be rescheduled and decriminalized. "Of particular significance," the report noted, "would be investigations into the treatment of glaucoma, migraine, alcoholism and terminal cancer."

Nixon, in the midst of a reelection bid, dismissed the Commission's recommendations. Whoosh goes The Memory Hole.

In 1973, as the Watergate crisis triggered congressional interest in some unsavory CIA operations, Nixon's CIA Director, Richard Helms, saw the writing on the wall and ordered all MKDELTA/ULTRA files destroyed. By the time the Senate began investigating CIA behavior in 1975, nearly all traces of MKULTRA had—officially at least—been systematically erased. Whoosh goes the Memory Hole.

At the time of our arrest we knew none of this. We were certainly aware of the use of marijuana laws as a societal control mechanism although now the focus had shifted a bit to encompass not only blacks and musicians but also a new emerging facet, the counterculture, a broad collection of individuals which included white, middle-class college students who called themselves "hippies"—a term which accurately described Robert and me during our college days in Florida. But cannabis had been long absent from the medical scene. The Shafer Commission recommendation on therapeutic use, brief and buried in the report, was barely known to the public. The NIDA report to Congress, provided to us by Phyllis Lessin, had cursorily dismissed the plant's vast history of medical use with a single line. "In many parts of the world," the section began, "marijuana has been, and still is, used as a folk medicine." Five thousand years reduced to "folklore."

Whoosh.

5. PROVING IT

Robert's phone calls to Drs. Mario Perez-Reyes and Robert Hepler bore fruit in mid-October 1975 when both men responded positively to Robert's request to become a research subject. It was welcome news in an otherwise desolate time. The police had "stolen" Robert's medication and obtaining marijuana was hard. Robert's vision was clearly suffering.

Although we couldn't know it at the time we were actually having an incredible run of luck. The federal government had been put on notice as early as 1970 that marijuana use caused a regular drop in the intraocular pressure. But by late 1975 there were just two researchers in the entire country exploring this phenomena on human beings and both programs were winding down. Perez-Reyes in North Carolina was concluding a study on the effects of intravenous (IV) cannabinoids on intraocular pressure, attempting to confirm early studies conducted at UCLA which demonstrated a direct pressure reduction in the normal eye following use of marijuana or several different marijuana derivatives. Across the country, in Los Angeles, Robert Hepler was beginning to wrap-up his research on marijuana's ocular effects. His primary focus was not marijuana's effect on the elevated eye pressures of glaucomics but rather the general physiological effect of marijuana on recreational users of the drug. He had managed to convince the federal government that there should be some follow-up with respect to the proposal that marijuana may be helpful to those afflicted with glaucoma. That small study, along with the larger epidemiological study of "normals," would shutdown by the end of the year. Perez-Reyes would not be far behind.

Had we been busted even three months later this entire story would be a moot point. Fate, it seemed, had a definite hand in things...a phenomenon that would seem to mark our entire adventure.

Robert's first excursion into the world of marijuana research was not particularly promising. It began on the day after

Thanksgiving in November 1975. NORML was proving very helpful and managed to find the funds to fly Robert to Raleigh-Durham, North Carolina. He was met by Dr. Perez-Reyes at the airport and was whisked away to what he later termed "a trip down the rabbit hole."

Perez-Reyes was among an elite circle of researchers in America permitted to employ the derivatives of marijuana on human test subjects via injection or oral transmission. He was linked to The Triangle Research Center, a large conglomerate of government offices and laboratories where, among other things, various components of marijuana were synthesized and made available to researchers throughout the world.

Perez-Reyes had extensive experience with many marijuana derivatives but his current experiments focused on delta-9 tetrahydrocannabinol (THC), delta-8 THC, cannabinol, and cannabidiol. Delta-9 THC is commonly referred to as marijuana's "psychoactive" ingredient, the part that makes people high. In fact, other ingredients in marijuana also have psychoactive effects but on a much milder scale. Perez-Reyes had observed that marijuana, or a collection of its active ingredients, could indeed aid in the reduction of intraocular pressure (IOP), confirming the UCLA results. But Perez-Reyes went on to demonstrate that delta-8 THC could provide the same measure of IOP reduction with less psychoactive impact. He had observed this in approximately twelve paid volunteers, all "normals"—healthy with no glaucoma.

Robert was Perez-Reyes' first glaucoma patient.

Perez-Reyes' study was focused solely on IV administration of marijuana, an aspect that did not deter Robert's enthusiasm for involvement. Before his travel to Raleigh-Durham we speculated on what it would be like to "shoot up" marijuana derivatives. Robert was about to find out.

> *While the assistant attached an elastic band around my arm and various electrodes to my upper body to measure metabolic rates, Perez-Reyes explained the procedures he would follow during the experiment. "Once every five minutes I will come in and ask you to describe your feelings. You will get very high," he was speaking carefully and looking at me intently. "Take as much of the drug as you feel comfortable with. If you feel you are losing control, call out and we will stop at once. As*

soon as we stop you will begin to come down again very quickly. Do you understand? This is very important." I nodded. *"THC can hit you like a train. Do not be embarrassed to call out. Okay?"*

After a last check of serum and delta-8 THC containers, Perez-Reyes wiped my arm with a cool alcohol swab, and a long thin needle sliced perfectly into a vein.

The final step before beginning the experiment was measuring my eye pressure, which Perez-Reyes recorded in the 20s, not as high as they could have been but well above the normal range.

After once again reminding me to call out should the experience become too threatening, Perez-Reyes joined his assistant in a corner of the room, out of my sight. I waited, staring at the offensive florescent light overhead, trying to feel the beginnings of promised euphoria. Perez-Reyes came and went like Carroll's rabbit. Every five minutes, as promised, he would pop into my field of vision and ask how I felt. Each time, I responded there was nothing to report, no distinctive feelings of euphoria, no marked changes in the psyche. Nothing.

On Perez-Reyes' fourth entry, he reminded me with a gentle smile that he could quickly stop the experiment and eliminate any adverse reactions. In a flash I comprehended the game. All this time, some twenty minutes or so, Perez-Reyes had simply run serum into my vein. There had been no THC. This was the investigator's control. But the repeated warning gave it away. With new anticipation, I awaited the introduction of some unknown glory.

Perez-Reyes' assistant appeared on the next five-minute check. This seemed to confirm my assumption that the real test had finally begun. I replied that I felt nothing but asked for a glass of water that was quickly produced.

The assistant disappeared and I continued to wait. I was not prepared for the event that followed.

Perez-Reyes returned to the table followed by his assistant. Once again he asked me if I felt anything unusual. I considered the question carefully. *"No, nothing distinctive."* Perez-Reyes reached over and carefully pulled the needle from my arm.

"Mr. Randall, I do not know what is wrong. You say you do not feel high, yet I have given you 10 milligrams of THC. You do not feel odd or strange, nothing is abnormal to you?"

"Nothing distinctive or overpowering," I replied, confused by the doctor's frustrated excitement.

Perez-Reyes pulled a chart from a nearby bookcase and held it before me. "Let me explain what has happened. This is my chart for experiments dealing with eye pressures. I gave these people 6 mg. of delta-8 THC and every one of them noted profound alterations in their thought processes. Some could not tolerate a full dose, some had a negative response. But you tell me you feel nothing after 10 mg. What am I to think?"

I gazed at the chart. I had the sinking feeling that I had somehow sabotaged the experiment. Worse yet, my hoped-for court evidence was teetering in the balance.

Perez-Reyes once again inquired about my mental state. "You say you are not stoned?" "No, I'm not stoned," I replied. Perez-Reyes had me lay back on the table and once again measured my eye pressure, fumbling a bit as before but when he finally recorded the IOP my hopes soared. From the dangerously high 20s, my eye pressure had plummeted to a normal range. The hoped-for court evidence once again loomed in my inner vision.

In fact, the North Carolina evidence was never presented in court. Despite the reduction in eye pressure, the lawyers were concerned about the researcher's lack of federal approval to conduct experiments with glaucoma subjects. Legally, it was felt, Perez-Reyes was on shaky ground and evidence from his experiments could 1) muck up the case, and 2) get Perez-Reyes into considerable trouble.

The UCLA testing was considerably more extensive in scope. Robert traveled to Los Angeles, once again with the help of funding from NORML, on December 7, 1975 and would not return to our Washington home until December 18th. During that time he was housed on the "Marijuana Ward" at the UCLA Neuropsychiatric Institute.

The ward was home to the UCLA Marijuana Research Project and for nearly five years had housed teams of six to twelve research subjects, all male and all between the ages of 25-45. A battery of physiological and psychological tests were conducted, all designed to reveal the harm of marijuana use.

After five years the studies were winding down. Despite massive efforts by some of the best researchers in the nation to pinpoint the "harm" of marijuana the overall consensus was just the opposite. Marijuana, it seemed, was relatively benign.

Dr. Robert Hepler, an ophthalmologist, was attached to the study. He and his staff dutifully noted alterations in pupil size before and after marijuana use. Expecting to find an enlargement in pupil size the ophthalmology team found just the opposite—a barely perceptible, but clinically significant pupillary contraction, a common side effect of several glaucoma control medicines used to reduce ocular pressures.

Hepler made the critical connection and began measuring eye pressure as well as pupil size of the research subjects. The results were striking. After smoking marijuana there was a sudden, often very significant decline in ocular pressure. While many drugs increase intraocular pressure only a few are known to effectively lower it. As early as September 1971, Hepler communicated his findings in a letter to the Journal of the American Medical Association (JAMA). He wrote,

> "The purpose of this letter is to present preliminary data concerning the most impressive change observed so far, namely, a substantial decrease in intraocular pressure observed in a large percentage of subjects.
> …The possible implications, including the mechanism of action, and even possible therapeutic action in the treatment of glaucoma, are obvious."

In 1973 Dr. Hepler received government permission to expand his study to include a small sampling of glaucoma patients. Unfortunately finding glaucoma patients—generally in their sixties and seventies—willing to smoke marijuana was difficult. Attempts to advertise for patients even got Hepler in trouble with the professional ethics board of the California Medical Association. The handful of glaucoma patients willing to participate in the study were all marijuana-naive, first-time smokers. To further complicate matters, glaucoma patients—unlike the young male subjects held captive in the Neuropsychiatric Institute—could not be incarcerated and closely monitored over extended periods. Despite these difficulties, Hepler found marijuana, when smoked, was highly effective in lowering the elevated ocular tensions of glaucoma patients.

After five years of study involving hundreds of normal subjects, and brief, confirmatory tests on ten glaucoma patients, Hepler felt he had a fair understanding of marijuana's IOP lowering properties. But, what Hepler really needed to confirm his conclusions was a glaucoma patient who was not marijuana-naive and whose IOP could be carefully tracked over a period of days. He was despairing of ever finding such a candidate when Robert Randall called in October 1975.

Robert and Hepler had an instant connection. Robert was greatly impressed with the physician's thorough assessment and willingness to "level" with Robert about the seriousness of Robert's glaucoma. The doctor spent almost an hour examining Robert's eyes and candidly told him, "It's a wonder you see anything at all," Hepler replied. "There's a great deal of injury, and almost no healthy tissue left." Hepler would come to appreciate Robert's curiosity and intelligence declaring at one point, "I just wish my medical students picked up this stuff as fast as you."

The testing on Robert was meticulous and extensive. For a full day he was tested on various combinations of conventional glaucoma medications and his intraocular pressures were measured every two hours. Hepler was accomplishing two goals: 1) satisfying himself that Robert's glaucoma was indeed unresponsive to readily available, legal medications, and 2) establishing a baseline diurnal curve of Robert's eye pressures

Intraocular pressure is measured by a process called tonometry and calibrated in terms of millimeters (mm) of mercury (Hg). Normal IOP for most individuals is between 10 and 20 mm Hg and can vary slightly in each eye. Upon waking, Robert's 8 a.m. pressures were around 17–18 mm Hg—high normal but acceptable. By 10 a.m., however, the pressure had already risen over 20 mm Hg—above the accepted limits of "normal" pressure. By noon his IOP was around 25 mm Hg, and during the afternoon it remained elevated in a range of 24–33 mm Hg. Then, around 6 p.m. the IOP began to rapidly increase. By the 8p.m. pressure check it exceeded 30 mm Hg, and by 10 p.m. it was nearly 40. Despite the best glaucoma control drugs known to modern medicine, Robert's IOP was dangerously elevated for 12 of the 14 hours tested.

On the second day Robert was introduced to the federal government's infamous marijuana cigarettes. The "joint" was perfectly rolled, looking very much like a tobacco cigarette without a filter. In fact, the tobacco companies had donated a cigarette-rolling machine to the federal government to produce the thousands of "joints" required for the five years of research at UCLA

Robert smoked the cigarette under the observation of two medical students. His anticipation was great but the effect of the cigarette was similar to the effect he felt the previous month in Raleigh-Durham: nothing, no feeling of euphoria, and no sense of being "high." And when his eye pressure was taken there was no drop in the elevation. Robert inquired if the cigarette was a placebo and the evasive comments of Hepler's aide seemed to confirm the guess.

Later that day he returned to the "smoking room" with the two medical students who gave him another perfectly rolled cigarette.

"That first joint was a placebo, right?" he asked.

One of the students nodded and leaned forward with the cigarette. "You can tell because the real marijuana cigarettes have a small "M" printed on them. See?"

Robert strained to focus, and finally saw a discreet, nearly invisible "M" in exactly the same place tobacco cigarettes were imprinted with a brand logo.

The effect was not as he hoped nor was it what Hepler expected. Robert reported only a "slight buzz" and his eye pressure was dangerously high at 30/23, just about where it had been the day before.

The third day of testing, December 10, was a repeat of the first, a day of continuous pressure readings with no placebos, no pot. Robert's ocular pressures were steady, predictable, and high, dangerously high, especially in the evening.

On the fourth day Hepler added a pill form of synthetic delta-9 THC and at last Robert displayed a physiological reaction the researchers expected but not what Robert expected.

> *Clearly, something impressive was happening. Time was slowing; extending. My heart was racing; my mouth desert dry. I had entered an unevenly vibrating universe and the resulting anxiety was nearly overwhelming. After some reflection I suddenly realized being "high" was fun. What I was experiencing, while powerful and oddly appealing, was not fun. Indeed, it was just the opposite of fun. I was working desperately hard to maintain an outward shell of tranquility.*

The THC, while definitely mind-altering, had no effect on Robert's eye pressures so, on the next day, the researchers increased the dose, from 20 to 30 mg.

> *Once again the regular routine of pressure readings dominated the day. Once again there was failure. My eye pressures remained locked into the steady diurnal curve that was plotted four days ago upon my arrival at UCLA.*
>
> *My lack of "high" was confounding to the researchers. The 30 mg of THC produced even less psychic anxiety than the previous dose of 20 mg. It was North Carolina all over again. Just as with Perez-Reyes, I began to have the feeling I was somehow savaging the experiment.*

Dr. Hepler was as perplexed as Robert. For years he had carefully measured a consistent drop in eye pressure following marijuana use. Robert was jarringly out of sync with all of his research.

On Monday Robert sat down with Hepler, his aide Bob Petrus, and tried to sort things out. During the discussion Robert revealed that he had experienced the same reaction in North Carolina with Perez-Reyes and the infused THC.

> *"You didn't get 'high' on infused THC?!" Hepler was disbelieving. "Do you know how much THC you received in North Carolina?"*
>
> *"Between 10 and 12 mgs. over 40 minutes. Dr. Reyes said it was twice as much as he'd ever given anyone else."*
>
> *"And you didn't feel 'high'?!"*
>
> *"No. No 'high.' Perez-Reyes was so concerned by my lack of reaction he stopped the test. I think that was a mistake."*

"At that dose, by infusion, I can see why he stopped the test. ... Let's review. You didn't get 'high' on infused THC. And you didn't get 'high' on oral THC. Is that right?" Hepler was systematically eliminating possibilities.

"That's right. And I haven't gotten 'high,' not really 'high' on the couple of marijuana cigarettes I've smoked since I've been here."

"You smoked a joint with 2 % THC an hour ago. Do you feel 'high' now?" Hepler was struggling to put it together. Why was I different?

"Not 'high.' Maybe I'm THC tolerant. Is that possible?" I was also searching to explain why marijuana, which worked so well for so long at home in Washington, would suddenly stop working at UCLA.

Hepler paused. "Maybe you're not hitting your therapeutic load."

It was the "Eureka!" moment, the time when all the difficult pieces come together and the solution becomes crystal clear. "Therapeutic load" refers to the amount of drug necessary to trigger a therapeutic effect. In Robert's case he was not receiving enough marijuana to lower his eye pressure. Having smoked marijuana daily for almost two years Robert's body needed a higher dose of the drug to achieve the therapeutic benefit of lowering intraocular pressures.

Hepler and his aide began talking excitedly and asked Robert to wait while they made some calls. When the two men returned twenty minutes later it was with a determined look.

Petrus led Robert to a private room and began unloading ten small manila envelopes containing marijuana cigarettes from his pockets. He then gave Robert a series of instructions on how to record serial numbers, a stopwatch to measure the time it took him to smoke each of the "joints," and instructed the intrigued young man to smoke as many of the marijuana cigarettes as he needed to become "high."

For the next hour I dutifully opened manila envelopes, recorded serial numbers, took my pulse and timed how long it took to smoke each new joint emblazoned with the "M." I was half way through my third joint when I paused just long enough to realize I was 'high.' But, I reckoned, why stop at three? By the time I finished the sixth joint I was absolutely, unmistakably stoned. Utterly blitzed. Still, in keeping with the spirit of the experiment, I pressed on. I was finishing my seventh joint when Petrus reappeared.

When the aide measured Robert's eye pressures he could barely contain his excitement. "Your IOP is 17/17!" Petrus was gleeful. "Let's see. That's nearly 10mm below your baseline; about a 35% reduction!" The experiment worked.

Petrus and Hepler were exuberant. Robert, happily stoned, could not stop smiling.

"So, it was a therapeutic load problem," Hepler said triumphantly. "We just weren't getting enough marijuana into you. And, clearly, something other than THC or in addition to THC is helping to lower your pressures. Seven joints of 2% THC," he calculated, "means the most THC you could have gotten was around 14 to 16 mgs., and half that was lost in the process of smoking."

"Marijuana works?" I ventured.

"It seems marijuana works very, very well," Hepler, now also smiling, replied.

For the next two days Hepler and Petrus devised a series of procedures that confirmed the theory and refined the process. Having resolved the problem of therapeutic load Dr. Hepler was able to quickly establish a proper dose schedule for Robert—three joints every four hours (while awake) to control the dangerously elevated intra-ocular pressures.

It was precisely the kind of data needed to prove that marijuana worked.

Precisely the kind of data to submit in court.

6. BUILDING THE CASE

Robert arrived home from UCLA on December 19, 1975, the holidays descended upon us and before we knew it the American Bicentennial Year had begun. It was a curious portend and would provide an interesting backdrop for the coming events.

During the first week of the New Year we compiled the raw data from Robert's UCLA tests into a presentable format. There was no denying the failure of conventional medications nor the near-miraculous results when legal quantities of Uncle Sam's weed were added to his medical regimen. On January 16th we presented the data to the lawyers.

The lawyer and an associate were reading through the charts and summations of the UCLA data. After five months of repeatedly explaining marijuana's beneficial effect on Robert's glaucoma there was, at last, some specific data on which a case could be built. "Bobby" had proved it. We waited expectantly.

It was a dismal day and the dreary view from Paul Smollar's window provided a bleak backdrop to the expectant air in the small office. On mid-winter days Washington can be especially gray. The incessant brightness of the overhead fluorescents did little to lift the somber mood. The five or ten minutes it took for the lawyers to absorb the report seemed an eternity.

Paul finished the last page and looked across the desk. "Bob," he said quietly, "this is history!"

It was an instant of glorious communication. Bobby was gone, replaced by a newly respected Bob who wasted little time in stating his demands.

"It's not enough to win the case. We want to sue someone. Without a guarantee of legal access to marijuana nothing is gained. I need a noncriminal supply, at a reasonable price." Robert had thought this through.

Paul looked delighted. All the implications, each facet of the thesis asserted a fascination and within seconds the lawyer and associate were engaged in a flurry of rapid incantations. Like patients in a hospital bed surrounded by doctors and interns, we listened to our future discussed in Latin terms and judicial procedures with familiar words such as "publicity," "history," and "great case" punctuating the discussion.

Robert edged his way into the conversation and soon the three men were engaged in a free-for-all brainstorming session. Fantasy gave flight: quash the Superior Court with a federal injunction or ask Congress for special action?

"Sue the bastards!" I said. All three turned in my direction. "The government has mindlessly set out to destroy Robert's sight. Sue them! The historical evidence is there, the current research is there, and now we have the UCLA data. Let's get their attention and sue for $17.76 million."

Paul looked upon me kindly and said he was uncertain the government could be sued for acting to prevent an illegal act. I returned to my supportive role as the conversation expanded into Robert's UCLA experiences with different doses of marijuana cigarettes. The lawyers were intrigued and conversation flowed back to the question of what to do about marijuana supplies. Paul observed that a "not guilty" decision would do nothing to resolve the problem. Perhaps a judge would go so far as to allow cultivation but it seemed doubtful and if Robert ever left Washington, D.C. how would that affect his situation?

"Why not ask the government for their marijuana?" It was my second attempt to become part of the party and this foray was far more effective. The men were stopped in mid-conversation. For a moment there was silence. Paul spoke first, struggling to reject the idea on legal grounds. Robert, much to my dismay, tried to support him. But the harder they tried the more rational, obvious, and suitable the question became. As Paul walked to the elevator with us he continued to talk excitedly about the prospect of making Uncle Sam provide the pot, "straight from the farm in Mississippi." As the elevator car arrived he briefly congratulated me for my suggestion. It was a nice gesture on the lawyer's part, but as the elevator descended I wished aloud to Robert that the lawyers would spend more time considering my suggested lawsuit for $17.76 million.

We were cocky and confident following that meeting. Without a clue as to what lay ahead we naively felt the curtain had come down on Act 1 and we greeted the lawyers' enthusiasm as resounding applause for a job well done. But there was work ahead—the play was far from over and the act had barely begun.

Our trial was scheduled for March 15, 1976, a date that gave us some pause. It was, after all, the Ides of March, the day on which Caesar had been brutally slain so many years before. It is also the day when, by tradition, the buzzards return to Healy, Ohio. Neither occasion promised much hope and as we moved through January and February we would often make jokes about the cataclysmic date that loomed in our future. We were trying hard not to believe in omens but, in retrospect, perhaps we should have.

Never mind, Fate was orchestrating a curve ball that would save us from the buzzards. The daggers, unfortunately, were not quite sheathed.

Dr. Hepler provided a strong, positive letter summarizing the UCLA findings and supporting Robert's medical use of marijuana, which he called a "special substance." Attention then turned to Robert's personal ophthalmologist Dr. Fine. Would he agree with the conclusions that Hepler had reached? In September 1975, just after our arrest, Dr. Fine had boldly committed himself to supporting the facts and, after looking over Hepler's notarized conclusions, Robert said the physician had the look of a man burdened by the receipt of what he had asked for. Discussion turned to preparation of a similar document for Fine, eliminating the sections on research and drawing a conclusion, based on Hepler's authorized research, in which Fine would agree to prescribe marijuana, if it were legal. Fine stalled and stalled and stalled. February was slipping away and our court date was fast approaching.

After considerable delay Paul offered to intervene. The result was unexpected. It was suggested another round of medical tests be conducted, this time with the highest possible doses of conventional medications. The site? Johns Hopkins University in nearby Baltimore.

Robert felt betrayed, stabbed in the back by both Paul and Fine. Who would pay, he asked? Fine said he would arrange for Hopkins to carry the cost and made it quite clear that without the Hopkins tests we would not have his support. How would we be able to conduct the tests and analyze the results before the trial date? Not to worry, said Paul. A request for continuance had already been filed.

It was the fatal blow. Robert was going to Baltimore. On the Ides of March, instead of Superior Court in Washington, D.C., Robert would be at Johns Hopkins University's Wilmer Eye Institute.

Robert's experience at the Wilmer Eye Institute was a low point in our still embryonic adventure. His experience at UCLA gave him an expectation of collegiality that was not present in Baltimore. To the Wilmer physicians Robert was a patient and patients do not participate, or for that matter even comment, on their own medical care.

He was subjected to a brutal round of medication administration. Every available conventional medication was administered at the highest possible dosage. It was a nightmare.

For five days I was "tested." Neither my eye pressures nor my relationship with the doctors improved. Johns Hopkins was not about me—it was, in fact, about lawyers and doctors, ophthalmologists in particular. I was at Johns Hopkins strictly for Dr. Fine. He desperately wanted something else to lower my eye pressures so that he would not have to testify on my behalf. He could not bring himself to believe that with all modern medicine had to offer it was a weed, a smoked weed, that was the key to my medical treatment. This simple fact went against everything Fine had been taught.

There were only two differences between Dr. Fine and the Hopkins residents: age and familiarity. Fine was probably twice the age of the Baltimore residents. More importantly he knew me, had treated me for more than three years. Our dealings were tempered by this fact. In the Hopkins residents I saw ophthalmologists in training and what I saw was a conspiracy of conservatism, a willingness to accept only what they were taught and nothing more. It was only in Hepler that I had seen the curiosity and drive for knowledge that separates practicing physicians from true caregivers and even in Hepler there was some waffling. In the course of my twenty-year adventure these observations would remain as steady and predictable as marijuana's ability to lower my eye pressure. Many ophthalmologists, unlike physicians who treat cancer, AIDS, pain or paralysis, have little if any interest in the unknown.

But Hopkins did have its rewards. It was at Johns Hopkins that I met my first glaucoma patient. In all the years with Fine I had never spoken with the other patients in the waiting room. Nor did I meet any patients at UCLA. At Chapel Hill I didn't stay long enough to even see another patient. At Johns Hopkins things were different.

The glaucoma patient Robert met was Vincent Mustachio, 53, a factory worker from West Virginia. He had come to Hopkins for his third glaucoma surgery. Mustachio had glaucoma in just one eye and it had responded to conventional treatment for nine years. Then things went haywire and his pressure became severely elevated. His doctor sent him to Wilmer Eye Institute for filtering, a surgical procedure in which a hole is poked in the eye to allow the aqueous fluid to escape and, hopefully, lower the pressure. In Vince, like many others, it had failed.

Now they would try, for the second time, a procedure called a freeze. Using an agent chilled to $-60°$ the chamber above the eye is frozen and, it is hoped, the ducts regulating the input of aqueous humor are numbed into inefficiency. If successful the resulting scar tissue will help curb the ability of the pressure to increase.

The first "freeze" was a failure and Vince's pressure elevated to 70 mm before they sent him back to Wilmer. This time they would use an agent chilled to $-80°$. Vince was not looking forward to it.

Robert peppered the man with questions about the procedures, genuinely fearful they would become a part of his own future. Vince was friendly and accommodating.

In the midst of this general conversation, Robert was astonished when Vince Mustachio began to tell him about the night at the factory when "a couple younger fellows asked me if I wanted to smoke some marijuana." Off they went to the parking lot.

"It was kinda interesting, that marijuana." Vince explained. "But, believe it or not, it reduced the pressure. Usually the pressure gets so bad at night that I wake up with a headache. The night I smoked marijuana I woke up feeling just fine."

I stared at the man on the bed across from me. I couldn't believe my ears. Not only was Vince the first person with glaucoma I had ever met but now he was explaining to me how helpful marijuana was.

"It was good for my glands too," Vince rubbed his crotch area. "Took away the swelling and pain. The pressure in my eyes only went away for maybe four, five hours. My glands, they felt better for a month!" Vince chuckled. "Prostate. You know," waving again at his crotch.

I gave a nod of understanding and leaned back on my bed in thought. I wasn't sure what to say. Vince indicated he had used marijuana even before the filtering procedure. He knew it lowered the pressure but he had surgery anyway.

"Vince, why didn't you keep on using the pot? Maybe you wouldn't have needed the surgery." It was a gentle probe.

There was a pause. "Don't like the high," Vince responded.

As I watched Vince in agony following the surgery I knew his explanation of disliking the "high" was not a complete answer. The euphoria that can accompany marijuana use could not be worse than the suffering this man endured. In the days following Vince's surgery I probed for a deeper reason and, with time, it emerged. Vince feared arrest and, most of all, he feared losing his job.

When the management at Vince's glass factory found out about his glaucoma Vince's job had been changed. After 27 years with the company, and five additional years at Pittsburgh Plate Glass, Vince Mustachio was told he "lacked experience and education" for advancement. Indeed, the company suddenly discovered Vince was unqualified for the job he had held for several years. His wage was reduced and his hours cut. Vince was hanging on for dear life. At home were two preteen children and a wife. The last thing Vince needed was a narcotics arrest or even a hint of wrongdoing.

So, Vince Mustachio was trapped in a world of ever-increasing medical problems brought on by the failure of prescribed medications and modern surgery. How differently would Vince have felt about marijuana's "high" if the doctor could have prescribed it for him? And how different would the outcome be? These question haunted Robert.

> *I remained at Hopkins for nearly six days. It was a dismal, depressing, sometimes brutal exercise in denial. It wasn't me that was in denial. It was the medical community. They brought out the big guns, leveled them straight at me, and missed every time. None of the conventional medications managed to lower my eye pressures to an acceptable range but they did manage to irritate my eye causing it to spasm and twitch. The drugs increased my urinary output, caused diarrhea, altered my concentration, induced nausea, caused sleeplessness, and blurred my vision. Despite all that, I can truly say Hopkins opened my eyes. I did not want to be like Vince but more importantly I did not want there to be other Vinces.*

In that long, barbarous week there was one ray of hope. It, too, came on the Ides of March although the seed had been planted nearly four years before in June 1972. Robert and I attended an anti-Vietnam War demonstration on Capitol Hill, just eight blocks from what would be our home three years later. We arrived as the festivities were winding down. The crowd had generally dispersed but a small group was still clustered on the stage, sitting Indian style in a huge circle, surrounding a radiant and resplendent Joan Baez, folk singer and activist. She was dressed in a brilliant white shirt and blue denim overalls. Her smile was dazzling and the aura about her was captivating.

As we approached the group the folks sitting nearest to Baez suddenly got on their feet and left. We quickly slid into their spot. I had my camera and began clicking away. One resulting picture captured Joan Baez and Robert, side by side.

Now, I am a great believer in "cosmic circles"—events or encounters that continually loop back on themselves to form the link in the chain of our lives.

Early in 1976, as it became clear that our legal case would become very expensive very fast, we talked about contacting musicians and rock stars for possible funding. I immediately remembered the picture of Baez and wrote her a letter, including a copy of the photo.

On March 15th as I rattled about our apartment, trying to adjust to Robert's absence, the phone rang. I was fully expecting to hear Robert's voice. Instead it was a woman asking if this was Alice O'Leary. When identity was confirmed the caller identified herself. "This is Joan Baez."

It can be safely said that I never expected this call. Dumbfounded, all I could muster was a contemporary but lame, "Far out!" It is a moment of inarticulateness that will haunt me forever. No doubt it was a reaction Joan Baez had encountered before.

After recovering from an in-artful beginning, I thanked the singer for her call, explaining I never anticipated such a personal response to my letter. The singer responded that my letter was "beautifully written" and asked "How is Robert?" She seemed genuinely concerned to hear he was hospitalized and promised a monetary contribution.

The conversation was brief. I explained we needed considerable financial and organizational assistance and Joan Baez suggested we try the Quakers or perhaps Amnesty International. I realized there was little more the woman could say. What could she possibly know about medical marijuana? Her call, with its explicit conveyance of support, was more help than any organization could do for us, at least at that point in time. After more pleasantries, she was gone.

A few days later we received a check for $100, which was immediately delivered to the lawyers. The money was a very small part of what we owed but the source was impressive. In fact, it would be the only contribution we ever received from the music industry until fifteen years later when David Geffen would support our work with AIDS patients.

On that cold March day, however, the world seemed brighter and warmer for just an instant because someone of stature had been touched by our story. For me it was an affirmation, a closing of a cosmic circle that signaled we were on the right path.* Each of us, in our own way, received an affirmation that week. Come hell, high water, or even the Ides of March, we were committed to our course. Neither of us ever looked back.

---

* Little did I know that the cosmic circle with Joan Baez was not yet closed. That would come 25 years later, as Robert lay dying in Florida.

7. LOOSE ENDS

With Hopkins behind us and the trial rescheduled, we settled down to the task of tying up loose ends.

The criminal case seemed well controlled. With UCLA and Hopkins we had secured the scientific evidence that supported Robert's claim of medical need. One remaining question was the troubling aspect of the charges against me. The lawyers clearly could build a case on Robert's behalf but what defense could Alice claim? It was agreed Robert could fall on the sword and swear the four plants were his and his alone but it was a perilous course and involved outright perjury. I did smoke. Without the benefit of a marriage certificate Robert and I could be compelled to testify against one another. It was a messy aspect of the case that would not be resolved until the trial itself.

Following the January meeting with Paul the case had become two separate actions. There was the criminal case and then the matter of ongoing, legal supplies of marijuana. Paul had run with my suggestion of asking the government for their marijuana and had chased down the various petitions, forms, codification, regulations, protocol demands, policy assessments, and procedural and administrative requirements needed for permission to use the government's marijuana. The early enthusiasm for demanding "Uncle Sam's pot" was quickly diminished by a growing mountain of legal work necessary to satisfy government demands.

While Robert languished at Hopkins, Paul made a call to the National Institute on Drug Abuse (NIDA) and found a sympathetic soul who led him to believe that all would be simple and quickly dispatched. Paul was assured NIDA would happily provide Robert Randall, that poor soul, with the marijuana he needed. Paul was elated and easily convinced. We wondered how anyone could be so naive. If NIDA was so willing to help, where had they been since December? The good folks at NIDA were well aware of the undeniable UCLA findings with respect to Robert's needs. Yet no one had offered assistance until the lawyer called with a vague insinuation of "legal petition." When a lawyer calls, offer to cooperate—Bureaucracy 101.

There is only one way the government will be moved to compassion. It involves public exposure and it is accomplished via The Media. As early as September 1975, Robert had realized media attention would offer personal protection, the modern day equivalent of seeking sanctuary in the church. But the timing was critical. Too much exposure prior to the trial would burn out the circuits and reveal strategies too soon. So we waited for the proper moment, continually rethought the options, and trusted the Fates.

Fate, it seemed, was an accommodating partner to the tale. In late February, just two weeks before the soon-to-be-postponed court date on the Ides of March, we received a call from Karen Spadacene, an old college friend then working at the Washington office of the Australian Broadcasting Commission (ABC). Karen wondered if Robert would have any interest in meeting with Jeffrey McMullen, a rising young star of the government-financed television network. McMullen was doing a story on the release of the *5th Annual Report on Marihuana and Health*, the report Phyllis Lessin had promised to send some months before.

The report was released in early February with some fanfare. The director of NIDA, Robert DuPont, held a press conference to announce marijuana didn't seem as bad as everyone thought and it seemed to have some interesting medicinal properties. This bombshell was big news in a town still reeling from the candid comments of First Lady Betty Ford who acknowledged that all of her children had probably smoked pot and she would have tried it herself if it had been widely used when she was a teenager.

McMullen came to Washington from his New York office to tape a segment called "The American Way" for the Australian version of "60 Minutes," a show called "Weekend Magazine." He had already decided to focus the story on the health and medical aspects of marijuana and had arranged for an interview with Dupont. After listening to Karen's retelling of our story, he realized he had serendipitously found the "human" angle to the story—someone battling the government to get a medically needed but legally prohibited drug. It was a perfect match.

On March 4, 1976, Robert met Jeff McMullen at a nearby gift shop where they filmed Robert-buys-rolling-papers and Robert-walks-in-his-neighborhood shots. Then they settled down in a nearby park, across the street from Washington Police Precinct #1, to film a few questions. It was all over very quickly and Robert's first filmed interview was "in the can."

The ABC interview was perfect. It gave Robert an initial taste for the power of his story. We could see the effect it had on the film crew, Robert could sense the power in Jeffrey's questions. The fact that it would be telecast halfway around the world was okay too. It wasn't time for local or national coverage of Robert's story. There were still some loose ends to tie.

Chief among them was Dr. Fine. Robert was fiercely loyal to the ophthalmologist and felt he had benefited from the physician's steady, conservative approach to care during the previous three years. But those same qualities were now becoming a roadblock.

The primary issue in the spring of 1976 was the doctor's refusal to acknowledge the UCLA results and the utter failure of the doctors at Johns Hopkins. After the Hopkins fiasco Fine prepared a legal statement that would be submitted to the government and the Court. The last line stated that surgery was the last alternative for controlling Robert's intraocular pressure. Robert tried to control his temper as he read the document.

> "Well, Dr. Fine, it seems okay except for this last line. You say surgery is the last alternative available which can control my intraocular pressures. I don't really like the impression that leaves. After all, the UCLA tests show there is another alternative."
>
> The doctor squirmed a bit. "Well, young man, you have declined surgery."
>
> My exasperated glance made Ben Fine squirm even more. From our first meeting, long before the ophthalmologist heard of my use of marijuana, Fine had emphasized his dislike of surgery as long as medications could control the pressures.

> *Seeking some retort, Fine snatched a piece of paper from the desk "And, of course, the conclusion at Johns Hopkins is the same." The physician handed me the letter from Gary Diamond, pointing specifically to the last page, "it is our conclusion that maximal medical therapy ... was not successful in controlling Mr. Randall's pressures."*
>
> *This time my glance was withering. I was annoyed with Fine's efforts to split hairs. "But there is another medicine."*
>
> *"Oh, well, yes there is your 'special substance.' "*
>
> *I sincerely wished that ophthalmologists could learn to say marijuana.*

It was an awkward and uncomfortable meeting. Robert left Fine's office with a promise that the doctor "would work on" the affidavit. Fine did work very hard but not very fast. He would drag his feet and delay until well past any reasonable point of expectation. Our trial date, scheduled for May 7, would be postponed for a second time because of Fine's inability to state the obvious and sign on the bottom line. He would occupy innumerable hours of time in those few weeks between the first of April and the first of May all over a simple statement of facts: yes, I treated Robert Randall, nothing worked until he went to UCLA, based on those findings marijuana might be worth looking into. Simple. So simple it made our heads spin.

Finally, on May 10th, Dr. Fine signed the much-needed affidavit. After weeks of wrangling with Fine and foot-dragging by Paul, Robert drafted a three-page statement for Fine that incorporated the fundamental points. How innocuous that document seems today.

Meanwhile Paul had managed to carve out a petition to the federal government seeking permission to use marijuana in the treatment of Robert's glaucoma. It was far from perfect and only added to the loose ends but it was filed May 21, 1976. Eight weeks later we would be in Court.

8. TRIALS AND NEGOTIATIONS

As we slid into July 1976 the whirl of activity surrounding our case was reaching cyclonic proportions. On a day in early June, as we waited for the photographer from *The Washington Post*, Robert turned to me and said, "These are the last quiet moments of our lives." The building cacophony was certainly indicating that he might be right.

Robert's handling of the media was the key to our success in moving the issue beyond Robert's individual need for a specific medication to a national debate about the medical use of marijuana. A carefully timed article in *The Washington Post*, which appeared on June 8, led to interviews with all the major TV stations in Washington and follow-up stories by United Press International (UPI) and a smattering of smaller outlets. The stage was set. Trial was set for July 16.

At the start of the day it seemed everything had come together beautifully. The court date was sandwiched in between the closing of the Democratic Convention in New York and the opening of the Summer Olympics in Montreal. Hepler had agreed to testify and, with Keith Stroup's help, funds had been procured from The Playboy Foundation to cover the cost of the airline ticket, hotel room, and expert witness fees. As we arrived at the court building in the early morning we were greeted by Jim McManus of CBS news, complete with film crew, sound crew, and courtroom artist. Metromedia News arrived slightly later. Yes, it was going beautifully, we thought.

But six hours later things weren't as rosy. It was 4 p.m. Jim McManus was nervous. The deadline for feeding transmission to New York was close at hand. From across the hall Robert and I watched as McManus sent a sound technician off to make a phone call. It had been a long, long day of going nowhere.

The technician returned shortly and advised McManus, quite loudly, that New York was intrigued. "Stay as late as necessary and feed whatever possible." Robert and I heaved a sigh of relief.

All day we had waited for the District of Columbia court system to find a courtroom and a judge. The case had been given priority status because of the presence of an out-of-state expert witness, Dr. Robert Hepler of UCLA. But "priority" seemed to mean nothing to the slow-moving wheels of the D.C. judicial system.

The first half of the day had been pleasant. McManus regaled the small group with talk about his years at the Nixon White House. The artist, Aggie Whelan, told some fascinating tales about the trial of Nixon's Attorney General, John Mitchell. Everyone wanted to know about Robert's experiences with the federal government's marijuana at UCLA.

But as the hours dragged on everyone grew weary. There had been endless hours, it seemed, of frustrated silence.

At 4:15 John Karr, our lawyer, emerged from the clerk's office, beaming from ear to ear. The time and place had been set: Monday morning, July 19, at 10 a.m.

CBS and Metromedia gathered their gear and headed down the hall. Robert, John, Paul, and I piled into my aging VW and set off to the offices of Karr and Graves, where Hepler had patiently waited all day. John had planned to summon the doctor as soon as a court had been assigned rather than force the ophthalmologist to wait around in the corridors. Now it would be Monday before Hepler testified.

"We'll head over to the Lawyer's Club for drinks and dinner," John announced "Paul, make sure Hepler's reservation can be extended at the hotel."

"He won't be able to stay, John." Robert uttered the words not as a warning but simply as a statement of fact. Paul agreed. Hepler had mentioned a tight schedule, an ailing wife, and four small children. John lapsed into a sulky silence.

When Hepler confirmed the inability to stay John swung into action, picked up the phone and called the judge who was scheduled to hear the case on Monday. Pleasantries, explanations, and then the Big News. "Well, Judge Washington, the only solution I can see is a deposition. Uh-huh, yes sir. All right. Thank you."

It was 4:45 p.m. on a Friday afternoon in mid-July. We could not believe John had pulled this off yet soon we were back in the VW heading across town to The Old Pension Building, a monstrous brick structure on the edge of Washington's newly opened Judiciary Square subway stop. Built in the 1870s to service Civil War veterans, the Pension Building is a cavernous arena where the maimed and mangled had once collected their country's tribute. Taken over by the District of Columbia, it had been configured into smallish courtrooms and other administrative offices.

The VW pulled up to the curb. No cameras, no sketch artists, no reporters greeted us. Hustling along the sidewalk, we worked hard to keep up with John Karr who, unhesitatingly, made his way to Courtroom 38, presided over by Judge James A. Washington. We were the first to arrive.

The courtroom came to life in fits and starts. Courtroom reporters, delighted with overtime, arrived quickly and would pack slowly when the procedure was done. A bailiff sulked in and looked at us with disdain. Overtime was not enough to pay for the inconvenience of this session.

The prosecutor and assistant arrived. A surprisingly young and angular man in a plaid suit, the prosecutor placed his briefcase on the communal table and extended his hand, "Richard Stolker," he said with a smile. I recoiled from the man but Robert firmly shook his hand.

It was 5:30 p.m. when the judge arrived. "What purpose has brought us together at this late hour, Mr. Karr?" John explained the need for a deposition and Stolker objected. "Depositions are taken only for the convenience of someone at a distance from the court." The attorney argued. "Dr. Hepler was here. If he was not willing to stay then the judge could issue a court order compelling the physician to remain in town until Monday."

For ninety minutes the attorneys argued back and forth. Judge Washington seemed determined to let the prosecutor run through his full range of arguments. Finally, at 7 p.m. the judge had heard enough. The doctor was here. The defendants had requested priority several days before the trial date and it had not been heeded. The State was at fault. Hepler should not be further burdened by the State. The deposition would proceed.

Shortly thereafter, Hepler took the stand. John began with the foundation questions. How long at UCLA? Nine years as a full professor. And what awards and citations? The question completely stymied the doctor. You could almost see Hepler trying to recall a citation from the Lion's Club or perhaps an award from the Eagle Scouts. Hepler replied that he had none.

John then proceeded to mismatch the date of Hepler's research by five years, placing its beginning in 1975. Hepler, tired and tense after a long day, could not find a way to set it right. Paul began to scribble in large block letters on a legal pad. Robert was doing the same. I reached across the table for the *1975 Marihuana and Health Report*, opened it to the page describing Hepler's research and held it out to John.

The flurry of activity at the defense table prompted a sense in John that something wasn't quite right but he remained as smooth as silk and proved quick on his feet.

"Dr. Hepler, is the report mentioned in this government publication a report you published?"

The assistant to Richard Stolker caught her breath and leaned into the prosecutor. "He is the one," she whispered loudly, "He's the same H-E-P-L-E-R!!"

Robert shot me a look and we almost laughed aloud. Hepler's name had been a matter of public record in the case papers for some weeks and the prosecution had to wait for this moment to figure out if he was the H-E-P-L-E-R. There could be hope after all.

For the next hour things went smoothly. John led Hepler through the definition of glaucoma, an explanation of IOP, a brief review of Hepler's research, how Robert had first contacted the doctor, and what the tests at UCLA revealed. The testimony was compelling and well presented.

At 8:00, the judge called a short recess. We wandered into the cavernous center hall. The day's fading light was still visible outside. A gentle rain was falling. It was a quiet moment after a long day, a day not yet over.

The prosecutor was green and began his cross-examination with a curve ball. "Are you a forensic chemist, Dr. Hepler?"

Clearly confused, Hepler acknowledged that he was not.

"If you are not a forensic chemist, how can you tell us about marijuana?" The silence in the courtroom went well beyond the normal silence one would expect during a trial. There was a stunned quality among all that watched. Even Stolker's assistant seemed a bit green about the gills. Hepler could find no answer.

Feeling his oats and mistakenly thinking he somehow had the good doctor on the ropes, the prosecutor moved on.

"Where do you get your marijuana from, Dr. Hepler?" The voice was shaded in suspicion.

"The government."

"Which government?!" It was more a demand than a question. "Are you authorized to conduct this research, Dr. Hepler?"

"Mr. Stolker!" It was Judge Washington. "This line of questioning seems a bit extreme. We have already seen that Dr. Hepler's research has been published in the official reports of the Department of Health, Education and Welfare. It strikes me as highly improbable that such an agency of the government would accept and publish the findings of a scientist who was not fully authorized to proceed with such research. Unless you have clear evidence to the contrary I suggest you accept Dr. Hepler as an expert witness and proceed with a line of questioning more germane to the case."

Humbled but not bowed the prosecutor bumbled his way through an embarrassing display of cross-examination for almost two hours. The clock was nearing 10 when he finished lamely, "Do you know marijuana can cause chromosomal damage, Dr. Hepler?"

"No. I know there is some evidence to suggest that but it has certainly not been proven."

The state, thankfully, rested.

John Karr rose with two final questions. Playing off the tenor of Stolker's last question John asked, "Do you know marijuana lowers intraocular pressure, Dr. Hepler?"

Hepler understood and took the bait well. "Yes, absolutely. The evidence proves incontrovertibly that marijuana consistently lowers the intraocular eye pressure in humans."

"Would you prescribe marijuana for Mr. Randall if it were legal?"

"Yes."

It was over. With one final bit of formality Judge Washington looked squarely at Robert and me. "Be in court at 10 a.m. on Monday morning or forfeit your constitutional rights, face issuance of a bench warrant, and loss of bail."

As we recovered during the weekend the first "feature" article on Robert's case was released in *The National Observer*, a now defunct newsweekly. *The National Observer* was a combination of breaking news stories and analysis. Robert's story was the lead, prominently featured above the fold and headlined "Pot Could Save His Sight." A large photo accompanied the article.

The *National Observer* piece was terrifically sympathetic. Not a single government official would be quoted by name but the reporter, Daniel St.Alban-Greene, succinctly summarized the prevailing attitude of the moment: the government might allow Randall to use marijuana but only in his doctor's office. Robert's response to that proposed solution was to threaten a lawsuit.

Greene also neatly captured the real problem with Robert's request:

> Yet there is a broader issue involved here, as Randall well knows: his initiative—if successful—could be a long step toward legalizing marijuana—first for therapy, eventually for unrestricted use.

> Obviously I have a very high stake in getting access to marijuana," he reflects, in his verdant, second-floor living room. "At the same time, I'm totally cognizant of the broader implications. I'd be happy if other people with glaucoma would petition the government, too, or at least make their views known.

> It's time for marijuana to be discussed rationally.

The die was cast. Dan Greene's article was the first to link the question of legalization with medical use but it would not be the last. The link was anticipated but in that summer of 1976 it was not the foremost thought in our minds. As Robert succinctly noted:

> The big problem is getting people to understand without my becoming either a pathetic figure or a hero. I'm neither. I'm simply a human being placed in this odd situation because of a convoluted law.

On July 19th we gathered again in courtroom 38. The morning was droning on as prosecutor Richard Stolker presented the case of *U.S. v. Randall/O'Leary*. The arresting officer, Patrick Mooney, was first on the stand. He managed to "misstate" numerous "facts" about the location of the plants and the layout of the apartment. Among the items he admitted into evidence were several over-exposed photographs of mail arranged on a table in the living room. These constituted "evidence" of who lived at the apartment. No one seemed to care that the overexposure rendered it unreadable.

Mooney was followed by another detective and then a Forensic Chemist from the DEA, David C. Noll. Next up was Lesley Ray Brett, a narcotics detective for the D.C. police. Incredibly it seemed that Stolker was going to use Brett to counter Hepler's testimony. He moved through a series of questions designed to have Brett declared an expert witness. He then turned the detective over to John Karr for cross-examination.

Under cross-examination it seemed Detective Brett had not read any scientific books or articles, relying instead on the popular press and the DEA for "that kind of information."

In a masterstroke of judicial interpretation, Judge Washington allowed Brett as an expert but not a medical expert. Hepler's testimony, for the moment, was unchallenged.

Next on the stand was Margot Kelly, our landlady. Margot was not pleased to be called as a witness. Born in Germany she emigrated after the war and was happily building a real estate empire in Washington, D.C. Margot had no desire to deal with authorities any higher in the government than the appraisal office.

Margot Kelly looked nervous as Stolker approached her like a snake oil salesman. Oozing pseudo-charm he first established that she owned the property and then asked Margot who lived at 709-A 8th St. SE on August 23, 1975?

"Mr. Randall and Ms. O'Brien."

Stolker automatically moved to correct the woman, "You mean Ms. O'Leary?"

"Objection!" John said the word so forcefully that it startled Robert and me, who were giggling at Margot's frequent error. The woman had never bothered to properly learn my name and, after more than two years, we had given up trying to correct her.

"The prosecutor is leading the witness, your honor."

"Sustained."

Stolker was flustered. Margot was clearly confused. At the defense table John momentarily beamed at Paul. Robert and I were befuddled.

I leaned into John and whispered, "John, she always gets my name wrong." John dismissed me with a wave of the hand that was sharp and clearly said, "Shut up."

Stolker backtracked and asked Margot if the occupants of 709-A 8th St. SE were in the courtroom. When she acknowledged they were, he had the woman point them out and verbally instructed the record to show that Mrs. Kelly had pointed to Robert and I.

He then asked Margot if there was a lease for the apartment. "Of course," Margot responded, a bit indignantly. "Do you have a copy of that lease?"

Margot nodded and opened her purse. Large and white, it was a constant feature of Margot's appearance. We had often wondered what it contained and now we would learn. We watched in fascination as papers and keys emerged from the seemingly endless depths of that purse.

At last she produced the lease. Stolker asked her to read the names on the lease. "Robert Randall and Richard Talcott."

Robert and Richard had leased the apartment in 1973 but Richard had moved to New York six months later and Robert had asked me to share his life and apartment. It never occurred to us to change the lease. Stolker blanched. "Talcott? Who is Mr. Talcott?"

"Objection."

"Sustained."

Stolker looked done in. "Your witness."

"I have no questions, your honor."

"You may step down, Mrs. Kelly."

Margot was barely off the stand when John leapt to his feet. "Your honor, I move that the case against my client, Alice M. O'Leary, be dismissed. The government has failed to prove she resided on the premises in question."

We were stunned but no more so than Richard Stolker. A brief argument ensued. Stolker pointed to the pictures of mail. Unreadable, noted John. Furthermore, Ms. O'Leary's name was not on the lease and the landlady stated a Ms. O'Brien lived there.

"Your honor," John concluded seriously but with a wicked glint in his eye, "For all we know, Mr. Randall may have a fetish for Irish women. That is certainly no crime."

Stolker was not amused. "Your Honor, Mrs. Kelly," he seemed to choke at the Irish name, "Mrs. Kelly visually identified Ms. O'Leary as living with Mr. Randall."

John quickly countered, "Your honor, that is not adequate proof of a crime." His Honor agreed. With a few words and a quiet tap of the gavel I was free to go. "We will take a ten-minute recess." It happened so fast we could barely react. We had worried for months about my defense and now, in an instant, I was free. John was ecstatic and looked like a ballplayer who had put one out of the park. Even the judge seemed pleased as he gave his gavel a genteel tap and smiled in our direction.

I was removed from harm's way and now it was full steam ahead with Robert's defense—not guilty of possession of marijuana by reason of medical necessity. That was the goal, pure and simple.

The trial was delayed for two days while attorneys prepared written arguments about the admissibility of Hepler's deposition.

The trial resumed on July 22 when testimony was taken from Dr. Fine, Judge Washington ruled that Hepler's deposition could be used, Robert testified, and the closing arguments were given. Stolker's ability to stun the assembled spectators continued well into his closing argument when he railed against the "smokescreen of medical testimony," rhetorically asked if "the known risks of surgery are worst than the unknown," and concluded that "treason is a victimless crime."

John focused on the facts. Robert Randall incontrovertibly had glaucoma, which was not controlled by available medications. Two ophthalmologists indicated they would prescribe marijuana if it were legally available. Government-sanctioned tests had shown that marijuana did indeed lower the intraocular pressure of Mr. Randall to within the safe range. If Mr. Randall did not use marijuana, did not break the law, he would go blind. It was, John said, an act of necessity. He reached deep into the legal foundations of our system, to the English Common Law and the Magna Carta. He spoke of the legal tenet of "necessity," those rare instances in which one must break the law because to do otherwise would bring greater harm upon the individual than the law itself was striving to prevent.

Judge Washington listened intently. We would later learn he was the former Dean of Law at Howard University. This was not an average case and, through the mysterious workings of fate, we had not drawn an average judge. The argument intrigued him but his questions gave little clue as to his leanings. He was a careful, measured man, who gave great weight to each side.

Finally all the words had been spoken and the trial was over. Judge Washington said he would consider the case over the weekend. Court dismissed. Now we waited.

The case got wide media coverage. Jim McManus had reappeared on Monday, July 19th. Film was fed to New York and we appeared on the *CBS Evening News* with Walter Cronkite. McManus' report was straightforward, well done, and handsomely embellished with sketches by Aggie Whelan. Cronkite, of course, made no comment on the case but the sheer fact that he had selected it gave the situation some weight. The mantle of credibility which Walter Cronkite could bestow was a testament to a medium—television—that was still young in 1976.

The "weekend" would stretch on for weeks and we could only wait for Judge Washington to render the decision. There was more press coverage as Dan Greene's article was reprinted in several major newspapers, most notably on the front page of *The Chicago Tribune* on August 1, 1976, just under the banner with huge letters "He Smokes Pot—to Save Eyesight."

It was getting very interesting.

As we waited for Judge Washington to render his decision our focus shifted to the petition filed with the federal seeking legal access to marijuana for treatment of Robert's glaucoma.

The system of drug control—which was a triumvirate of the National Institute on Drug Abuse (NIDA), the Food and Drug Administration (FDA) and the Drug Enforcement Administration (DEA)—never anticipated a request from a lone individual who had clearly demonstrated his need for marijuana. There was no program in place to accommodate such a request and during the summer of 1976 the three agencies spent many hours attempting to resolve "the Randall problem."

Phyllis Lessin, whom Robert had first contacted in September 1975, became his primary contact during the long weeks of negotiating an answer to the petition. It certainly wasn't in her job description to assist patients seeking medical access to a Schedule I drug, but that was the problem—it wasn't in anyone's job description. In the summer of 1976 the federal agencies were improvising and since no one knew what to do we were able to accomplish a lot.

Robert visited Phyllis at her office in the Parklawn Building in mid-August of 1976. NIDA had a proposal: to establish a quasi-research program that could receive supplies of marijuana and then distribute them to Robert. It was the barest skeleton of a solution but before any further progress could be made it was imperative to find an ophthalmologist willing to be the "researcher." Robert's personal ophthalmologist, Ben Fine, had said he would "rather not." Robert and Phyllis had spent many hours contacting nearly every ophthalmologist in Washington, D.C. No one was interested.

In the August meeting Phyllis was blunt. Robert had to bring pressure to bear on Dr. Fine. "He's your best bet," she argued "He knows your case and he's a reasonable man."

Robert was sure it wouldn't work. "Phyllis, Dr. Fine has no interest in becoming a researcher for FDA and NIDA. He's made that very clear."

The young bureaucrat was quick with her reply, "But he doesn't have to be a researcher in the pure sense. That's the beauty of the special 'Compassionate Exemption.' " Phyllis and NIDA had a new angle. The agency would develop and hold the research license, minimizing the amount of paperwork the ophthalmologist would be forced to file. "Fine can treat you just as he always did but once a year he would need to file a report with the FDA outlining your situation. Nothing more than what he's doing already but with a copy to us. It's perfect."

It was perfect—too perfect. NIDA and FDA were doing the best they could to resolve the issue and punt the problem on to someone else, the "researcher." Robert knew what the intent was and he knew his doctor. "But Fine won't want to handle the stuff." he protested. "The DEA says he'd need a 750-lb. safe in his office to store the marijuana. Fine won't do that."

Phyllis was remarkably persistent. "Look, we can take care of that problem if Fine really objects. We can find a local pharmacy, maybe something at NIH." The young woman began to wander, thinking aloud.

Robert was not convinced. "I don't know, Phyllis. I'm still worried about the DEA. They could make Fine's life hell."

Phyllis leaned towards him and lowered her voice. "You don't have to worry," she murmured, "You even have people there working for you. It really is an amazing thing."

Robert was in awe and would later write:

It was a bureaucratic seduction scene. The temptress and the tempted. I wanted to believe the young woman but something gnawed at me, something wouldn't let me believe the friendly gesture.

Phyllis pressed on, explaining that a true evolution in government policy was at hand. If I could convince Fine to act as the physician and file the protocol, an entirely new precedent would be established. "That's the best part, Bob. Other doctors will be able to use this special exemption and the prototype we're developing allows for up to 50 patients per doctor."

It was an intriguing idea, one that appealed to me. The press coverage was prompting letters and phone calls from all around the country. I was already hearing from other patients who medically needed marijuana. Maybe the notion of helping so many others would appeal to Fine as well.

How young and naïve we were but no more so than the bureaucrats in NIDA and FDA who wanted to make this thing work. It was 1976, a time of hope and openness. To cite a cliché, we had been to the moon...surely we could get marijuana to a young man who would go blind without it. Right?

9. DEUS EX MACHINA

Phyllis Lessin worked very hard to craft a solution and by early September Dr. Fine had agreed to her proposal that NIDA would act as the primary researcher and the doctor would report his findings on an annual basis to the federal agency.

On September 7, 1976 it all began to unravel. When Robert called to "check on things" he could tell there were many people in Phyllis' office and her tone was tense.

"Look, I know we've worked hard to get Fine on line," the young woman began, "but it isn't going to work. The folks at the upper level here have vetoed the idea of NIDA holding the research license with Fine acting as the researcher. He has to sign an Investigational New Drug (IND) application."

Robert couldn't believe it. In the intervening weeks since he and Phyllis met in August, he had been in awe as the pieces seemed to come together and Fine agreed to help. Everything was set. Now this.

"But he won't agree Phyllis, you know that. No one in town will." Robert was angry. "We've been through every ophthalmologist in Washington. There's no one. Does anyone there understand I'm running out of time?"

Robert had been without marijuana for more than a week. The tricolored haloes and white-outs were coming with great regularity and he had begun to wonder if it wasn't the government's plan to force him into surgery.

"We know your situation, Bob." The agitation was extreme on both ends of the link. "You've made it very clear."

Phyllis was tired of Robert's insinuations that she didn't understand his situation. From her perspective he clearly didn't understand hers. She had worked hard to resolve this, had spent the entire morning on the carpet taking a lot of heat for her perceived actions "beyond the scope of NIDA's mandate." She had even offered to resign but the upper level management at NIDA would not accept her resignation.

As she relayed all of this to Robert he softened. It wasn't good to attack your friends.

"Is negotiation over NIDA's position in this matter possible?" Phyllis conveyed the question to the mysterious voices in her office. There was indecipherable murmuring. "Maybe, but we're trying some other tracks. A number of us are meeting at NEI tomorrow to discuss the future of other requests such as this." It pleased Robert to hear they anticipated more requests but he held little hope for NEI. Phyllis continued, "NIDA has got to observe its Congressional mandate in this area. We cannot extend into therapeutic evaluation."

"Phyllis," Robert began softly, "it is unwise for me to delay in moving toward medical control of my situation."

The NIDA bureaucrat understood what he was saying. Without some positive action by the federal government to release supplies of marijuana he was looking at a very risky surgical procedure, one that would likely blind him. Phyllis knew how tenuous his sight was. But there was little more that she could do.

The sense of tension lifted. "Yes, I… we understand that. We are moving with some speed . . ."

"Phyllis, is NIDA flexible at this point?" Robert pressed once more. He needed to know if the avenue was closed or merely blocked.

"Look, the decision came from us …from very high up. But it has been a confusing day. I think there is some flexibility at policy level. Especially if NEI can enter at a future date and relieve NIDA of the administrative responsibilities."

"Would congressional intervention help?" Robert had been working with an aide in Senator Jacob Javits office. Perhaps a call from Senator Javits' office might be persuasive.

There was more murmuring from Phyllis' office guests. "No, at least not today. Maybe tomorrow. It's good you informed us such a thing might happen. We will pass the information along."

"Phyllis, I won't allow this to go on much longer." Robert realized his words were close to a threat but he felt certain the young woman understood it was not aimed at her personally.

Still awaiting the decision from Judge Washington and weary to the bone from waiting for government action on the petition, Robert was quite sincere. Things had to be resolved.

"I understand, Bob. Hold back another day or two while the dust settles a bit here. I'll call you tomorrow."

It was a moment of darkest despair for Robert:

For a moment I felt queasy and cursed myself for allowing the feelings of hope to build in the last few weeks. I should have known it was too good to be true. They were going to blind me. They were going to win.

I picked up the phone and called Paul but the attorney had little to say. John Karr was on vacation and Paul couldn't possibly take any action while John was away. "What you're talking about, Bobby, a civil suit, would be major bucks. How are you going to pay for that?"

I hung up the phone and stared straight ahead.

So close ... We were so close ...

I called Alice to relay the news. Her disappointment and concern was a welcome salve against a brutal day but it didn't alter the situation. "I'll see you in a couple of hours. I'll make some more calls. Maybe I can find some medicine." She was gone and I was alone again. I wondered how Alice would pay for whatever medicine– marijuana–she might be able to find. The rent had depleted the bank account. The lawyers were harping about cash. Fine and several other doctors were owed for visits. Even Johns Hopkins had been calling–the promised arrangement to pay for my week at the Baltimore facility appeared to have fallen through and collection agencies were being mentioned. How much longer could we keep this going?

In the ancient Greek and Roman theater there was a device employed called *deus ex machina*—literally "the machine of the gods." Arriving on some form of stage machinery, either as a cloud from above the stage or, more likely, as a chariot from the wings, a deity would arrive to intervene in the action or neatly resolve a complex story line. Robert couldn't know it but his *deus ex machina* was about to enter the plot and its conveyance would be a ringing telephone. It was Phyllis.

"I hope this excites you as much as it does me." Phyllis said. Her fatigue from earlier in the day was gone. She seemed genuinely thrilled.

"I called NEI and one of the folks over there told me about a new research application for marijuana and glaucoma. It's just been received so it's a bit behind yours but we can speed things along and I've talked with the doctor. He's willing to sign onto your request and treat you. It's unbelievable!"

The young woman was talking very fast and Robert—shaking off his despair—was having a hard time understanding why she was so excited. "Phyllis, I'll be honest with you. I can't afford to move somewhere else for eye care."

Phyllis stopped him in mid-sentence. "Bob, you don't have to move. The doctor is at Howard University. You know, up there on Georgia Avenue?"

He couldn't believe it. "Phyllis, are you saying you've found a doctor in Washington who is willing to treat me and prescribe marijuana?!"

A giggle slipped from the other end of the line. "Uh huh. He's waiting for your call now. His name is John Merritt."

Dr. John Merritt was Robert's *deus ex machina*. The two men met the next day, September 8, 1976, and connected easily. Merritt answered all Robert's questions, and when he asked if he was asking too many the young doctor responded, "No, glaucoma is so unknown. The only way to learn is to listen." In Robert's journey through the ophthalmology world there had only been one other doctor who had said such a sensible thing, Robert Hepler.

By Friday, September 10, Phyllis Lessin had John Merritt's signature on the IND she had originally prepared for Fine and NIDA. It was her crowning achievement and her last act of kindness on Robert's behalf. NIDA removed her from the case that afternoon and forbade her from participating in any future inquiries of a therapeutic nature.

Throughout the country the story of "Man asks for pot to save sight" was rippling across newspapers. The cat was out of the bag. Marijuana's medical use was no longer an abstraction buried in some dull governmental report. A real person was asking permission to use the illegal stuff and others with similar ailments were paying close attention. They were wondering if marijuana could help Uncle Harry's vision or Cousin Sue's chemotherapy. And they were calling the agencies, just as Robert had. NIDA was nervous, the whole of the federal drug establishment was nervous.

The removal of Phyllis didn't change any of this but it was the first step towards reestablishing the stonewall of silence, the initial effort to regain control.

Not surprisingly the matter would drag on for several more weeks. By late September all was signed and sealed. The marijuana, Merritt told Robert, was in transit, arriving any day now via the U.S. Mail. This point was most remarkable. After months of jumping through hoops and hurdles to obtain this "dangerous" Schedule I drug, after Merritt was forced to purchase a 250-lb. safe to securely store the "dangerous" substance, the "dangerous" drug would arrive by parcel post.

It all seemed terribly anti-climatic. But, that was, of course, an illusion.

On October 5, seeking to get ahead of the story and gain the upper-hand, the government released the news of Merrit's IND program at Howard University to UPI. The story spread like wildfire across the country and portrayed the government in a very favorable light.

> Acting on the appeal of a man who claims he needs marijuana to keep from going blind, federal drug regulation agencies have approved human clinical tests of "pot" for the treatment of glaucoma, government spokesmen said today.
>
> The unusual "compassionate" approval for closely controlled studies by a Howard University professor may involve up to 50 patients, who either will be given marijuana capsules or be allowed to smoke "pot" to relieve pressure within the eyeball.
>
> For now, however, the study has only one patient, Robert Randall, 28, who is fighting a criminal marijuana charge in a court case here.

The story went on to provide some background on glaucoma and Robert's tests at UCLA and Hopkins. It also sang the praises of government agencies cooperating together. "It was a compassionate get-together. We responded to Randall's appeal and to his doctor's appeal."

As the weight of the now publicly confirmed IND settled across America's consciousness the very practical aspects of supply—where and how—began to command attention. Where would the government's marijuana be stored and how would Robert access it? This point would become the stickiest and nastiest of all.

Robert's intentions were clear. He wanted to receive marijuana like any other drug, by prescription from a pharmacy. In the weeks of wrangling over the petition and the eventual IND, this point was constantly shuffled to the background. Whenever Robert would raise the issue he was instructed not to worry about it.

But now it had to be worried about and the DEA, the federal agency most concerned with the drug's security, became the principal actor in the evolving drama. They had already forced Dr. Merritt to purchase a 250-lb. safe that was bolted, from the inside, to the floor of his office. Here Merritt would store the supplies of marijuana used by the other patients in the research program.

Robert's case was different. From the initial filing of the petition the intent had been to obtain marijuana for use as a conventional medication. Now, as the IND was approved, the hour of reckoning was at hand.

Initial alarms had been raised by Ed Tocus of the FDA when he told Dan Greene in July that take-home supplies of the drug would never be allowed. Permanent hospitalization was discussed but quickly dropped when the obvious stupidity of such a suggestion was echoed back to the government officials who raised it.

The next scenario had Robert reporting to Howard University whenever his intraocular pressure needed control. The tests from UCLA had clearly demonstrated his need for ten marijuana cigarettes a day, most of them in the evening hours. The prospect of traveling to Howard ten times a day was as laughable as lifetime hospitalization. The DEA then proposed that Robert purchase a safe in which to store the marijuana. To demonstrate the extent of their flexibility he was offered two options: a 750-lb. freestanding safe or the sportier model chosen by Merritt, 250 lbs. bolted to the floor from the inside.

Robert made several points: 1) either model involved a considerable expense of money, 2) our landlady would probably not appreciate the damage that could be caused by installing either of the models, and 3) the only time marijuana had ever been stolen from us was when the police busted us in August 1975.

The final gambit was played during an emotional conversation with Phyllis on the day the UPI story appeared. It was unknown who released the story but Phyllis clearly blamed Robert and the months of constant pressure finally made the young woman explode in anger accusing Robert of being ungrateful and jeopardizing the program just to "save the world."

"And there's another thing," the tone of the introduction made Robert brace himself for the onslaught. "You'd better back off this idea of taking the marijuana home. The DEA and FDA have already agreed you can only be allowed to take home supplies if you agree to complete silence about it. No one must know ...for your own security."

The gauntlet was cast. Robert could have the marijuana he medically needed but he must shut up, not tell a soul, keep quiet —"for [his] own security."

Robert sought the advice of others about this latest offer from the feds. Several friends counseled him to take the marijuana in whatever way he could get it. Some said the government had the upper hand and was "looking pretty good." To refuse the offer and attempt to regain momentum via the media could jeopardize the entire arrangement.

The lawyers argued for patience and their suggested tack was reinforced by a new friend, Creighton Burns. Creighton was the reporter for *The Age* of Melbourne, Australia and I had been working as his research associate for more than a year. He had become an ad hoc advisor to our endeavors.

Creighton loved politics and saw, from the first, that this was predominantly a political question. His assessment was pragmatic and honed from years of political observation around the globe. With the wisdom of one who is comfortably detached, Creighton observed that the bureaucrats were "acting just fine" and noted he would "fire a damn bureaucrat that didn't make this difficult for you. They hire only 'safe people,' at least in the places where Robert is being discussed. They'll never move as fast or as completely as a mindful person has a right to think. And," he added soberly, "they probably don't like Robert telling them what is and what isn't acceptable."

Creighton's ultimate advice was that of the lawyers— patience. But he added an important caveat. "Don't get publicly forced into anything. Someone wants this settled, that's obvious. Don't muck it up with public statements until you understand what's going on."

It was good advice. In the days following the initial release of the news story about Merritt and Howard University, Robert's standard response became "No comment." Using the still pending criminal trial as an excuse, he was able to put off reporters from throughout the country. NORML had issued a press release following the unexpected UPI story and this had triggered an intense round of media interest including the return of Jim McManus from CBS, *Newsweek Magazine*, *The New York Times*, National Public Radio, *The St. Louis Post Dispatch*, *The L.A. Times*, and more. To each Robert said "No comment," citing the pending court decision, now scheduled for October 20th. It was easier than he originally thought. The news media, especially the print reporters, sensed a growing story and didn't seem to mind the delay. Robert encouraged the reporters to contact the government officials in charge of the case and promised "off the record clarification" of any confusing points. This proved an efficient way to glean important facts and better understand the dynamics of what was happening within the agencies.

On the October 20th our lawyers informed us they had "gotten things a little confused." There would be no decision that day. It was, in fact, the day Judge Washington returned from vacation. Worse yet, the judge had returned from vacation and gone immediately to hospital. A diabetic, the judge was having "some trouble." Our spirits plummeted at the news.

The days ticked by. The judge left the hospital but there was still no decision nor were there supplies of marijuana from the federal government. Inch by inch we seemed to be moving towards the final scene of Act I but in true theatrical style the most dramatic scenes were yet to come.

10. GIVING THANKS

The day after the presidential election of Jimmy Carter Robert received a call from a reporter at WMOD radio with news that Judge Washington's clerk was hinting at a decision in the case by week's end. When Robert called Paul hoping to get confirmation of this latest tease the news he received was devastating.

Without even an "hello" Paul launched into the conversation. "Bobby, we haven't double-checked this yet, it's being done now." The words seemed right, confirming there may be a release of the decision but there was an unnatural strain in Paul's voice. "Bobby, I don't know …on your court decision," the words were hesitant. "From all we know, well, it's impossible right now. Bobby, all we really know is that Judge Washington had a diabetic seizure early this morning. He was on a flight of stairs at the time, collapsed, and broke his neck."

Robert quickly absorbed the possibilities. "Is he dead?"

"We think he's alive." Paul anticipated Robert's next question. "We don't know the status of the decision. Something was said about dictation but we don't know if he had dictated it or was about to." Paul, sounding sorrowful, rang off with the promise to call as soon as "anything new is learned."

The decision, in fact, had been dictated and was on its way to the typist. But an unsigned decision was no decision at all. If Washington failed to recover we would be back at square one.

Meanwhile news reports about Robert's case had begun to appear throughout the country. A story ran in *The L.A. Times* and was soon syndicated nationwide. *Newsweek Magazine* featured the story in its November 8 issue under the banner of Medicine. *Jet Magazine* ran a small blurb about the Howard program and mentioned a "28-year-old man fighting criminal charges."

Momentum was building and the prospect of redoing the criminal trial was not a comforting one. We soon learned Judge

Washington had survived the fall but was paralyzed. Would it be permanent? Would he be able to certify somehow that his decision was done and would have been signed?

The other aspect of Robert's case—legal supplies of marijuana—was also stalled. Despite the public perception that his petition had been granted Dr. Merritt was still awaiting supplies of marijuana from the federal government.

On November 12th Robert traveled to Howard University for a meeting with Dr. Merritt. The young doctor was in fine form. The press stories were generating all kinds of interest and he was relishing the attention.

Robert's pressures were high, 33/31. "Here, I want you to try this." Merritt handed him a capsule, the color of oxblood. Robert knew it well—THC. He wanted to say, "It won't work," but realized Merritt had to play through the role of researcher. He quietly swallowed the pill.

For the next hour Robert endured the anxiety producing effects of THC then Merritt retrieved him for a second pressure check which revealed no change in the IOP.

The doctor motioned Robert to a chair in the corner. Merritt wanted to talk.

For the next hour we talked about Merritt's plans in a frank and revealing fashion. Merritt was on the move. With the Howard program barely open Merritt was already making other plans. He talked about NEI, budgets, future research. There was a cockiness that was unsettling to me. There were references to "enemies" and some veiled comments on my behavior, my willingness to be "so insistent," to want things "my way."

It was all remarkably friendly but as I considered the young doctor before me there were warning bells ringing softly in the background. Merritt's intentions were not mine. For all the impulse of his emotion and his concern for patients, Merritt was willing to absorb methodological constraints–double-blind studies, placebo doses–all in the name of science and goodwill with the upper echelon at NEI. Merritt was not only on the move, he was on the make.

It was late on Friday afternoon and the rambling talk had gone on too long. Merritt walked to his desk, opened a drawer, and handed Robert a clear, rectangular box filled with 45 marijuana cigarettes.

"Now look, Robert, the final clearances, certificates, whatever, haven't come through yet. If you tell anyone about this take home ...about this outpatient supply, it's my ass and your sight. You understand?"

Robert understood all too well. Taking the box from Merritt's hand, he looked the doctor straight in the eye. "But we're working on it, right?"

"You can be a real pain in the butt. You know that?"

As I exited Howard and hailed a cab I was awe struck with the stillness of the moment. More than a year after the saga began, here I was triumphant, and there was not a single camera, no waiting microphones, just a creaky D.C. cab finding one too many potholes and reminding me of my treasure each time my hip pocket hit against the vinyl seat.

I'd done it! I'd won.

It would not remain a quiet victory for long. The news leaked and soon Jim McManus of CBS news was covering the story. Robert smoked one of his legal marijuana cigarettes on tape. The resulting footage was nearly magical in its conveyance. It undoubtedly ruffled some feathers in the federal government but it also buried the question of you-can-have-it-if-you-don't-tell, at least for the moment. The government had tried to draw a line in the sand but the uniqueness of the story was inescapable. "Bob Smokes Pot! And It's Legal" screamed one headline accompanied by a photo of Robert blowing smoke in the air. Photographers love smoke in the air, especially illegal smoke.

Twelve days later the final scenes of Act I would play out. Judge Washington, still recovering in the hospital, signed the decision in *U.S. v. Randall*.

By the time Robert arrived at Karr & Graves Paul was already busy on the phone with reporters. He handed the decision across the desk and covering the mouthpiece he said, "Last page." Familiar with the office layout, Robert slipped away to the conference room.

Robert appreciated Paul's shortcut. The decision was hefty, twenty pages of legal opinion. Robert sat down and flipped to the last page.

> Upon the basis of the foregoing discussion, the Court finds that defendant, Robert C. Randall, has established the defense of necessity. Accordingly, it is the finding of this Court that he is not guilty of a violation of D.C. Code 33-402, and that the charges against him must be hereby DISMISSED.

Breathing a sigh of relief Robert quietly began leafing through the pages, skimming the section on "Facts" and moving quickly to "Opinion." His eyes darted through the paragraphs snatching bits and pieces.

> Penalizing one who acted rationally to avoid a greater harm will serve neither to rehabilitate the offender nor deter others from acting similarly when presented with similar circumstances.

The words were an elixir. It was far more than we had hoped for. It is a masterpiece.

Signed from his hospital bed, Judge James Washington had provided a detailed, cogent, perhaps airtight argument in support of his decision. It was eloquent and seemed flawless. Each part of the argument resonated as the former law school dean carefully defined the concept of necessity, an ancient seldom used common law tenet, and then applied the concept to Robert's medical need. Coining the term, "medical necessity," Washington determined that Robert had a clear and unequivocal right to use marijuana to treat his glaucoma.

> The evil he sought to prevent, blindness, is greater than that he performed to accomplish it, growing marijuana in his residence in violation of D.C. code.

Washington even went so far as to proclaim "Medical evidence suggests that the prohibition [of marijuana] is not well-founded."

Robert couldn't fully comprehend it in one sitting but he knew that an important precedent had been established.

He paused for a moment and looked out the window. A light snow was falling. Tomorrow was Thanksgiving Day and Fate had given us plenty to be thankful for. His thoughts slipped away to the judge, still hospitalized from the fall. "Thanks," he said quietly.

Robert Randall had won and the world was quickly finding out about it. John Karr and Robert gave several interviews to the local TV and radio stations. When he arrived home he found a pile of messages from reporters throughout the country. The UPI newswire was carrying the story far and wide.

Friends were notified and arrived with champagne and congratulations. Throughout the evening the phone rang with friends or press. Families were notified and there was much happiness.

By midnight the last guest was gone and the last call from the press answered. Finally alone, Robert and I settled into our own celebration.

Section II:

Changing Laws

11. ALONE IN THE LIFEBOAT

As the dramatic and eventful Bicentennial year was drawing to a close, Robert's story virtually exploded upon the American consciousness. We began to hear from individuals who were similarly afflicted and we heard from others with diseases such as multiple sclerosis, epilepsy, and cancer chemotherapy patients. All these individuals had stories to tell and all had a need for medical access to marijuana.

The media blitz was intense and sustained. In the three months following his acquittal Robert spoke with countless reporters and radio stations. He traveled to New York to appear on "Good Morning America," gave a press conference in the fabled Playboy Towers Hotel in Chicago, posed for *People Magazine*, and taped numerous other TV segments. Robert was invited to several state legislative sessions where he testified about the medical benefits of marijuana and displayed his small plastic vials filled with government joints. Legislators would jockey to have their picture taken with "America's only legal pot smoker."

In February 1977 he taped a segment of "To Tell the Truth," a long-running TV game show in which celebrities ask questions of three panelists in an effort to determine which one has the unusual occupation or talent, in Robert's case "Legal pot smoker." He fooled no one. The celebrities, most notably Nipsy Russell and Peggy Cass, showed a sophisticated knowledge of marijuana. Even the elegant Kitty Carlisle was able to select Robert from the panel.

Robert Randall wasn't exactly a household word but his situation was well known. Invariably someone would exclaim, "Oh yeah! You're that guy, that guy with the eyes." It became a running joke with us as we made our way through those incredible first months.

The atmosphere was bright with promise. Sanity, it seemed, could prevail. There was a new president, Jimmy Carter, whose young staff was peppered with marijuana smokers. Keith Stroup knew many of them and was optimistic that changes would come, and soon. Stroup spoke in glowing terms of Carter's nominee for drug policy advisor, Dr. Peter Bourne. Now, with such a well-placed contact in the White House, it seemed the possibilities for expansion of research and medical access to marijuana were opening like the petals on a rose.

This impression was reinforced by an editorial that appeared in *The Washington Post* just ten days after Robert's acquittal entitled "Drugs and Public Policy." The December 6 editorial decried the lack of research into marijuana's medical use, cited Robert's case specifically, and concluded:

> All this [uncertainty] is the clear result of permitting the criminal sanction to blind the rest of us to the fact that this substance needs a great deal of investigation in all aspects, hazards as well as benefits, so that we can protect ourselves from the former and gain what we can from the latter. None of this is happening now.

We were so overjoyed with our success, so confident of a new day dawning, that we didn't see the storm clouds gathering. Another editorial, this one across the continent, would issue a different opinion in the early days of 1977. Appearing in the Spokane, *Washington Chronicle* under the headline "Pot Users Try New Angle," the editorial noted:

> Claims that use of marijuana retards glaucoma, an eye disease that usually leads to blindness, is the peg on which the National Organization for the Reform of Marijuana Laws (NORML) will hang its hat in a national campaign to decriminalize use and possession of the drug.

The editorial would conclude with an ominous warning. "Opponents to decriminalizing marijuana should go to work immediately on building up a strong case against NORML."

Within six weeks of the decision in Robert's case the battle lines were drawn in the war for medical marijuana. Those lines continue to this day, dug in like the weary trench soldiers of World War I facing an endless barrage of attack and counterattack. Caught in the no man's land between warring factions are the patients, still waiting for sanity to prevail.

On March 3, 1977, Robert appeared on the "Tomorrow Show" with Tom Snyder. The Snyder program, which followed Johnny Carson's immensely popular "Tonight Show" on NBC, had a loyal following, especially in the West where time zones presented the show at a more reasonable hour. Snyder was a skillful and playful interviewer. Robert and Snyder connected well and the show sailed along smoothly. When Snyder cajoled him to "light one up," he did so. It was the first time he smoked "live" on camera. Robert would later reflect in our 1998 book on the importance of the Snyder show.

When I began my journey through the maze of federal bureaucracies I was focused on Robert Randall but as my story seeped into national consciousness in 1976 I heard from others with numerous afflictions. At first it was just a trickle of correspondence and phone calls. The dual victories of November 1976–legal access and acquittal–turned the trickle to a torrent. The Snyder show amplified the interest even more.

Alice and I responded to each call or letter with increased despair. There was a growing sense of obligation and responsibility to others, but what to do?

The logical answer was to file more petitions, to try and do for others what had been done for Robert. But the circumstances were vastly different. Realistically we could not mount the type of effort that had been successful in Robert's case. It was costly, time consuming, and far too dependent upon the petitioner doing an extraordinary amount of "legwork." Moreover, doors that had been open when Robert began his effort were now shut hard. Federal agencies were on their guard. There would not be another Robert Randall any time soon.

It would be better, we reasoned, if we organized the patients into a concerted effort. On April 26, 1977, we filed a petition with U.S. Attorney General Griffin Bell that was signed by 13 seriously ill individuals including a schoolteacher from Ohio, a craftsman from Missouri, a prisoner from

Florida, and a cancer patient from Pennsylvania. Also included was Robert's roommate from Johns Hopkins, Vincent Mustachio. We asked the Attorney General to schedule open hearings to consider the reclassification of marijuana and allow its medical use.

In the spring of 1977, such an action by a diverse group of individuals generated another round of media attention and had the desired effect of shifting the focus beyond Robert. Local news stories appeared wherever a petitioner happened to reside.

In Kansas, *The Wichita Eagle* featured the story of 62-year-old Ara Cron, a glaucoma patient and retired schoolteacher, who lamented she was "too old to get the drug" but pleaded for an opportunity to try it. She left it clear the opportunity did not necessarily have to be legal. She cited a long family history of glaucoma and her concerns about risky surgery. Ara's story would, in fact, generate a "donation" of marijuana from a concerned citizen. She tried smoking the drug and her husband Gerald measured the results with a tonometer. They were impressive, dropping from 40+ mm of pressure to readings in the high teens. This was enough to convince Ara's doctor who began pursuing an IND application of his own and was pleased with the cooperation promised by the FDA and NIDA.

It seemed Robert's case was opening the doors for others. But that was an illusion. There would be no expansion of medical marijuana users and the wheels were already in motion to shut down Robert's access.

In May 1977 Robert traveled to California and was a panelist during the Medical Marijuana session at the National Conference on Drug Abuse (NCDA). The session was particularly well attended. There was a great deal of interest in America's Only Legal Pot Smoker and the conference received a tremendous media push as a result of Robert's presence.

Among the other panelists was Dr. Robert Peterson, a NIDA official who once told Robert "you'll never make it through the bureaucratic layers." The NCDA crowd was clearly sympathetic to Robert's criticism of NIDA's failure to aggressively research marijuana's therapeutic applications. Peterson was forced to defend the agency's policy. After the panel, as Robert was being ushered away by a conference organizer, Peterson stopped him for an instant and asked how he could manage to travel to San Francisco on just a week's supply of marijuana.

In fact, Robert had a nine-day supply but federal officials were under the impression that Dr. Merritt would release no more than one week's supply at a time. Ever since Robert's appearance on the "Snyder" show, there had been discussions about "Randall's take home supply" and increased mobility. The upper echelon of Washington's drug bureaucracies was annoyed with his public exposure and growing notoriety. The bureaucrats had ignored the initial press rush, assuming his celebrity status would fade. But now it was obvious that Robert was doing everything he could to feed the fires of interest in medical marijuana.

On May 12, as Robert made the press rounds in Los Angeles, a little known committee of the FDA, the Drug Abuse Research Advisory Committee (DARAC) was meeting in the Parklawn Building. It had "invited" Dr. Merritt to "discuss" his research program but the discussion quickly shifted to Robert's personal conduct. After considerable talk, Merritt was asked to leave the room and a secret vote was held. Merritt was then informed that Robert would no longer be authorized to possess any more than a daily supply of marijuana. When Merritt protested he was told, quite bluntly, that DARAC could revoke Merritt's research license if he failed to cooperate. Moreover, there were criminal liabilities that could be invoked.

Merritt delivered the news to Robert the next day, May 13. Robert immediately called Ed Tocus, his contact at the FDA. Tocus was not surprised at the call but he was taken aback at the extent of Robert's knowledge. With the delivery of Merritt's bombshell, it had not taken Robert very long to put the pieces together.

While in California Robert had telephoned Dr. Hepler to pay his respects and update the ophthalmologist on his ocular condition. Hepler mentioned a phone call from a "Washington committee that was making some inquiries" about Robert's "personality traits." Not surprisingly, Hepler refused to answer such inquiries. The committee had called Hepler shortly after the "Snyder" show.

Robert asked Tocus outright if it was the same committee that had met with Merritt. Tocus confirmed it was. From that point the conversation took a chilling path. Robert recalled the conversation in this writing:

> "Under the DARAC policy of daily supply I'd become a medical prisoner of the District of Columbia." I spoke slowly and with a measured tone. I wanted to be certain that Tocus answered the next question without any emotional overtones. "Do you expect me to stay in Washington until I go blind?"
>
> There was barely a pause. "That, I believe, was the intention of at least some committee members in voting to restrict your supply." Tocus' reply was delivered with such calm that it shook me to the bone.
>
> "Look, I have three joints left. That's enough for this afternoon. Today is Friday and Merritt has made it clear he will not be available this weekend. So, if provisions are not made to resupply me before this evening, you, DARAC, and the FDA will be in court on Monday morning."

It was a stupendous bluff. We had no way of backing up such a threat. We were still in debt to the lawyers from the criminal case and there was little hope of finding anyone else on such short notice. But it worked. Robert's supplies were reinstated. DARAC had seriously overstated its power. As an advisory committee it could only "recommend" policy to the FDA, and the regulations did not allow such recommendations to become true policy until the minutes were published in the federal register and a public hearing was held. That was months away. The FDA was acting in a totally improper manner by implementing DARAC's "recommendation" without any review. Their braggadocio had been as bold as Robert's.

It was the first overt attempt to "corral" Robert's legal access but that unique position had already been threatened, in writing, by the drug abuse advisor to the President of the United States.

In mid-April 1977, sensing that his days as America's Only Legal Pot Smoker were numbered, Robert decided it was time to play the Bourne card. Throughout the latter part of 1976, Keith Stroup had often advised Robert to contact Dr. Peter Bourne, who was then associated with the Drug Abuse Council, a D.C. think tank funded by the Ford Foundation. But Robert was already working with another individual at the Council, Jane Silver, and he wasn't sure what more Bourne could do for him in that turbulent year of 1976. Now, in the spring of 1977, Bourne was President Carter's newly installed drug policy advisor.

Since entering the White House Dr. Bourne had become less sympathetic to marijuana issues. As President Carter's drug abuse expert and special assistant to the President for Health, Bourne seemed to be leaning towards continued spraying of the herbicide Paraquat on Mexican marijuana plants. But he had remained silent on the matter of marijuana's medical use and this gave us some hope.

So in April 1977 Robert wrote a letter to Dr. Bourne ostensibly to inform him about our petition effort with the other patients. But Robert also used the opportunity to outline his own position to the Presidential advisor:

> I have had limited desire to attack those agencies responsible for my access to marijuana. While the system of marijuana management itself seems ill conceived and mal-administered, I did receive a measure of justice. I had reason to believe, for a time, that adjustments would go forward.

Later in the letter he would write,

> The present system pits public policy against human biology. The human reaction to this conflict of values cannot greatly enhance the authority of the law and creates the possibility of ill-informed individuals engaging in attempted medical self-treatment.

> The Schedule I prohibition has almost no benefits. It has been a failure in discouraging the recreational use of marijuana and a success at denying an expansion of our medical knowledge. It has the double disadvantage of denying millions of individuals

the civil rights which are theirs and of denying additional millions of their biological well-being.

On June 6, 1977, Dr. Bourne responded. His letter was very clear.

> As a physician, I understand and have great empathy with the issues you raised. I can assure you that my feelings are shared by hundreds, perhaps thousands, of physicians and researchers who have fought to bring relief and discover new treatments and cures. The responsible agency staffs and researchers involved in the marijuana and glaucoma issue all share with me a great feeling of compassion and are pledged to pursue the question. However, this compassion cannot be allowed to over-shadow the basic questions.

Bourne then elaborated on the need for research and the problems with the cannabinoid eyedrop. Finally he got to the heart of the matter.

> I understand that technical questions remain about your status under the law in that you are not really legally authorized to possess marijuana to treat your glaucoma. Under the law, the researcher (Dr. Merritt in your case) is authorized to possess and administer it. If you disregard some of the conditions of the study, it may be jeopardized. I understand that the agencies involved have not authorized your take-home supply but have chosen to overlook it in their compassion for your case. Publicity in the case has forced consideration of tightening up the dispensing of your supplies.

Dr. Bourne was clearly threatening to use Robert's medical need in an attempt to constrain his right to speak. It was medical blackmail. Bureaucrats can threaten and bluster through procedures and phone calls, but are seldom reckless enough to issue them in hard black and white.

Within three days of the Bourne letter there came a second indication from the government that Robert's legal access may be in jeopardy. As Bourne had noted, there was some question about Robert's status with respect to legally possessing marijuana. Our lawyers had appealed to the U.S. Attorney General for clarification and a statement of immunity. The appeal was forwarded to the Drug Enforcement Administration and, not surprisingly, the agency refused to extend such immunity.

The warnings were now unmistakable. Either Robert could keep quiet and retain his marijuana or he could talk and the marijuana would be taken away. His sight or the right to speak.

We were entering perilous waters.

Two weeks later the government upped the ante even further when it demanded, via Dr. Merritt, that Robert sign a research consent form similar to that he had signed when he was Hepler's subject at UCLA.

"Ten months, man!," exclaimed Merritt. "Ten months you've been receiving this stuff and now they want a consent form." Merritt was angry. "I swear, I don't understand those people, I don't understand them at all."

But Robert understood very well. Consent forms aren't signed by patients; consent forms are for research subjects. By getting Robert to sign a form, the FDA would be codifying its control over his care.

The form Merritt presented to Robert was ominous. It would bestow on the FDA the following authority:

1.) Robert's marijuana could be replaced with placebo doses, regardless of the medical consequences.

2.) The agency reserved the right to determine when "enough" research had been conducted.

3.) The FDA had the right to determine which type of "THC vehicle" (smoked, pills, eye drops) was appropriate.

The trap was transparent. "I can't sign this," Robert said and looked at the physician.

"You agreed to sign it last November." Merritt was not pushing, only making an observation.

"No. We agreed it wasn't necessary," Robert replied firmly. Merritt said nothing but handed Robert his week's supply of medication. "I'll let the FDA know your decision."

FDA was not pleased and demanded that Robert sign the form. His solution was to type a Statement of Duress which he took to Merritt's office. Before signing the Consent Form he scratched through the offending paragraphs and then signed the document.

Merritt looked on dubiously. "I don't think that will work, Bob."

"Well, maybe this will." Robert removed the Statement of Duress from his pocket and asked Merritt to watch as he signed it. He then asked Merritt to sign as a witness. Merritt shook his head as he signed the statement. "You're pushing it."

"No, they're pushing it, Dr. Merritt." Now it was Robert who was angry. "I was clear from the first about my need for marijuana. I am not a research subject. I've been through research and it showed I need marijuana." Robert was speaking with certainty. "I will not give up my rights to satisfy a bunch of bureaucrats who can't acknowledge the truth."

"Okay, okay." Merritt took the duress statement and stapled it to the consent form. "You stay here, I'll call Tocus."

It was a long fifteen minutes in Merritt's outer office. Robert was pushing and he knew it. But he also knew he had never agreed to daily supplies and wasn't about to backtrack now. NORML's general counsel had indicated there would be reason to sue if the government rescinded Robert's supplies. If the statement of duress didn't work then he would go immediately to NORML from Howard. He didn't like the option but there were no others he could see at the moment.

The door opened and Merritt emerged, smiling slightly. "You win," he said. "Tocus agrees to accept your edited consent form and your statement of duress IF you promise not to release either to the press or make any comments about this."

Robert smiled. "See you next week."

In that same week Robert would receive a call from one of the petitioners, Ara Cron, and the news was not pleasant. Despite her doctor's willingness to sign the necessary IND papers, NIDA and the FDA bungled and delayed his request for permission to use marijuana in treating Ara's glaucoma. The anonymous gift of marijuana, sent as a result of her story in the *Wichita Eagle*, had lasted two weeks and was gone. Without marijuana Ara's IOP had risen to its old levels. She and Gerald didn't know where to buy more, didn't know who to trust, didn't know where to turn. For weeks they pleaded with Robert Peterson at NIDA and Ed Tocus at FDA. Senator Bob Dole intervened on her behalf but still the agencies stonewalled.

Trapped in red tape, Ara underwent surgery on June 1 for one eye and June 3 for the other. The operations were successful within the medical definition of success. Ara's IOP was under excellent management, but much of her sight was lost due to complications following surgery. It was a chilling example of the power the agencies could invoke, the same agencies now demanding control over Robert's medical future.

The next few months moved along uneventfully and the silence from the agencies was ominous. Robert continued to speak with the press and the story continued with a steady momentum.

In late November, just after the one-year anniversary of Robert's court victory and securing of federal marijuana supplies, he received a call from Dave Anderson of UPI.

"There's a story on the wire. I'd like your comment."

The 3 p.m. wire story, dateline Wichita, carried Ara Cron's story to the nation. It had been triggered by Robert's recent anniversary—one year of legal marijuana smoking.

Deep within the wire service copy was a passing mention of Dr. Merritt's study followed by a brief paragraph which read, "But he is phasing out the program until he moves to another city."

"Would you care to comment?" Dave Anderson asked.

"No," Robert said. "It's the first I've heard of anything like that. It must be a mistake." Dave doubted his wire service would make such a mistake. But when the UPI wire on Ara repeated at 5 p.m. the paragraph on Dr. Merritt's plans was missing.

The next day Robert traveled to Howard for a routine visit. Everything was typical. Pressures were taken, Merritt gave him the weekly supply. Then he drew Robert towards a small office. "We need to talk," Merritt said.

"Is it true you're leaving Washington?" Robert asked preemptively. "A UPI reporter called and. . ."

After taking a deep breath Merritt said, "The UPI story is true. I was hoping to tell you first, but someone leaked the news. I've received a grant, a big grant, from the National Eye Institute to study marijuana's effects on glaucoma." Merritt nervously shifted. "But they won't give me the grant if I stay at Howard," Merritt said. "Instead, the NEI wants me to do the study down in Chapel Hill at the University of North Carolina."

"North Carolina. Like Research Triangle Park, North Carolina?" Robert asked.

"That's right."

"And they'd prefer that you give me up as a patient, right?"

"That's right. I mean, it would be impossible for you to keep up weekly visits if I'm 350 miles away." Merritt was trying to seem sensible.

"Maybe we could stretch out the time between visits." Robert was trying to remain calm.

"I don't think they'd allow us to do that," Merritt replied with the certainty of a man who had already explored the option.

"Well," Robert said, realizing his fate was sealed, "a big grant from NEI, and a promotion at a new school like the University of North Carolina is too good to turn down."

"It certainly is," Merritt smiled, self-satisfied by his coup. "It certainly is."

Having failed in their numerous other attempts to "rein in Randall" the government finally found the weak link—Merritt. The bureaucrats at the DEA, FDA and NEI were willing to pay Merritt a very hefty price to disrupt Robert's legal access—$95,000 per year for 3 years plus a professorship at UNC. With Hepler no longer involved in research, Merritt would have an exclusive right to explore marijuana as an ocular therapeutic. Generous federal funding, a new professorship, and all the professional credit he could handle. It was, simply stated, an exceedingly tempting offer and Merritt had taken the bait, hook, line and sinker. Robert would later write:

Merritt would continue his study of marijuana and glaucoma for a number of years at UNC, publishing numerous articles in scientific journals that underscored marijuana's ability to reduce intraocular pressure. He was genuinely interested in the medicinal properties of marijuana but I've always felt he erred in leaving Howard. In North Carolina he became part of the effort to develop synthetic forms of the drug that could be used instead of the natural substance. An admirable goal but one that does little for those with an immediate need, like myself and the countless others who contacted him for help when he was at Howard. Over the years we lost contact with one another.

As he began to prepare for his move to North Carolina Merritt promised to make some inquiries on my behalf to locate a new doctor. I'd been down that road before and didn't have much faith that things would work out. I was in serious trouble, again.

12. SQUARE ONE...AGAIN

In December 1977 Robert was not only a featured speaker at the 5th Annual NORML Conference, he was a feature. Everyone wanted to meet "the only legal pot smoker in America." Lawyers, researchers, activists and some just plain loony people would cluster around him. Private conversation was impossible. As soon as he would stop moving the small cluster of following sycophants would stop too, respectfully a few feet behind, and simply stare at him, many with an adoring smile. It was, to say the least, a bit unnerving.

We found a corner table in the darkened cocktail lounge and settled in for a much needed break. But it didn't last for long.

"Mr. Randall?"

We looked up from our chairs to find a hairless young man—tall and thin as Lincoln—holding out a gigantic hand. "I'm Lynn Pierson. We spoke on the phone?"

I could see that Robert was extremely weary but he invited the man to take a seat. "I was wondering if you could help me get medical marijuana," he said.

"Why don't you tell me something about yourself, first," Robert replied.

"We discussed this on the phone," Lynn was impatient.

"I talk to a lot of people. Refresh my memory." The edge in Robert's voice revealed just how weary he was. "Tell me what you want."

"Legal marijuana," Lynn replied with a hint of annoyance.

"Everyone wants legal marijuana. Why do you want it?" After a year of listening to people Robert could be curt but Lynn did not flinch.

"I have cancer," he said.

"*And . . . ?*"

I was starting to wonder if I should intervene. Robert was normally patient and polite but his weariness was getting the better of him.

"And I need your help." Lynn was direct and his request for help had a touch of attitude.

"Tell me your story, Lynn." I spoke calmly and honestly. Lynn may have spoken with Robert but I didn't know him.

The outline of Lynn's story was written in his frame. At 25, cancer and chemotherapy had eaten his bulk and rendered him bald. Diagnosed in 1975 with testicular cancer, Lynn was being treated at the Albuquerque Veterans Hospital. He'd had surgery—"they cut off my nuts," Lynn explained, with a quick look in my direction to make certain he did not offend—but the cancer had spread. So the doctors told him chemotherapy was his only hope. The first dose of Cisplatin—then one of the newest, most highly toxic anti-cancer drugs available—left Lynn sick and vomiting for days.

"It was terrible," Lynn recalled. "I couldn't eat, couldn't even smell food without vomiting. There was constant nausea. I knew I wouldn't survive that kind of chemical torture. And it was real hard on my family too."

Lynn returned to the V.A. hospital and told his doctor "no more." He could not, would not, tolerate the debilitating nausea and vomiting caused by Cisplatin. He bluntly told his doctor he would rather die.

The oncologist's reply shocked the young man. "Have you tried marijuana?" The physician pulled out an issue of *The New England Journal of Medicine* and showed Lynn an article by Drs. Stephen Sallan and Norman Zinberg. "These Harvard doctors report marijuana can reduce the side effects of chemotherapy. You're a young man, Lynn. You can find yourself some of this stuff. Give it a try before you give up."

"It was a miracle," Lynn said. "A few puffs of pot took the nausea away. And there was hardly any vomiting. Then I got real hungry. Hell, I ate so much I actually gained some weight."

"So," Robert interrupted, "you know marijuana works, and you know how to get it. Why go through all the hassle of trying to get it legally, Lynn?" I listened to Robert give advice that in 1975 had made him furious. But we could tell by looking at the lanky New Mexican that there was probably a good chance, despite the chemo, that Lynn was dying.

Lynn paused and chose his words carefully. "I have—had—a friend who needed help," Lynn said and went on to talk about an older man whom he had befriended at the

Albuquerque V.A. Hospital. The two had much in common: the same diagnosis, the same mutilating surgery, and the same intense negative reaction to chemo.

"I told my friend about how marijuana helped," Lynn said. "And his doctors urged him to try pot. But he refused. He was sick and afraid. He said he'd never broken any laws and wasn't going to die a criminal."

"So he suffered and died," Robert said, his voice softening. "And that's why you want to get legal marijuana?"

"Yeah." A silence fell across the table. I knew Robert was thinking about Vince Mustachio, the glaucoma patient he had met at John Hopkins. He understood what Lynn was saying.

I picked up the conversation thread as Robert quietly considered the young New Mexican. "When did your friend die, Lynn?" I gently asked.

"About a month ago. Then I heard about this conference, and remembered seeing Mr. Randall when he came to Santa Fe to testify before our legislature. I thought maybe you could help me."

"Why didn't you talk to me after the hearing?" Robert asked, recalling the hearings in February 1977.

"You looked busy. There were a lot of people around. I was sick. It wasn't the right time," Lynn explained.

We continued chatting idly about family. Lynn was married but had no children. He was born in Kansas but grew up in New Mexico and had many connections, including some prominent friends in the legal system. Lynn had thought about going to court to receive marijuana but he wanted to do something bigger, something more inclusive.

"I was thinking about a study, like the one you're in." I could feel Robert bristle at the implication he was in a "study" but he remained silent. "That way others could get supplies, too. I know my doctor would help. He's the one who . . ."

"Lynn!" Robert interrupted with a flash of insight. "You've got something I don't have."

"What's that?" Lynn asked.

"A state legislature," Robert replied, his voice reflecting the excitement of this insight. "Maybe we should pass a law."

"Maybe we should," Lynn said smiling.

It was a "Eureka" moment, one of those split seconds in which things become crystal clear. In the animated cartoons from the 1940s and '50s, it is that moment when a light bulb materializes above the cartoon character's head.

Lynn returned to New Mexico and immediately began a two-track approach. He contacted a lawyer and explored the possibility of going to court to obtain marijuana. But he also began making phone calls to legislators and state government offices. Throughout the holidays Robert and Lynn talked regularly on the phone, getting to know one another and outlining a political strategy. New Mexico state representative Tom Rutherford, a NORML supporter, was interested and anxiously asked for legal language. While Representative Rutherford's support was helpful, Robert advised Lynn to seek help on the Republican side of the aisle. New Mexico was, and is, fiercely conservative. Robert knew the legislation wouldn't fly without help from the Republicans.

While Lynn toiled away in New Mexico, Robert's own situation was looking bleak. Merritt was leaving and Robert needed to secure a doctor who could assume responsibility for his care. When Merritt first announced his departure Robert had held some hope that everything might work itself out but in late December talks with officials at NIDA this illusion was quickly shattered.

"What's the problem?" Robert Petersen at NIDA asked. "You know how to get marijuana. And, believe me, unless you buy a psychedelic trip van and start selling pot to school kids no one in this town is ever going to bust you again. So, what's the problem?"

The message was clear. The bureaucrats did not care if Robert smoked pot but they were determined he would no longer do it legally. If he went blind, well, that's life. It was a risk the bureaucrats were prepared to take. It was a well-calculated assault based on the simple assumption that he could not assemble the considerable resources—the doctors, the lawyers, the funds—needed to challenge them. It seemed, at the time, a very safe bet.

Things were no more promising on the lawyer front. NORML, an organization awash in attorneys, could not find one lawyer willing to take what was certain to be a complicated, time-consuming, financially unrewarding case. There was, after all, no criminal charge. Instead, this would be a purely civil matter and no one was sure what kind of legal argument could compel the United States to provide Robert with medical access to an officially prohibited substance.

Even though NORML was unable to help with respect to a lawyer for Robert's impending civil suit, it was helpful in other ways. In December 1977, just before the NORML conference, we approached Keith with the idea of establishing the Medical Reclassification Project, a kind of "task force" working out of NORML. The organization agreed to the idea and in January 1978 I began working daily out of the NORML office on M St. NW. We were hearing from more and more individuals—many funneled through NORML—who wanted legal access to marijuana for medical purposes. It was placing both a financial and personal strain on us. NORML had the existing infrastructure to respond to these individuals and it had a network that could allow us to continue generating the type of positive press attention that had so bolstered our efforts in 1977. Additionally we reasoned that my work could buffer Robert in some ways. He was reluctant to affiliate formally with NORML but there was no reason I couldn't.

As one of my first projects, I reprinted a report issued in October 1977 by the Hawaiian Public Health Service (HPHS). It was the first state-sponsored report on marijuana's medical use, with a summary and bibliography of contemporary research. It would become a valuable tool in the coming months.

Not surprisingly, the HPHS recommended more research but one recommendation was surprising and remarkably compassionate. Because glaucoma eventually results in blindness, the task force further recommended that persons suffering from glaucoma who are unresponsive to conventional medications not be prohibited from using marijuana to control their disease.

By mid-January, Dr. Merritt was packing up the last of his boxes and preparing for his move to North Carolina. Robert would see him for his last formal examination on January 13. He had prepared a ten-page affidavit that he presented to Merritt

"What is this, anyway?"

"It's an affidavit." Robert explained. "It reviews my last 14 months of treatment, describes how marijuana is medically used to control my eye pressure, and reaches some conclusions about the nature of my care. I think you'll find it very matter-of-fact." It was, of course, a test. How far had Merritt defected?

"This is to help you if you have to go to court?" Merritt was wavering.

"That's right," Robert replied. "We can refine it when—if—I get an attorney. But I thought it would be wise to make a clear record before you leave town. I don't want to have to track you down in North Carolina."

"That makes sense," Merritt said. "And I don't see anything in this affidavit I disagree with."

"Fine. But give it a careful read. I'll call tomorrow to correct any mistakes or get a signed copy. Oh, if you sign it make sure there's a notary. This has to be notarized," Robert was insistent.

Merritt looked up from his desk and smiled. "I'll see you tomorrow, Robert."

Merritt signed the affidavit and vanished into his new world. He gave Robert all of his remaining marijuana, about 100 joints in all. It wouldn't last long but it was a magnanimous gesture. Robert was truly sorry to see the young doctor go:

He'd appeared out of nowhere, offered help when no one else would and been a very good doctor. For over a year Merritt had protected me from the most blatant bureaucratic abuses but, as his departure drew near, some part of me wanted to protect him. I couldn't understand why he was surrendering his secure position at one of the nation's leading universities for a pocketful of promises.

With Merritt's defection I realized the bureaucrats were willing to pay nearly any price to shut me up. I was causing too many waves. Doubtless, Merritt had even used me as leverage to secure the best

possible deal from NEI and FDA. In the end it was simply too good to turn down.

Realizing that he needed to reach out publicly if he was to get any help, Robert typed and retyped a press release. The final result was a lumpy, all-too-wordy four-page diatribe. He was less than satisfied, but nevertheless he made multiple copies, mailed many, and then delivered others by hand to the National Press Building.

The result was silence. Getting legal marijuana, we learned, was news. Losing it was being just like everyone else and that is not news.

It was looking grim when Dave Anderson from UPI called.

"We spoke last year about the DEA petition and more recently about Ara Cron?" the reporter had a good background on the story. "I've just been handed this release. Is it true—is the government really trying to take away your pot?"

He and Robert met that afternoon. After listening to the story, Dave reviewed the facts—"this press release certainly contains a lot of information," he noted—then said, "I think my editors will be interested. Have any other outlets picked it up yet?"

"Not yet," Robert said without trying to seem anxious.

"Fine," Dave said. "By the way, what are you going to do when your government pot runs out? Are you going to go back to the streets to buy pot?"

An obvious, but dangerous question. After a few seconds, Robert coyly replied, "I'm going to do what any sane person would do. I'm not going to go blind."

Dave jotted down the quote and smiled.

In the last week of January 1978 the number of legal medical marijuana users in America would double—to two.

In California, Judge Don Work of the El Centro Superior Court issued an order allowing the release of confiscated marijuana supplies to a 21-year-old cancer patient named Craig Reichert. The young man, confined to the Scripps Clinic in La Jolla, was terminally ill. For more than two years he had battled a rare tumor, which was cancerous and had developed near his kidneys. Like young Lynn Pierson, Craig had been told to try marijuana to help with the nausea and vomiting that resulted from his cancer treatments. When his parents saw how much it helped their son they took steps to secure the drug legally by meeting with the local judge.

Following the meeting, and after speaking with the doctor, Judge Work issued a string of unprecedented orders immunizing Craig, his family and medical caregivers from arrest and authorizing the local sheriff to deliver confiscated supplies to the hospital.

It was a stupendously gutsy decision.

Robert and I were elated. A genie, once released, cannot be put back. Even if the bureaucrats succeeded in cutting off Robert's supplies the public awareness of medical marijuana was spreading and new avenues of access seemed to be opening.

On the same day that we learned about Craig Reichert, Dave Anderson's story hit the wire and was picked up by dozens of newspapers, including *The Washington Star*. The capital's only evening newspaper gave the story Page 3 prominence. Accompanying Dave's article was the now infamous photograph of Robert puffing legal marijuana. The caption under the photo said it all. "Robert Randall: 'I'm not out to pick a fight. I'm out to save my sight.' " The media machine kicked into high gear and the phone started ringing as reporters looked for comments on the Reichert case and, later, Robert's own situation.

The story ignited new interest in Lynn Pierson's efforts in New Mexico and in legislation that was introduced in Hawaii that recognized marijuana's medical utility. The firestorm of media interest was a tonic to Robert. He spent hours talking on the phone to radio stations across the country. For two days he was constantly fielding calls, doing on-air interviews, and scheduling future radio talk.

In the midst of this flurry of calls, Peter Meyers, NORML's in-house lawyer, managed to break through. "Robert, I've been trying to reach you for hours." It was an age before call-waiting or voice mail.

"Look," Peter rushed on, "I received a call from an attorney at one of those legal factories on Connecticut Avenue.

He saw *The Star* story and has an interest in your situation. But," Peter said, "he won't call you because it would be unethical to solicit a client. So he asked me to call. His name is Tom Collier. If you're interested I've got his number."

Robert was interested, very interested.

13. STEPTOE STEPS IN

Peter Meyers wasn't kidding about a "legal factory." There were more than one hundred names on the Steptoe & Johnson directory in the lobby of their Connecticut Ave. office building. Washington, D.C. was a mecca for attorneys and there were many "legal factories" in the Nation's capital. Steptoe & Johnson, in 1978, was the city's third largest law firm.

Tom Collier was on the sixth floor.

It's fair to say that Robert and I were both surprised when Tom appeared. We were expecting someone older and grayer. Tom seemed close in age to ourselves—30-something. We would later learn he was actually several years younger than us.

Tom Collier had curly blond hair, longer than expected, and was in a rumpled white shirt rolled up at the sleeves. His tie was loosened. He was eager and engaging.

He led us through a maze of corridors into a cramped office where a single window faced the back wall of the next building. As we entered the small room it became obvious the floor and chairs were a critical part of Tom Collier's filing system. Not expecting my presence he had cleared only one chair. He carefully removed a pile of papers from the second guest chair in his office and we settled in.

For the next two hours we told Tom of our adventure. After we finished, Tom told us something about himself and Steptoe & Johnson.

"Steptoe thinks of itself as a conservative southern law firm," Tom began. Misters Steptoe & Johnson started the firm in West Virginia in 1913. During World War II, Mr. Johnson served as Assistant Secretary of War and later as Secretary of Defense under President Harry Truman. The Washington office of Steptoe & Johnson was established in 1945. Over the years Steptoe & Johnson had grown with the government and was now one of the top five law firms in Washington with a string of wealthy corporate clients and more than 150 attorneys on staff.

Tom Collier was a small-town Mississippi boy with big ambitions who always wanted to be a lawyer. After graduating from the University of Virginia, where he was president of the student body, Tom received his law degree from the University of Mississippi where he graduated with honors. He was a clerk for an Appeals Court judge in the 5th Circuit before he joined Steptoe as an associate.

Tom was a 3rd-year associate, midway through a seven-year apprenticeship. At the end of that time the Steptoe partners would review his work and promote him to junior partner or throw him out of the firm. A brutal system.

Having survived three years so far, Tom Collier was looking for a case he could control. Steptoe, he explained, prided itself on providing select clients with *pro bono publico* legal assistance.

"That means 'for the public good?'" Robert asked. "Without charge?" Our hearts had begun to race a little faster at the prospect.

"Yes, that's right." Tom Collier was looking for an interesting *pro bono* case that would appeal to the senior partners and excite the interest of other associates. He thought Robert's case was interesting.

"Clearly," Tom said, "the government is manipulating your medical care to curb your free speech rights. And, clearly, they are willing to blind you to achieve their goal. This could be an important case. But it would require a great deal of effort."

This young attorney had hit the nail on the head and was extending the possibility of a major Washington law firm coming to Robert's aid. Steptoe & Johnson was altogether different from anything we had experienced. Perched at the pinnacle of the legal profession the firm was huge; rich, well-staffed and deeply connected. How, we wondered, would a corporate, well-connected, obviously conservative "southern" law firm respond to the idea of medical marijuana?

Tom seemed to be reading our thoughts as he carefully explained the need to propose Robert's case to a committee that would vote yea or nay on extending help. The young attorney was honest and straightforward, offering hope but making no promises.

By the end of the two hour meeting Robert, Tom and I were comfortable with one another and there were good feelings as we parted.

As the elevator doors closed on Tom standing in the 6th floor lobby I turned to Robert and uttered the only word possible.

"Wow!"

It would be two long weeks before Steptoe & Johnson agreed to take Robert's case. Like any corporate entity, Steptoe & Johnson had its own bureaucracy and Tom's request would make its way through the corporate structure.

We didn't know it at the time but we already had a powerful ally at Steptoe. *The Washington Star* article had been first seen by a senior partner, Jane McGrew. Ms. McGrew had served as counsel to the Shafer Commission and gone on to specialize in pharmaceutical regulation and law. It was Ms. McGrew who had first drawn Tom's attention to *The Star* article.

Nor could we have any idea of the depth of commitment that Steptoe & Johnson would bring to the issue of medical marijuana. They would stand by Robert for the next two decades, as this story will reveal. In the early years of our adventure Robert would often use the metaphor of a lifeboat when he described his experience as America's Only Legal Pot Smoker. To extend that analogy, Steptoe & Johnson became the lighthouse that offered hope to many. Their integrity and professionalism made the critical difference on so many occasions. We cannot repay or ever thank them sufficiently.

14. NEW MEXICO

Our efforts in Washington to re-instate Robert's marijuana would soon be eclipsed by the remarkable accomplishments of Lynn Pierson, the young New Mexican who we met in December 1977 at the NORML conference.

Robert and Lynn became a formidable team. Lynn was a quick study and a natural politician. Shortly after the NORML conference Robert sent the young man a three-page letter outlining his views of what could be accomplished in New Mexico.

> *I warned Lynn against "the fast and splashy route" or "the folk hero trip." I counseled the young New Mexican to stay focused. "The media is after a story and you, as the story focus, have a great deal to do with the type of focus received." I reminded Lynn of Andy Warhol's oft-quoted comment that everyone gets fifteen minutes of fame but admonished the New Mexican that, "The issue of marijuana therapeutics cannot be resolved in fifteen minutes. Keep yourself in a good position and don't worry, the media will come because it is NEWSWORTHY."*

On January 28 the first news report of Lynn's efforts was published in *The Albuquerque Journal*.

"There was little hesitation in Lynn Pierson's voice," the story began, " 'I'm not supposed to be alive,' he said, his voice revealing a trace of pride in a wave of humility."

The article was a relatively "soft" news piece, an interesting story about a man with a problem. There were no inflammatory comments, no heroics. It was a simple, homespun story about a local fellow who had some ideas about passing a law.

Lynn, Robert concluded, "A damn quick study."

New Mexico, despite its immense geography, is a very small place. People actually know people, and politics is personal. In the late 1970s there was only one media market— Albuquerque—with small outposts of print in Santa Fe, Silver City and Las Cruces. Blessed with vast distances and a small population, New Mexico was one of the first states in America to be wired for cable TV. So electronic media generated in

Albuquerque covered the entire state. In political terms New Mexico was a compact, comprehendible place—a community.

In February 1977 Robert smoked legal marijuana for the media in Albuquerque, then spoke before a committee of the state legislature in Santa Fe. On that day, somewhere in the back of the room, was Lynn Pierson.

Now, less than a year later, Lynn was approaching the same legislature for help. Lynn was a native son—which counts for a lot. After our meeting in Washington, Lynn returned home, continued chemo and, despite terminal illness, drove almost daily from his home in Albuquerque to see legislators in Santa Fe.

Open, engaging, and obviously in need of help, Lynn walked—some would say "stalked"—the halls of the state capitol building. The New Mexico legislature was comprised of nearly 100 Senators and Representatives. Lynn spoke personally to nearly every one of them.

His dogged determination captured their attention and his obvious need would soon win their trust and affection. "It's wrong," Lynn would tell them, "that cancer patients are throwing up because our government won't admit marijuana has medical benefits." They could find no way to disagree.

At the outset it was a message Lynn delivered alone. Soon, however, his doctors realized Lynn was serious about passing a law and quietly began phoning legislators to confirm Lynn's observations and express their support of his goal.

Robert advised Lynn to seek help from both Democrats and Republicans. That advice was soon amplified by a more illustrious voice—the Governor. Lynn had easily won the support of Senator Manny Aragon, a Democrat who had sponsored an unsuccessful decriminalization bill in 1977. Senator Aragon discussed the issue with New Mexico Governor Jerry Apodaca and the Governor told Aragon that if he and Pierson could win the support of Senator John Irick, a staunch anti-marijuana hard liner, then they could almost be assured of success in the legislature.

Without hesitation Lynn descended on Senator Irick and explained how marijuana had prolonged his life and helped him tolerate the dreadful chemotherapy treatments. Senator

Irick, initially skeptical, was clearly moved by the young man's courage. He told Lynn "If you get over 50% of the Judiciary Committee we'll figure out something."

The Committee met at the end of January and heard from several witnesses including Lynn, his doctor, a pharmacist from Albuquerque, and Rev. M. Buren Stewart, Lynn's minister and senior pastor from St. John's United Methodist Church in Albuquerque. Rev. Stewart told the committee, "Lynn is trying to help himself and humanity. He is not asking for decriminalization but that [marijuana] be reclassified for doctors to give it for treatment." The proposal sailed through the Committee and Lynn secured Irick's support although the Senator fell short of cosponsoring the bill. For Lynn, and the Governor, it was enough to have Irick's vote.

Nearly all of this was accomplished without much public comment. But, once the Judiciary Committee endorsed the concept in late January Lynn became a bona fide celebrity in the compact media world of New Mexico. He was a natural interview—likeable, determined, absolutely certain he was right. In the press Lynn's quest quickly became a Don Quixote story—dreaming the impossible dream, tilting against windmills. Lynn captured hearts and minds easily. New Mexicans embraced his cause with an almost mystical fervor.

New Mexico politicians were not Washington bureaucrats. They rushed to Lynn's defense and he suddenly became the public face of a State that was absolutely certain compassion could overrule regulation. New Mexico entered the medical marijuana issue with all the hope and optimism that marked the opening of the American West.

After the Judiciary hearings the real work began on the bill. In order to get the initial hearing, Lynn and Aragon had borrowed the recently introduced Hawaiian bill and submitted it to the Judiciary Committee. The bill flatly recognized marijuana's medical value in treating life- and sense-threatening diseases like cancer and glaucoma. It ended the medical prohibition and authorized marijuana's licit medical use under a physician's supervision. It was a start and marked a radical departure from the absolute prohibition of marijuana. But it was merely a broad sketch. It lacked the fine detail necessary for conformity to state and federal law.

It also failed to identify a source of supply for the drug. For Lynn this was the critical point. Without a legal source of supply he knew that other cancer patients, like his friend from the V.A. Hospital, would never be provided with marijuana.

The bill was sent to the New Mexico Legislative Council Services for fine-tuning. It was unlike anything the Council had ever seen. Many questions were raised in staff meetings. The staffers, intent on helping Lynn and others in New Mexico, turned to Washington for guidance, Expecting sympathy and understanding, perhaps even kudos for this "groundbreaking legislation," the New Mexicans were surprised at the reaction they received.

The bureaucrats in Washington were myopically focused on shutting down Robert Randall and slow to realize the erosion that was taking place throughout the country. Their initial responses to New Mexico's Legislative Council Services were blunt and abrasive. New Mexico, the bureaucrats asserted with a haughty certainty, could not abandon the medical prohibition. It was not allowed. Besides, they added with smugness, where will you get the marijuana? Going for the obvious, New Mexico officials noted marijuana was grown by the federal government so couldn't they just get some of the government's pot? No, said the feds. Government marijuana would only be given to government sanctioned "research programs." New Mexico did not have the authority to use the government's marijuana. It couldn't be done. Period.

This was really nothing new to New Mexicans; they were accustomed to "going it alone" and weary to the bone of government intrusion. If Washington wouldn't help then they would help themselves. The Legislative Council Services turned to Lynn for guidance but Lynn was too ill. He knew what he wanted and had little patience with bureaucrats—state or federal—who told him marijuana couldn't be gotten legally. He advised the Council to speak with his friends Robert and Alice.

We began to converse regularly with the folks in New Mexico, raising possibilities, brainstorming ideas. It was new territory for us, too. We didn't have an answer but we were at least willing to explore the options, which was more than the federal bureaucrats had been willing to do.

For a few days we explored the Reichert model, the California judicial decision that released confiscated stocks to a cancer patient. Supply was not a problem, the Council reasoned, because there was plenty of marijuana in New Mexico sitting in the offices of sheriffs and local police. Instead of burning it as contraband why not meet urgent human medical needs and devise a system of drug "destruction" via authorized use?

The Albuquerque Journal seemed to agree when it weighed in with an editorial entitled "The Case for Marijuana" which concluded, "As a civilized society, we should do what we can to help make those who suffer from dread diseases more comfortable. Denying Pierson marijuana thwarts that ideal."

The editorial sent shockwaves through the Washington drug bureaucracies.

As the idea of using confiscated marijuana was floated publicly, the Washington bureaucrats who had been so rude just a few days before suddenly were initiating calls to "their colleagues" in New Mexico. They offered the opinion that the use of confiscated marijuana might be illegal. It certainly was unsanitary. After all, how could New Mexico possibly know if contraband pot seized from drug criminals was contaminated? The DEA was spraying illegal marijuana fields with Paraquat—a deadly herbicide. What might happen if a cancer patient got hold of Paraquated pot? Consider the liabilities.

Employees from the Legislative Council Services began to explore the process of testing marijuana for contaminants. Doubt began to set in. It became obvious that the use of confiscated marijuana did carry some risk. Testing supplies would be an arduous, and expensive, proposition.

Attention then turned to the possibility of growing marijuana in-state but DEA officials quickly squelched that idea pointing to the need for licenses and the expense of securing, harvesting, and preparing the plant.

For the first time since returning home from Washington in December 1977 Lynn became disheartened. The federal effort to re-impose fear began to have a corrosive effect on the enthusiasm for the legislation. For a while there was talk of simply authorizing Lynn to legally use illegal marijuana via a legislative "memorial." It began to look as though the federal government would block New Mexico's drive to legalize medical marijuana.

Things were falling apart when, through a series of brainstorming sessions with Anne Murray, a new friend at the Legislative Council Services, we hit upon a simple question: "Why couldn't New Mexico authorize a statewide research program that provides federal supplies of medical marijuana to cancer patients?" After all, the bureaucrats in Washington insisted it was the government's desire to have research on marijuana's medical use. So, why not give them research? New Mexico could help Lynn and the nation by answering some of the critical questions about marijuana's medical effects.

The compromise position made Lynn nervous and rightly so. "How can we trust the federal bureaucrats?" he asked. We had no answer because we knew the bureaucrats could not be trusted, but, in the final analysis, it was the only plan that could work.

The compromise bill, now entitled the New Mexico Controlled Substances Therapeutic Research Act (CSTRA), swept through the necessary committee hearings in both assemblies and was rushed to the floor for a final vote. In the House it was enacted by a lopsided 53-9. In the Senate the vote was even more impressive: 33-1.

"It was a rout," Lynn shouted into the phone. "We whipped 'em good." Lynn was loving it. "I bet I get government marijuana before you do," he told Robert. Not wishing to experience the bad luck of tempting fate, Robert declined the bet.

To underscore the urgency of their historic measure the Legislature forwarded the newly enacted bill to the Governor Jerry Apodaca for his immediate signature. It was the first "emergency legislation" enacted since the outbreak of the Korean War. Lynn, the legislators felt, should not have to wait for care.

Ignoring the threats of faraway bureaucrats, Governor Apodaca invited Lynn to the bill-signing ceremony on February 21, 1978. After signing the measure, the Governor turned to Lynn and said, "Okay Lynn, you can start smoking it legally now."

It was just ten weeks since we had met Lynn and decided to pass a state law. Cameras flashed, wires ran, and, all across America, ink and megawatts proclaimed that the end of marijuana's medical prohibition had arrived in that most unlikely and conservative of states, New Mexico.

The New Mexico law was a dagger thrust into the heart of federal policy. Lynn's crusade created a landmark law fully supported by inhabitants in the Land of Enchantment. Seemingly without reservation the people of New Mexico wanted Lynn to get his government pot.

"We done good," Lynn said.

"We've done very good," Robert replied. "Now, all we have to do is get the feds to hand over the marijuana."

That's all.

15. BACK IN THE LIFEBOAT

While Governor Jerry Apodaca was signing the New Mexico Controlled Substances Therapeutic Research Act into law, Robert was seated in one of Steptoe & Johnson's impressive conference rooms overlooking Connecticut Avenue and the city of Washington. The firm had agreed to take his case on February 10th and Tom Collier immediately began to coordinate legal strategy. Robert and the young lawyer had one or two preliminary meetings and then Robert was called in to meet the "team."

"This is a huge case," Tom said. "Unless they agree to a settlement we'll have to sue three federal agencies—the DEA, FDA, NIDA—and two cabinet Departments—Justice and Health, Education & Welfare. This is going to take weeks organize."

While dismayed by the prospect of a long delay, Robert was more than pleased with what Tom had accomplished thus far. Seated around the table were five bright, young, and highly aggressive attorneys who, after years of laboring to advance corporate power, were eager to apply their talents to aid an afflicted man in search of justice.

"This is John Bates—constitutional law, Jim Young—bureaucratic procedures . . ." Tom made his way through each one. Robert quickly learned Tom was an exceedingly competent lawyer but his true talent was in coordinating the talents of others. This was the first real test of Tom's ability to marshal Steptoe's tremendous resources and direct the crafting of a large, important case. The firm's partners would closely monitor Tom's progress. Success was his only option.

Robert became an integral member of the team when Tom charged him with collecting affidavits from the doctors. Tom had seen Dr. Fine's affidavit from the 1976 case and was impressed when he learned it had been written by Robert. The young lawyer asked Robert to do the same with Drs. Hepler and Merritt. Robert was delighted to be put to work, especially on the affidavits since it gave him control over how the facts were articulated.

It was soon decided to expand the affidavits to include the stories of other patients who had found marijuana helpful in treating glaucoma. Tom reasoned that such affidavits would demonstrate to the Court the extent to which government restrictions were harming the public and the difficulties faced in trying to obtain marijuana. Robert drafted affidavits for some of our first allies—Vince Mustachio and Ara Cron—as well as some new friends including Jim Ripple of Arizona, a 65-year-old retired cowboy whose wife, Mildred, had called me at the Medical Reclassification Project in early January.

The Playboy Foundation agreed to provide some funding for "out-of-pocket" expenses that might be associated with the case, just as they had with the criminal trial.

Despite all this progress one critical element in the case—a doctor—was missing. Without a physician to supervise Robert's use of marijuana there was no case. He returned to Dr. Fine and once again began the slow dance of persuasion. The good doctor waffled, as usual. It was, in the immortal words of Yogi Berra, "déjà vu all over again."

My work at the Medical Reclassification Project (MRP) was proving to be both timely and interesting. By early March 1978 the New Mexico bill was already law and Hawaii, plus a number of other states, were considering bills, many of them carbon copies of the New Mexico legislation.

Robert had already testified before numerous state legislative committees during his year as America's Only Legal Pot Smoker but I had been working primarily behind the scenes. The MRP would change that. On March 2nd Robert would be in Hawaii testifying on behalf of that state's proposed legislation but the nearby state of Maryland was also holding hearings on that day, in Annapolis, and I decided to attend.

It was a short drive from Washington, DC. The small hearing room was hardly filled. Just a few members of the Judiciary Committee and a handful of witnesses, including me, bothered to attend the hearing on hastily proposed legislation which would reclassify marijuana to recognize its medical utility in the State of Maryland. I spoke briefly and submitted the Hawaiian Report as evidence of the drug's therapeutic potential. I also highlighted the recent signing of the New Mexico bill and focused on the drug's ability to help cancer chemotherapy patients.

My testimony was followed by that of Meredith Sykes, a lovely 25-year-old woman whose composure gave little clue to the disease, multiple sclerosis (MS), that was beginning to ravage her body. Meredith had been making some headlines of her own by publicly discussing marijuana's beneficial effects on the unwanted muscle spasms that are a hallmark of that illness. She had persuaded Dr. Denis Petro, a neurologist and FDA scientific review officer, to attend the hearing and back up her claims of therapeutic utility. Petro had reviewed the current and historical literature, determining that "Ms. Sykes' anecdotal observations seem to be rooted in science."

Meredith, Dr. Petro and myself testified as a panel. We were followed by a second panel comprised of law enforcement officials and a representative of the U.S. Labor Party, a right-wing organization backed by Lyndon LaRouche. All spoke forcefully and with great animation against the measure to reclassify marijuana, using inflammatory language and farfetched projections of imminent harm.

The chairman warmly thanked the second panel and quickly moved to table the measure. His motion was seconded by an aging representative who declared, "If this bill is enacted hippies will go out and get cancer just so they can smoke pot!" The appalling nature of the statement, coupled with the spiteful delivery, left me numb.

Later that same day, in the Scripps Clinic at La Jolla, California, Craig Reichert lost his battle with cancer. In the news accounts of his death, Reichert's family publicly confirmed that legal access to marijuana had made Craig's last days easier, helping to quiet the violent attacks of nausea that followed his chemo.

Before he died Craig confided to his fiancée that one of his last wishes was to thank the man who had made his final days so much easier, Judge Don Work. "He always said he couldn't believe it had happened," his fiancée told the press. "But that afternoon he told me he wished he could get out of bed and go out there and talk about this."

It would be four days later that I learned about the young man's death. Upon hearing the news my thoughts flashed back to the Maryland legislator and his absurd contention that "hippies will get cancer just to smoke pot." The cruelty seemed almost overwhelming. I had never met Craig Reichert, and had spoken only briefly with his mother. Nevertheless, it seemed as though a friend had died. For nearly six weeks Reichert had been America's Only Legal Pot Smoker. Now he was gone.

On March 15, 1978 a joint, two-day meeting of the Controlled Substances Advisory Committee and the Drug Abuse Research Advisory Committee (CSAC & DARAC) convened at 9:00 a.m. Robert, Tom and myself were among the attendees.

A year earlier, in a private meeting, DARAC had been plotting to restrict Robert's access to care, curtail his travel, and limit his speech. We had been barely aware of their existence, let alone the impact they could have on Robert's life. The FDA was packed with little committees of this sort, "public" advisory groups that the public knew nothing about.

Things were changing, however. It was the era of sunshine-in-government and the FDA had been forced to make public the meetings of its "public" advisory committees. There was some grousing about this but the law was the law.

When Tom Collier first learned about the meeting he felt it was important for Robert to address the committees and begin laying the groundwork for the lawsuit. It was, Tom explained, one step in the process of exhausting administrative remedies. "The court will insist we try every possible avenue of resolution." Robert wasn't pleased but he prepared written testimony and made certain he had enough copies for the committee members and the press.

The meeting droned on. The tedious talk, long delays, and glaring florescent lights took its toll on Robert's vision. He was frugally making his way through an extraordinarily generous gift of some prime Arkansas marijuana and had brought only one joint to the hearing. Anticipating that the committee would take up the issue of marijuana therapeutics at the appointed hour, he had used the medication far too early in the day and by late afternoon his ocular pressures had elevated to the point of rendering him white blind, totally unable to read his own testimony. It was nearly 5 p.m. before his name was called.

"My client," Tom Collier began, "is experiencing some difficulties. We request his testimony be postponed until tomorrow morning."

A simple request. But, after a brief discussion, the panel rejected any delay. Robert could barely see Tom's face let alone words on a page. The two conferred briefly and Robert suggested an ad-lib presentation but Tom was insistent on sticking with the prepared testimony. There was little Robert could do. "This is my attorney," he said, "He will read my testimony for the record."

Tom finished reading the testimony and received a terse "Thank you" from the chairman. There was an immediate flurry of not-so-hushed talk from the panel members and we could hear terms like "media trick" and "outrageous" float across the room in our direction. It was clear some members of the combined panel viewed the episode as a staged affair, designed to milk sympathy from the assembled press members.

There was no way to dissuade the thought.

After three weeks of waffling, Dr. Fine, true to form, got cold feet and withdrew from the case. Tom was very angry, feeling that Fine was cowardly and unethical. But Robert was surprisingly calm. He never expected Fine to reach the finish line with him. It would be his last encounter with the doctor who, in a very real sense, saved Robert's sight by playing straight. By not rushing Robert to surgery the doctor saved him from the fate of Vince and Ara.

On March 24th, the day after Fine's final defection, the heavens opened once again and brought forth a new doctor. He was a friend of Merritt's. Tom spoke with him in the morning and arranged an appointment for Robert in the afternoon.

Dr. Richard North was in private practice and had no opinion regarding marijuana's medical use in glaucoma therapy. But he was intrigued by the possibility and disturbed by the ethical implications of what Tom Collier had told him.

Dr. North was about Merritt's age, but they were very different men. Unlike Merritt, who had excessive nervous energy, Dr. North had an easy, pleasing manner. Merritt was intense and guarded. Richard North was open and loved to laugh. He seemed to enjoy Robert's cynical wit and the two men immediately liked one another.

North conducted an eye examination and, just like every physician who first examined Robert's eyes, he winced at the damage he found. Robert's eye pressures were above 30 in each eye.

"You're on your standard meds?" North asked.

"Yes. And my pressure will go higher towards evening." Robert explained. The two men spent some time discussing the UCLA findings and then Robert asked, "Would you like to see the difference marijuana can make?"

"I thought you didn't have any government marijuana," North replied.

"I'm out of government pot. But I have some high quality marijuana. Would you like to see it work?" Robert knew he was tempting North.

"Where could you smoke?" North said without hesitation.

"Oh, I'll just go out in the street. No one cares," Robert said.

But Dr. North cared. He was uncomfortable with the idea of a patient—his patient—wandering around the Adams Morgan area of Washington, DC smoking a joint. "Why not out back?" He led Robert to a fenced yard behind the office. "No one will bother you here. I have another patient coming. Why don't you relax, smoke out here."

When North was finished with his next patient he came to fetch Robert and they returned to the exam room.

"This is amazing," Dr. North said recalibrating his tonometer, then rechecking Robert's pressure again. "There's been a 50% decline in your eye pressure! It's now normal. In just over an hour. Does marijuana always work this well?"

"Always," Robert said. "If it didn't I'd be blind."

"Impressive."

"So," Robert asked, "will you be my doctor? I have lots of attorneys and a good legal case. But I need a doctor to monitor my condition, make reports and write script. Are you willing to help me?"

"I'd be pleased to be your doctor, Robert," North said without equivocation. "You understand I can't say much about marijuana—this is the first time I've seen it work. But, having seen this, to deny you care would be unethical. Downright unethical."

Dr. North, we learned, was an ethical man who responded to facts, especially facts he could measure on his tonometer.

By the end of March the affidavits were done and the last legal briefs were being evaluated. The legal argument, Tom explained, was tricky. "There is no constitutional right to sight," he said. "But that does not mean such a right does not exist."

"You clearly have a right to speak. The government cannot take that away from you. And," Tom said, "just as clearly—as the Bourne letter plainly shows—the government is trying to manipulate your medical care to control your speech. That's a start."

At this point, however, the law became theoretical. "Do you," Tom wondered, "have a constitutionally protected right to your sight?"

To us the answer seemed obvious. If "medical necessity" could be used as a defense to criminal charges, certainly the Constitution must, in some way, recognize the right of an individual to protect his sight—his biology—against government interference.

"Yes," Tom reasoned, "but does that mean you have a constitutionally protected right to see? Or, more specifically, to compel the government to provide you with a legally prohibited drug to retain your sight?"

This legal question deeply intrigued the Steptoe associates and multiple briefs were prepared in an attempt to locate and articulate a legal "right to sight."

The consensus was that by implication the Constitution must afford protection against undue government interference in medical care. A "right to sight" must exist somewhere between the right of parents to teach a child German (*Meyer v*

Nebraska, 1923) and the Supreme Court's recognition of a woman's right to abort a fetus (*Roe v. Wade*, 1973). "Certainly," Tom argued, "if a woman can elect—based on her innate privacy and biological rights—to abort a fetus, a man can elect to smoke marijuana to preserve his vision."

Having settled on this interpretation, of an implied right within an already accepted spectrum of rights, the associates returned to their law books to obtain citations to sustain the claim. "It is," Tom admitted, "less than certain how this might turn out in court. But, I think we can demonstrate the Constitution protects you from government actions that seek to control your speech by jeopardizing your sight. I'm fairly sure," he continued, "the government does not have a right to blind you for your speech."

The case was coming together and by the first week in April the suit was ready to be filed. Before rushing to court, however, Tom Collier decided to make one last "good faith" effort to resolve the case. So he began another round of calls into the bureaucracy. The result was not what we expected.

Ed Tocus, at the FDA, was suggesting an alternative to marijuana. A new, unapproved drug called Timoptic was in final Phase III testing. If research went well Timoptic could be approved by October. "Perhaps," Tocus suggested, "this new drug could help Mr. Randall retain his sight short of smoking marijuana."

Tocus provided Tom with the name of the company that produced the drug and a list of ongoing studies. "Perhaps we could get Mr. Randall into one of these studies? That might solve everybody's problem."

Robert was livid. Marijuana controlled his glaucoma—that was a well-documented fact. A doctor was ready to monitor his care. Hundreds of hours of research had gone into refining a credible legal argument. "I'm not going to become a government guinea pig!" he angrily told Tom.

"I'm not certain we have a choice," Tom calmly replied.

The team of Steptoe associates quickly assembled. All agreed: if a legal alternative to marijuana existed then questions of rights diminished into issues of preference. Robert could not "prefer" an illegal treatment over a legal therapy.

"But marijuana works. What if this new, unapproved drug doesn't work?" Robert protested.

"Then we have an even better legal argument," Tom replied.

Steptoe researchers scoured the medical libraries for information on Timoptic. It was derived from timolol maleate, a beta-blocker used in heart care. Merck, Sharp & Dome had developed a topical timolol eye drop under the brand name Timoptic. The results were outstanding.

On paper, Timoptic looked like a wonder drug. It lacked the myopia-inducing properties of most glaucoma drugs, and reduced intraocular pressure in 8 of 10 research subjects. Phase I and II testing revealed no alarming adverse affects. Now Timoptic was in final, Phase III testing. If no serious problems were detected, Timoptic would receive FDA marketing approval by fall.

The Steptoe associates did unearth the fact that about 14% of patients failed on the drug for unknown reasons. But all-in-all it did seem like a very promising drug. Like it or not, Robert was headed back to the research lab.

The closest test site was, ironically, at Johns Hopkins. But Robert had burned his bridges there and was refused admittance. The next closest test site was at Duke University in North Carolina, just up the road from the Research Triangle Institute where the government processed Mississippi marijuana into pre-rolled cigarettes and where Mario Perez-Reyes had infused Robert with pure THC in the fall of 1975.

Robert traveled to North Carolina in mid-April. The Timoptic study was being conducted by Dr. R. Bruce Shields. The middle-aged man did nothing to calm Robert's anxieties about the testing when he stated, "I understand the FDA has a particular interest in your case."

The first exam was routine. Robert's pressures were high, just under 40mm Hg. Shields administered Timoptic and did another pressure check an hour later.

"Excellent. Already responding," Shields triumphantly said. "Almost down to 20."

With that Robert was given a week's supply of the drug and sent home to Washington. The four-week plan called for Robert to travel to North Carolina once a week where Shields would evaluate the progress. The Playboy Foundation agreed to pay the travel expense. During the intervening days Dr. North would assess Robert's condition daily. This would eliminate questions regarding controls and provide an early warning if something went wrong.

For the first few days all was well.

"This is astonishing," Dr. North said. "Your IOP is 8. Just amazing."

The news, which at any other time would have been greeted with glee, deepened Robert's sense of impending loss. Having come so far was modern science about to steal the legal case and save the medical prohibition?

For the next three days Robert's eye pressures remained low but each day they inched up on the tonometer scale. On the third day the reading was 18. "I don't like the looks of this," Dr. North said, noting the increasing IOP readings. "We may be seeing a trend."

On the fourth day Robert's IOP was 22—above normal, in the danger zone. By the fifth day it was clear things were not quite right. The IOP was 26. "This could be tachyphylaxis, a rapid onset of tolerance to a drug's therapeutic effect," North explained to Robert. "You're developing a tolerance to Timoptic. If your IOP keeps going up we'll have to stop this study. These elevated pressures are endangering your sight."

Dr. North notified Tom Collier of the creeping IOP elevation. Both agreed to continue the experiment. "It's important," Tom explained, "to give Timoptic a fair trial."

On Robert's second visit to Duke, with pressures slowly rising, he hoped Shields would recognize the problem and terminate the experiment. But the doctor would not admit defeat. "This is a surprising result. You're taking the Timoptic every 12 hours as instructed?" he questioned.

"Yes," Robert replied. "Dr. North suggested tachyphylaxis?"

"Oh, I doubt that," Shields said, ignoring the evidence in front of him. "We had a case or two like that, but we shouldn't jump to conclusions. I'll see you next week."

During the entire second week Robert's IOP was above normal, constantly creeping higher. Dr. North became alarmed. "You can't tolerate much more of this without permanently damaging your sight," he said.

When Dr. North informed Tom Collier of the disappointing results, the Steptoe associates were galvanized into action. "We're prepared to file as soon as Dr. Shields determines Timoptic has failed," Tom Collier said.

By the third trip to North Carolina things were seriously out of control. "Your IOP is over 40," Shields said with mild alarm. "You are not responding properly to Timoptic." Shields' tone was accusatory, implying it was the patient, not the drug that had failed. "Are you taking your doses properly?"

"Yes. And Dr. North has administered many of the doses," Robert said, weary of the game being played with my sight. "I'm not the problem. Timoptic simply does not work. Does it?"

"No, it isn't working," Shields admitted. "But, I cannot allow you to leave with these pressures. You're in grave danger of losing your sight." He called in a nurse, spoke to her in hushed tones, then returned to me. "You'll be staying here tonight." It was not a question, but a command.

Robert was completely taken aback. "Why would I stay here?"

"The nurse is arranging for the first available operating theatre. We'll do your surgery this evening, and keep you here a few days for observation." Shields spoke the words with remarkable detachment.

"The hell you will," Robert replied. His tolerance was exhausted. "I am not going to have any damn operation. Not here. Not now. Timoptic has failed, right?"

"Yes," Shields sighed. "If Timoptic doesn't work nothing will work. If you don't have an operation—an immediate operation—you could be blind in a few days, maybe a couple of hours."

His scare tactics only increased Robert's fury.

"I am not—repeat NOT—having an operation," he was emphatic. "I am going home to smoke marijuana and get these pressures under control. My attorneys will contact you for a written statement."

As Shields continued to press, Robert abruptly stood up and headed for the door. "Thanks for your help. My attorneys will be calling."

It was time to file the lawsuit.

Three days after Robert's return from North Carolina, May 8, Tom filed the case.

It was, as Tom predicted, immense. The factual record, including affidavits, research reports, and correspondence ran more than 150 pages. The mean-spirited dialogue between Robert and the bureaucrats–including Dr. Peter Bourne's inartful threats–hung like a fuse at the heart of the brief. If the case went to trial the President's chief adviser on health and drug abuse, the DEA Administrator, and high-ranking FDA officials would be hauled before the court and compelled to publicly explain their threats. The press would flay them alive.

If the fact case was dense, the legal argument was equally thick, with a lean commentary interlacing constitutional claims to citations of federal statutes and relevant case law.

The final product was a handsome, intimidatingly large package held together by binding rings. The last piece of evidence was Dr. R. Bruce Shields' statement confirming Timolol's failure. Shields, however, omitted any written reference to his dire warning of Robert's imminent blindness.

Within 24 hours of filing suit the government offered to settle. We had won! But, oddly, it wasn't enough. Robert and I wanted to fight. For two years Robert had been bullied and threatened. Now, when its evil deeds were about to be publicly exposed the government folded like a house of cards. To hell with a settlement!

Tom wanted to fight too. But Tom Collier was learning to be a good attorney and a good attorney knows a settlement— on your terms—is better than a protracted courtroom battle fought to an uncertain outcome.

In crafting the settlement we agreed on a simple formulation: Robert's access to marijuana would be treated as any other medical prescription. The script would be written by his private physician and honored by a pharmacy. Beyond these elemental demands the settlement would strictly prohibit his involvement in future research. There would be no more Timoptic episodes. Finally, the bureaucrats could not use medical access to marijuana to restrict his right to speak or freedom to travel.

The proposed settlement compelled federal agencies to accept an anathema: A private physician writing script for marijuana and a pharmacy responsible for obtaining and dispensing supplies. The traditional patient-physician-pharmacy arrangement seemed so simple but it undermined the entire regulatory scheme. We were certain the government would reject the idea.

But in filing the lawsuit we had moved beyond the bickering of agencies. A U.S. Attorney was now in charge of the government's case and he accepted the settlement the next day. Tom then began hammering out the specifics with the various agencies. We can only imagine the scene at the FDA, NIDA, and DEA. We knew there were profound interagency frictions at work and there was much unhappiness, especially at the DEA.

Tom was skillful and resolute, demanding the best possible agreement for his client. Regulations that had seemed rigid and intractable fell away before the awesome power of the case.

To satisfy the FDA, Dr. North agreed to be an Investigational New Drug (IND) researcher. The usually complex, months-long IND process for marijuana vanished before the pressure exerted by Steptoe & Johnson. North received automatic FDA authorization to write script for marijuana.

Ed Tocus, when asked what the FDA would call this unusual process said, "Oh, it's a 'Compassionate IND' which allows for the medical use of a non-approved drug."

"Compassionate IND"—it was a term that had first surfaced briefly, in the summer of '76 but "compassion" had been dropped as hard-liners got the upper hand during that long summer of trial and negotiation.

It was, in fact, the first time the FDA authorized the medical use of an unapproved drug. The fact that marijuana was legally prohibited was ignored. It was a crack in the FDA structure with profound future implications.

16. SUFFER TO THEIR DEATHS

Robert's legal access to marijuana was once again in place, this time secured by the weight and influence of Steptoe & Johnson. He was back in the lifeboat but the cries of others needing help were growing louder. We knew that we must do something to expand legal access to other seriously ill individuals. It seemed our best bet was in the state laws. FDA continually harped on the need for research and in New Mexico legislation had been passed which would create a statewide program of research. Despite our battering by federal agencies we still believed we could give FDA what they wanted—medical marijuana research and plenty of it.

On May 25, 1978, two weeks after Robert's supplies were re-instated, he received a call from Lynn Pierson in New Mexico. "I'm glad you declined that bet," Lynn said, sounding weak. "I woulda lost big time. I'm still waiting and things don't sound too good."

Lynn was right. Things weren't good. Earlier that day I had talked with Anne Murray, a contact in the N.M. Legislative Council Services Office with whom I had worked for several weeks trying to make the signed legislation a reality. "It's all falling apart, Alice," the woman sounded very frustrated.

For three months officials in New Mexico had been working to obtain federal supplies of marijuana for Lynn and other cancer patients. They approached FDA in good faith. When the Washington bureaucrats asked for a "research protocol" the physicians at the University of New Mexico quickly complied. But the FDA found the proposal lacking. A second draft was submitted. And then a third.

New Mexico officials could not satisfy constantly expanding federal demands and began to feel like hamsters running in a wheel. Most frustrating was FDA's refusal to directly address the "problems" in the protocol. "You're not going to believe this, Alice." Anne went on. "When one of our doctors tried to clarify a point of procedure the reply from FDA was, 'You're getting warmer.' They treat this like it's a game."

Of greatest concern to Lynn was the attempt by FDA to impose "double-blind" testing. Under this plan fewer than half the cancer patients in New Mexico would actually receive marijuana. Others would be given placebo cigarettes or synthetic THC pills.

Lynn was furious. "I didn't fight so half the cancer patients in New Mexico would be tricked into getting phony pot."

Lynn's powerful friends in the legislature, the Department of Health and the media agreed. The law entitled cancer patients to receive medical marijuana. New Mexico did not intend to turn desperately ill cancer patients into U.S. government approved guinea pigs.

As Lynn had feared, the bureaucrats in Washington could not be trusted. Despite federal assurances of providing supplies of marijuana, bureaucratic resistance stiffened as other states began exploring New Mexico's historic legislation. If federal drug warriors could block New Mexico's request for supplies, other states would be less inclined to follow New Mexico's lead.

And there was ample reason to be worried about other states. As the Steptoe lawyers hammered out the last pieces in the *Randall v. U.S.* settlement, Robert was in Tallahassee, Florida, testifying on behalf of a New Mexico style marijuana-as-medicine bill. Similar legislation was moving along in Illinois and Louisiana. All three bills had a chance of passage in 1978.

State legislation, such as that passed in New Mexico, was not the only route that patients were using in their pursuit of legal access to marijuana for medical purposes.

Mildred and Jim Ripple, like Ara and Gerald Cron, had obtained some marijuana and discovered it worked on Jim's glaucoma. The elderly couple lived on a remote ranch in southeastern Arizona but that didn't slow down Mildred. She was determined to get Jim legal access and had even spoken with the officials in New Mexico about joining the neighboring state's program once it was authorized. New Mexico officials, frustrated with the FDA's refusal to approve the state's program, had sent her to the FDA. Let them speak with real people who have real problems, they reasoned.

Mildred did not hesitate to call the Washington agencies. And then she called again. And again. This regular bombardment of Washington bureaucrats with a cold, hard dose of reality would often cause some interesting revelations and Mildred became a conduit of Washington insight. In early July 1978, she telephoned the people in Washington, including Ed Tocus at FDA who told her the New Mexico program would never get off the ground because there wasn't enough marijuana. Mildred immediately called me at the Medical Reclassification Project to report what Tocus told her.

"Are you sure, Mildred?" I was having trouble comprehending what I had just heard.

"That's what Mr. Tocus said." The elderly woman was sure. "He said the FDA has destroyed its marijuana and only has enough for Bob Randall."

"The FDA doesn't have any marijuana," I said, trying to explain the difference between the FDA and NIDA.

"Not any more they don't!" The Arizonan woman was dead certain about what Tocus had said. "I don't know why they just don't grow more. But Mr. Tocus said Bob Randall was getting it all and they'd have to send pills to the New Mexico folks. Do you know if the pills would work for Jim?"

I couldn't make any sense of it but I was sure it was a warning flag. It was, in hindsight, the first glimmer of the "supply problem." New Mexico, a relatively small state in terms of population, expected several hundred patients in its program once it was approved by federal agencies. In 1978 three more states—Florida, Louisiana and Illinois— would pass laws similar to New Mexico's. These three states had much higher population numbers and would surely require more marijuana for their programs. More worrisome yet was the growing number of states that were preparing legislation for the 1979 legislative sessions.

The federal government was facing an awesome possibility—thousands of patients needing marijuana cigarettes. Ed Tocus' odd comments to Mildred Ripple were, perhaps, like the canary in the mineshaft, the first whiff that something was wrong. The bureaucrats were nervous.

For Lynn Pierson the summer of 1978 would be his last. Throughout July he fought on courageously, even traveling to Los Angeles to appear on the Tom Snyder "Tomorrow" show. He was hopeful when, on July 13th, the state certified Lynn as the first patient in the program. News accounts, including a story in *The New York Times*, reported that "the FDA was expected to approve the program and it could start in a little more than 30 days."

It was the *Times* article that led to Lynn's invitation to L.A. where he not only taped the Snyder show but also met Johnny Carson—a true highlight of the trip.

Robert saw the show and was shocked at Lynn's appearance:

> I had met Lynn only once, at the NORML conference in December 1977. Now, seven months later, Lynn had the look of a concentration camp victim. He was gaunt beyond words and there was a sallowness about his eyes that even the TV makeup couldn't erase.
>
> I looked at my friend and realized Lynn would not live to see his legal marijuana.

On August 11, Lynn collapsed at his home and lapsed into respiratory failure. The emergency rescue team worked frantically to revive him but by the time he was admitted to the hospital Lynn was comatose and brain dead. For the next four days Lynn's family would agonize over what to do. Lynn's brain waves were flat, his breathing controlled by a respirator. Finally, on August 15, Lynn Pierson died.

He was 27.

On the day of Lynn's death New Mexico officials exploded with pent-up rage against The System. Across the state there was outrage that Lynn had died without ever receiving the promised marijuana. This rage was expressed to Washington in no uncertain terms. Sensing a PR nightmare, federal agencies moved quickly to blunt the impact. Within three hours of learning about Lynn's death, the FDA verbally approved New Mexico's application for a statewide medical marijuana program.

Robert flew to New Mexico for the funeral and was startled by the emotions he encountered. State officials made a point of seeking him out, thanking him for all the help he had given Lynn and then venting an absolute contempt for the endless delays, the incompetence and sheer brutality of federal bureaucrats. Nevertheless there was a ray of hope. FDA had approved the program. Too late for Lynn, the mourners sadly noted, but at least he had not died in vain.

The day after Lynn's memorial service the FDA "clarified" its verbal approval and more demands were made by the federal agency. New Mexican officials realized they had been duped again. For a while New Mexican officials again considered confiscated stocks of marijuana but finally, with resignation, realized the use of such stocks posed immense legal liabilities.

It would take several more months and eight more patient deaths before New Mexico reached the end of its patience.

On October 27, 1978, Dr. George Goldstein, New Mexico's Secretary of Health, wrote a scathing letter to HEW Secretary Joseph Califano. If New Mexico's request was not approved, Goldstein promised to hold a press conference to publicly denounce the FDA delays as:

> ... neither morally nor ethically defensible. If DHEW's desire is to prevent programs such as ours from being implemented, please state that position publicly rather than prevent their implementation through indirect action and prohibitive procedures, while well-meaning citizens submit applications and suffer to their deaths wondering why they have not received the marijuana which they expected."

Finally, on January 26, 1979, New Mexico would receive its first shipments of marijuana and the long-anticipated research program would get under way. A few days later the New Mexico legislature would convene. Among their first acts was to name the statewide program The Lynn Pierson Therapeutic Research Program.

Lynn died without ever receiving his first legal joint but Lynn did not fail. Despite terminal illness he had been a powerful ally. His valiant efforts produced the New Mexico model for medical marijuana, a standard that would be taken to other states and adopted overwhelmingly.*

There would be new allies. The fight would go on. But Lynn was special. Pathfinders always are.

---

*Twenty-eight years later the New Mexico legislature would once again enact a law authorizing legal access to marijuana for those with life- and sense-threatening diseases. The bill was named the Lynn and Erin Compassionate Use Law, recognizing Lynn and Erin Armstrong, a young cancer patient who picked up Lynn's banner in 2004 and lobbied successfully for passage of the bill in 2007.

17. THE RIPPLES OF CHANGE

It was increasingly important to track the moves of the bureaucracies and we were learning that a great deal of information could be gleaned from committee meetings. I became conscientious in tracking the agendas of the seemingly endless number of government committees that had their finger in the medical prohibition pie.

DARAC, the committee that had plotted Robert's comeuppance in the first half of 1977, was of particular interest to us. In September 1978, perhaps hoping to escape the increasingly public meetings in Washington, DARAC members headed south for a meeting at the University of Mississippi. I was close on their heels.

On September 28, my 31st birthday, I stood in the middle of five acres of land affectionately referred to as Uncle Sam's Pot Farm. DARAC was taking a "field trip" and I was brushing shoulders with an elite group of farmers—the legal marijuana farmers employed by the U.S. government.

The 1978 crop was mostly gone, harvested just a week or so earlier. All that was left was a field of dark delta mud littered with broken stalks drying on black plastic tarps in the hot sun. In the center of the plot were a few plants of the *indica* variety, shorter and more bushy than their *sativa* cousins.

"Specialty items," noted Carlton Turner dryly. The director of the University of Mississippi Research Institute of Pharmaceutical Sciences (RIPS) was giving the DARAC members the grand tour. Turner referred to all marijuana not in his 5-acre fiefdom as, "Cannabis which has escaped from cultivation." There was not a hint of amusement at his turn of phrase. Marijuana, in his mind, was "a crude drug."

The farm was surrounded by a double fence of barbed and razor wire. Between the two fences was a path for guard dogs. Watchtowers with searchlights stood at the corners of the barren enclosure. It all seemed a bit excessive but was certainly serious in its appearance.

Looking about the acreage I was astonished at how small five acres could be. The cute references to the Pot Plantation had implied a huge operation, but it was tiny. Much of the land wasn't even tilled. At best there was just an acre under cultivation...and guard. "How," I wondered, "could this farm grow enough marijuana for New Mexico, Florida, Louisiana, and Illinois?"

The small group scuffed about in the dirt, posed for some pictures and then returned to the RIPS facilities where I met an aging southern gent; a professor of botany with a mane of snow-white hair and gracious Mississippi manners. Unlike Turner, who greeted inquiries with a tinge of paranoia, the old botanist was delighted by my interest in his arcane endeavors. Without hesitation he pulled out a large scrap-book to show me his favorite marijuana leaves from past harvests.

Officially, the Mississippi "Pot Plantation" began its work in the late 1960s. It was obvious, however, that the farm had been in operation much longer. The elder botany professor with his treasured book of long-ago harvested leaves suggested the pot plantation was decades old.

The farm had been an interesting sideshow but the real item on the agenda that had captured my attention was "Discussion of proposed protocols for Schedule I drugs." Jim Ripple's protocol had been submitted several months before and I was certain it would be part of the presentation.

Mildred Ripple, Jim's wife, had become regular correspondents with me. Mildred was feisty and determined to do everything it took to obtain medical marijuana for her husband. She was not going to let Jim go blind if there was something that could help him. Jim's family had a long history of glaucoma. His mother and a brother had been blinded by the disease, their eyeballs literally rupturing from elevated pressures. Mildred would not let that happen to Jim.

The elderly couple lived in the southernmost deserts of Arizona, three hours from Tucson, not far from the Mexican border. Their doctor was sixty miles away. Their remoteness seemed daunting but Mildred had painstakingly put together the necessary pieces to apply for permission to use marijuana. In July, Jim's doctor had submitted an IND protocol, copied almost word-for-word, from Robert's approved Compassionate IND.

To make certain that compassion prevailed, I discussed the case with Tom Collier who, in turn, discussed it with a friend in Arizona. Before long Mildred and Jim had the high-powered, Phoenix-based legal firm of Brown & Bain at their disposal.

Once Brown & Bain got involved the FDA became more helpful. Ed Tocus did not want a replay of Robert's case. A glaucoma patient—an aging, retired cowboy—suing the government for marijuana was certain to attract media attention and garner public sympathy.

Mildred lined up some political support as well, contacting Senator Barry Goldwater and asking for his help in expediting Jim's request. She also enlisted the support of Senator Muriel Humphrey, widow of former vice president Hubert Humphrey who had recently died of cancer. There had been rumors that Mr. Humphrey used marijuana during his chemotherapy treatments.

Now, in a non-descript room in Mississippi, Jim Ripple's fate was being discussed and it was tying my stomach in knots.

There was grousing from some committee members about letters from a lawyer and "those Senators." Repeatedly the committee returned to regulatory procedure and the inappropriateness of releasing an unapproved drug to a "single patient" who was clearly not part of any "viable research." There was more worry about precedents than there was concern about an ailing cowboy who had exhausted all conventional routes of treatment.

Finally I could contain myself no longer and, like a schoolgirl, I raised my hand to be recognized. "I am not sure it is appropriate for members of the public to make comments," I began politely, "but I think you have got to realize that marijuana is unlike other drugs that go through the IND process. I know this case you are talking about. I know the individuals involved and I know that the man has used marijuana illegally."

The committee listened respectfully as I spoke. "You've got to remember that marijuana is available to people. That is the big difference between it and the other drugs you are dealing with. I think it is far better for this man to receive marijuana through his doctor than to find it on the street."

"You say you know this specific case, the 65-year old man?" the DARAC chairman asked, with some surprise.

"Yes," I replied and then explained the human side of a case known to DARAC as Protocol K. The members listened, some with open amazement. Protocol K would survive DARAC and Jim Ripple's protocol would be approved in early October. But the Arizona cowboy would not get his legal marijuana any time soon.

My excursion to the "Pot Plantation" created more pieces of a puzzle that was presenting itself to us. There was Mildred's recanting of Tocus' curious claim that "all the marijuana has been destroyed." There were the references to a new drug called Nabilone at another joint-agency committee. What was that? And now there were these curious hints of a long established marijuana farm in the Mississippi Delta.

We decided to use one of the few tools given us by the federal government and filed a request under the Freedom of Information Act to see what we could learn about the government's production of marijuana and, while we were at it, we asked for minutes from any committee meetings at which medical marijuana had been discussed in the past two years.

The Freedom of Information Act materials arrived very quickly. The large packet contained detailed information on annual production, stockpiles of raw material and a complete inventory of finished, pre-rolled marijuana cigarettes. There was enough budgetary information to calculate the cost of production: about 90 cents per ounce to grow marijuana, with two-thirds of this cost going to security. The actual price of production minus security came to 30 cents per ounce.

Given these figures, is it any wonder pharmaceutical companies promoting expensive synthetic drugs have little interest in pursuing marijuana's therapeutic utility? Sure, marijuana might aid the afflicted. But how could a pharmaceutical company profit from such a cheap, easy-to-produce product? This was a bottom-line question that animated the prohibition. Beyond dogma there were dollars.

18. CRITICAL MASS

In the first quarter of 1979 the medical marijuana issue was virtually exploding across the country. There was a dizzying array of successes.

By March 22nd a total of sixteen states were considering medical marijuana legislation. A total of seven states had already enacted laws. There were the original four from 1978—New Mexico, Florida, Louisiana, and Illinois—plus recent successes in West Virginia, Washington, and Virginia.

Sixteen states considering laws plus seven laws already passed: twenty-three! Almost half the country actively considering medical marijuana! And that didn't even begin to include the indications of interest from other states, proposed or active lawsuits, and people like Jim Ripple, who were willing to fight the long battle for individual access to marijuana. Jim's supplies finally arrived in mid-January, just after New Mexico received its shipment. The retired cowboy was using the legally supplied marijuana with great success. His glaucoma was well controlled. Mildred was delighted.

It was an incredible period of time and we were sure the feds would never manage to get the lid back on the medical marijuana box. We were only partially right.

In early March I attended yet another of the monthly meetings of the Interagency Committee on New Therapies for Pain and Discomfort—a mega-committee comprised of 32 members from at least ten different agencies. The committee was chaired by Dr. Seymour Perry and had been meeting since late 1977 but the feds had not been eager to publicize its existence. I learned about it in mid 1978 from a well-connected Maryland citizen who was attempting to restore heroin to the list of drugs that doctors could prescribe for intractable pain.

The group "was formed in response to the expressed interest of the White House and Dr. Peter Bourne ... in the problems of pain and other discomforts of the dying and in fostering research on the possible pain-relieving characteristics of abused substances not approved for treatment in the United States."

Now, after nearly eighteen months of regular monthly meetings, there was an evident weariness. Medical marijuana dominated the discussions. There was no longer the patina of humanitarian concern or discussions of "helping the states" and "facilitating research." The darker forces, which advocated a tougher stance against marijuana therapeutics, were beginning to prevail. The focus was now on stopping the firestorm of medical marijuana legislation that was sweeping across the country. Words such as "discourage," "deactivate," and "defuse" were freely used. There was no effort to conceal the bureaucratic contempt for the efforts of the states.

But the bureaucrats had grossly miscalculated the strength of the medical marijuana issue. Viewing it as akin to marijuana decriminalization, the bureaucrats failed to understand the human dimension and, surprisingly, the support of conservative—true conservative—volunteers. Conservatives get cancer, too. Dixie Lee Ray, the Washington Governor who signed the nation's fifth marijuana-as-medicine bill, was one of them.

Indeed, it was conservatives—arch foes of centralized power—who became medical marijuana's most ardent proponents in the late 1970s. After 50 years of federal encroachment, conservatives were ready to reclaim state power and defend the sovereign rights of citizens to medical care.

And citizens were ready to demand it. In every state that considered a marijuana-as-medicine bill in 1979 the effort was propelled by a human-interest story. Some were small and lacked notoriety. Others blazed across the media skies, capturing attention, inspiring change. Here are just a few examples of the ways in which citizens demanded change:

• In Washington State the doorkeeper to the House of Representatives made it a point to tell every legislator about his wife's successful use of marijuana in combating the side effects of cancer chemotherapy. Washington legislators also took testimony from dozens of cancer patients who vigorously endorsed marijuana's medical usefulness.

• In Nevada legislators heard testimony from a 23-year-old woman blinded by the side effects of diabetes. She testified that marijuana helped ease the ocular discomfort she experienced and stimulated her appetite, which was helpful in controlling the diabetes. A Mormon judge who suffered from cancer initially requested the Nevada bill, enacted in June 1979. In testifying for the bill the judge said, "I, myself, because of my cultural background, would be reluctant to smoke marijuana. However, I might reconsider that cultural opposition if it appeared to be medically appropriate."

- In California, Patrick Mayer, a cancer survivor, would spearhead the campaign for that state's medical marijuana bill. Mayer, whose leg was amputated as a result of cancer, was an articulate young man who claimed to be one of the anonymous patients to first report marijuana's medical usefulness to the Boston oncologists in the early 1970s.

- A 50-year-old farmer's wife named Elva Emry inspired action in two states, Nebraska and Iowa. The Nebraskan cancer patient asked her neighboring state of Iowa for help in obtaining legal access to marijuana because medical facilities across the border were closer to her home. The request sparked legislation in both states. Iowa's bill would pass in June 1979.

- In Louisiana, Michael Pobuda, a 24-year-old victim of Hodgkin's disease, spent his final days of life struggling to implement the Louisiana bill enacted in 1978.

In that extraordinary year of 1979 there were many brave individuals who came forward to support medical access to marijuana. Many more quietly worked in the background, writing letters and making calls. But from our personal point of view the most compelling story of 1979 was Keith Nutt, a young man from Michigan who had the misfortune to contract cancer in his 22nd year of life but was blessed with fine parents who helped make his final days of life expansive and triumphant.

Like Lynn Pierson, Keith Nutt had testicular cancer. It was diagnosed in the spring of 1978. At the time he was living in Columbus, Ohio. His parents, Mae and Arnold Nutt, were living in Beaverton, Michigan. Keith had surgery to remove the cancerous testicle but, unlike Lynn, Keith did not immediately begin chemo. The doctors felt they had successfully removed the cancer. Keith tried to get on with his life but was unable to maintain his energy and, in the fall of 1978, he moved back home with his parents.

On January 1, 1979, Keith told his parents the cancer had returned. His remaining testicle was hard and enlarged. He saw a doctor the next day and was hospitalized that afternoon.

The second surgery was followed by extensive chemotherapy. Keith received Cisplatin and had severe problems with nausea and vomiting. His parents watched in horror as chemo took a rapid and devastating toll. Keith couldn't eat, couldn't bear to even smell food. His weight dropped dramatically.

For Mae and Arnold it was all too reminiscent of another son's illness. Keith's younger brother, Dana, had Ewings Sarcoma and suffered grievously during his short nine years of life. Keith told Mae he did not want to suffer like Dana. He vowed he would take his own life rather than waste away as Dana had. Keith extracted a promise from Mae that she would help him when the time came.

These were dark days for the Nutt family. Keith lost more than thirty pounds and grew weaker by the day. Mae was concerned she would be called upon to fulfill her promise to her eldest son.

Then she read in a local newspaper that marijuana could help cancer patients endure chemotherapy. Initially she scoffed at the idea but when she mentioned it to Keith he confirmed that other cancer patients talked about it. Mae needed no more encouragement. She began making calls to obtain more information, including packets from the Medical Reclassification Project.

Mae and Arnold read it all and were convinced. They began making inquiries to obtain marijuana for Keith's next chemo session but there was none to be found. Finally, they would "score" through an unlikely source—a Presbyterian minister who listened carefully to their story and arrived at their house late in the evening on the night before Keith's chemo with a small baggie of marijuana.

The next day, with some anxiety, Mae and Arnold watched Keith smoke the marijuana just as the nausea began to well up inside him. It was, they would later say, "miraculous." There was no vomiting, no nausea. Quite to the contrary, Keith's appetite improved as well as his demeanor and overall wellbeing. The aches and pains diminished. He was able to join his family for dinner—an act of sublime simplicity made possible by an illegal weed.*

As Mae watched her son improve she became enraged at the prospect of breaking the law to help him. She and Keith became vigorous and vocal advocates for the New Mexico style legislation that had already been proposed in Michigan. Despite his improvement, Keith was still very ill but he wanted others to know how helpful marijuana could be. Like Lynn, Keith was thinking of others.

On March 11, 1979, in the local *Bay City Times*, the Nutts went public:

> Keith Nutt of Beaverton doesn't care who knows he uses marijuana. It is the only thing that relieves the terrible nausea that follows chemotherapy treatments for cancer, says the 23-year-old man. Right now, Keith is still able to drive to his sources of marijuana. If the time comes when Keith can't get out of the house to buy the illegal drug, his mother, Mae Nutt, 58, says "that's where I come in! But it shouldn't be necessary to break the law to get help for a child who is very, very ill."

The story of Keith Nutt resonated across the Michigan countryside, invaded every nook and cranny of the state, gave focus to legislation which would easily pass in early October (House: 100-0, Senate:33-1). When Keith was too ill to travel to the State Capitol, Mae and Arnold would go alone and speak not only for their son but for all the sons and daughters who needed legal access to marijuana.

---

*The simple joy of eating was personified in a call I received from a man in South Dakota who had obtained marijuana for his cancer-stricken wife but he did not know how to use it. I explained the process and he called back thirty minutes later, in tears, because his wife was eating watermelon, her first food in days.

On the evening of Sunday, October 21, 1979, Mae and Arnold went to say goodnight to their son. They told the young man that Michigan's medical marijuana bill, the nation's 18th such law, would be signed the next day in Lansing. Keith was very happy that his efforts had made a difference. He smiled and said goodnight.

Early the next morning Keith Nutt died. That afternoon the bill was signed.

Mae and Arnold could have easily "retired" from the medical marijuana issue. No one would have criticized them for doing so. But they remained committed to Keith's goal of helping others and they were always mindful of the difficulties they had had in obtaining a drug that gave so much comfort. Before Keith's death, supplies of marijuana would arrive in all kinds of ways—the mailbox, the front door stoop, small bags passed along by friends. There was more than Keith could use so Mae began giving it to other cancer patients. She became known as Grandma Marijuana and her "delivery service" became the Green Cross. Mae would continue this work for several years after Keith's death, providing some comfort to cancer patients while Michigan's state program became mired in the same swamp of government obstruction that stalled New Mexico.

19. SOMEONE IS TELLING AN UNTRUTH

In the late 1970s the Internet was the stuff of science fiction and newspapers were still the dominant source of news. Clipping services—companies that scanned dozens of newspapers and then sent articles of interest to their clients—were the primary means of keeping in touch with events happening throughout the country. NORML subscribed to a clipping service and during the time that I had been working on the Medical Reclassification Project the number of medical marijuana clippings had been escalating each month. Many were simply duplicate copies of the same story, wire stories from the AP, UPI, or Reuters that were published in every paper in the country. The beauty of the clipping service, however, was its ability to provide clients with local interest stories and editorials from throughout the country.

In March 1979 a clipping arrived from *The Trenton Times,* the major paper for Trenton, New Jersey. In it was a picture of a woman seated on a window seat, wistfully gazing out the window. She looked incredibly fragile but her quoted words in the article revealed a fighter. "I demand [marijuana] and I'm going to get it one way or another!"

The subject of the article was a 57-year old woman who owned an antique doll store in New Hope, Pennsylvania. Her name was Anne Guttentag and she had been battling cancer for three years. The article was comprehensive, even providing the address of Anne's doll store in New Hope. She and her husband David, a law professor at Trenton State College, lived above the store. I immediately wrote Anne and offered the services of the Medical Reclassification Project.

In 1976 Anne had a radical mastectomy and hoped the cancer was stopped. It wasn't. In early March 1979 she had a second surgery for ovarian cancer. This procedure was followed by chemotherapy. Anne was given Cisplatin and Adriamycin. In the article she talked about her "nightmare."

I vomited until there was nothing left. Then I retched until my ribs and my back and my chest ached. Then I vomited again ... Hours of tortuous, degrading vomiting, feeling your insides tearing... My thoughts turned to death and how peaceful I could be.

Regular medications failed to stop the vomiting and when Anne learned marijuana might help she lost no time in trying to obtain the drug. She made calls to everyone she could think of, including the New Hope chief of police, trying to learn how the drug could be obtained legally. When no one could help her she called the press. A reporter from *The Trenton Times* (NJ) was happy to visit with her and the article made its way to my desk in Washington.

Anne was quick to accept my offer of help. I explained the Compassionate IND process and offered to help her doctor with the application process. By mid-April the IND papers had been forwarded to Anne's physician at the Thomas Jefferson University Hospital in Philadelphia. Application was made to the FDA in June 1979.

For the next five months, as Anne suffered through regular chemotherapy sessions, the FDA nit-picked the IND application, constantly returning the document to the doctor for changes, none of which related directly to Anne's proposed care. All "suggestions" were related to administrative matters or reporting procedures. Finally, in November, just in time for her last scheduled chemo session, Anne's doctor received supplies of the THC pill. The FDA insisted she try the THC before using marijuana. She tried the synthetic and complained bitterly about the dosage form and the effect. She had obtained some illegal marijuana and used it with great success. But the THC pills "were nothing like the cigarettes" she told me. "I feel so heavy, like I've been on a binge."

Her doctor immediately reported to the FDA that Anne had great difficulty keeping the pills down, a common problem. Both doctor and patient were hopeful, however, that the chemo sessions were finished and there would be no further need for THC pills or marijuana.

But the cancer wasn't gone. In January 1980 Anne was back for more chemo. The THC continued to fail but FDA insisted Anne's doctor try the pills six times "before deeming it a failure." Anne even agreed to give up her illegal use of marijuana during this tortuous round of "research."

"It was," she would later say, "a living hell."

In mid-March 1980, exploratory surgery was performed and though the cancer had shrunk it was still present throughout Anne's body. More chemotherapy was administered in April and once again the vomiting was awful. But Anne's doctor had good news. He had called FDA again and told them of THC's failure. FDA promised she would have the marijuana cigarettes she needed before her next treatment in May.

In April I received a call from an aide to the House of Representatives Select Committee on Narcotics. Medical marijuana could no longer be ignored. Since the enactment of Georgia's bill in February four more states had passed laws— South Carolina, Ohio, Minnesota, and Arizona. Another half dozen were considering measures.

It was not a surprise Congress was considering hearings. The surprise was that it had taken so long.

The aide was seeking general information and suggestions for possible witnesses. The aide noted he was particularly interested in any patients who "had used or were using marijuana for medical purposes, especially cancer patients. Do you know someone who might want to testify?"

"Well, there is a woman named Anne Guttentag."

Anne was invited along with another cancer patient, Richard Csandl, also from Pennsylvania. Richard had tried to obtain marijuana through the IND process and experienced great frustration. Ultimately, Richard abandoned chemotherapy after nearly a year of treatment. He credits illegal marijuana with helping him survive the oat-cell and small cell carcinoma that he was told in April 1978 would claim his life in 4-6 weeks.* After tolerating eleven months of chemo he simply

---

*Richard Csandl died in 1988. He was the founder of the Keenan House, a drug abuse rehabilitation facility in Allentown, PA.

walked away from the grueling medical treatments and began an aggressive program of diet and exercise. Robert completed this panel of patients. The Task Force listened respectfully as each told his or her story. There were a few questions focusing on the difference between THC and natural marijuana.

A panel of physicians, including Dr. John Merritt who was still teaching and researching at the University of North Carolina, followed the patients. All of the physicians on the panel expressed concern about the THC pill. The oncologists noted the absurdity of giving an oral medication to a vomiting patient. Beyond that they were concerned about the formulation of THC, its erratic performance and disturbing side-effects.

Then the Task Force heard from the government's representatives. Seven bureaucrats sat at the table to give testimony. It was the representative from NCI, however, who dropped the bombshell. Dr. John MacDonald, associate director for Cancer Therapy Evaluation, Division of Cancer Treatment, quietly announced that THC would be moved into the NCI's Group C program. "Under Group C," Dr. MacDonald explained, "a compound is considered to have documented medical efficacy for a specific indication and not be a research drug *per se*, although it remains investigational."

It was the first public indication of the government's strategy to end-run the unceasing drive by the states to enact marijuana-as-medicine bills by releasing THC. Group C had been occasionally referenced during the Perry Committee meetings but we had no understanding of the scale or impact. According to MacDonald, Group C drugs can be distributed to community/regional/comprehensive cancer centers as well as medical school affiliated hospital pharmacies. This would amount to 500 to 600 separate pharmacies scattered around the country making the drug available to nearly 3,000 oncologists. This amounted to virtual approval of THC.

Dr. Richard Crout, director of the Bureau of Drugs for the FDA, followed MacDonald's testimony. Crout's bombshell was even bigger.

"We have agreed with NCI that THC may be a candidate for Group C investigational status. NCI has therefore prepared an application for this classification that we received on May 12. In anticipation of this, we had already scheduled a discussion on placing THC in the Group C plan for FDA's Oncology Advisory Committee meeting to be held on June 26, 1980."

Still later in the hearings the NIDA representative would put the icing on the cake. "NIDA, in collaboration with NCI, is preparing to manufacture 500,000 THC capsules by July 1 of this year," he said. "And plans call for another 500,000 to be manufactured by January 1, 1981."

It was a done deal. The meeting of the Oncologic Advisory Committee in June was a mere formality, a rubber stamp. For more than two years the bureaucracies had been bombarded by constant demands to release marijuana for medical purposes. They had been stuck in the mire of ideological drug policy masquerading as science. The agencies had now found a way to extend the masquerade. Marijuana, they were saying, had no medical value but one of its components, THC, did.

The country would soon be flooded with THC and the government would happily blur the distinctions be-tween marijuana and its synthetic component. In short time THC would become known as the "pot pill," and the states were told they could have all the pot pills they wanted without having to pass those pesky laws.

But there were two problems—THC didn't work and the states wanted marijuana.

After the Congressional task force hearings, Anne Guttentag returned to New Hope with some new hope of her own. On June 6 she arrived for her scheduled chemo-therapy expecting the marijuana cigarettes. They were not there. She had been disappointed in early May but accepted it. Now, after her appearance before the Task Force and listening to the promises of bureaucrats who had said marijuana was easy to obtain by qualified researchers, now Anne Guttentag was very angry.

On June 8th Anne sat down to write the Task Force Chairman:

My dear Mr. Neal:

Once again I thank you for permitting me to speak before your committee on Narcotics Abuse and Control, May 20.

To bring you up to date, a prescription was issued for the marijuana in cigarette form in April. I have not received them as requested. I was treated again on June 6 with only the pills (THC) and Compazine. Needless to say both failed.

I'm about ready to give up. The fight to live is not worth going through this anymore. I feel no one cares, nor will any one do anything to help. Not when it took months to be given a pill that com-mon sense tells you will be thrown back up. And then to be made to wait months for the cigarettes that are known to work. I wonder if anyone realizes the anxiety that goes on?

I have stopped buying the marijuana illegally. My friend who got it for me and whom I felt confident would only supply good marijuana is dying from cancer of the brain. How's that for a finale? The government won't help and the one person that was helping is now a statistic—that one-out-of-four in this country dying from cancer.

Where is the group who told your committee that there was no problem with the paperwork and that marijuana was now easy to get? Show them this letter, for someone is telling an untruth.

Very truly yours, Anne Guttentag.

On July 24 Anne received her legal marijuana cigarettes—thirteen months after she asked for them. She called me to say "they made a BIG difference." Her voice was weary but triumphant.

Anne would have her marijuana cigarettes for the remainder of her treatments but the chemotherapy could not save her. Nevertheless, she spoke out often in the press and on TV, advocating legal access to marijuana.

We would speak for the last time on February 26, 1981. It was a painful conversation for both of us. "I'm going down, Alice. My mind is sluggish. I can't be sure of what I'm saying anymore." Her last months were a nightmare of medical and physical complications. I kept in touch with her husband, David, but Anne would no longer speak to me—she was letting go bit-by-bit. On August 23, 1981, the sixth anniversary of our "bust," Anne Guttentag died.

Section III:

Synthetic Solutions

20. LET 'EM EAT THC

With the May 20, 1980 announcement at the Neal Hearings of the Group C inclusion of THC, the bureaucrats had, at last, found their footing after enduring a groundswell of change. It was just 27 months after New Mexico enacted the first state law recognizing marijuana's medical value and there were already 24 state laws passed! It was only 3½ years since Robert had first received legal supplies of marijuana and become "America's Only Legal Pot Smoker." It had been an extraordinary period of rapid change.

In the face of an unexpected national referendum on medical marijuana, the bureaucrats had been forced to engage in their own capitulation. It is doubtful any of the agencies ever anticipated the wide-scale distribution of delta-9 THC but that is what had been forced upon them by the medical marijuana movement.

The federal agencies could not stop their ongoing political rout in the States but they could maintain some control through their absolute monopoly over the U.S. marijuana supply. Trapped in a public mask of "encouraging research with Schedule I drugs," the FDA freely promised federal stocks of marijuana to each state. This prevented the states from adopting extreme measures such as the use of confiscated stocks or exploring state-based cultivation programs.

The strategy worked very well in New Mexico but as the number of state laws increased the gap between static federal production and expanding state demands created a supply crisis. There was simply not enough federal marijuana to meet the demands from the States. Even the Council on Scientific Affairs for the American Medical Association (AMA) could see the writing on the wall. In a report issued in the first half of 1980 the Council advised, "It may become necessary to place additional acres under cultivation."

There were only two solutions: 1) expand federal marijuana production to meet accelerating patient needs, or 2) release a synthetic, pharmaceutically prepared solution.

Expanding U.S. marijuana production was the rational option. But this solution was bureaucratically unacceptable. The consequence of expanding marijuana production was obvious. Increasing U.S. marijuana supplies would increase state demands for supply. If this supply-demand dynamic took hold the government would, in effect, become the *de facto* pharmaceutical manufacturer of marijuana.

This outcome would challenge the very core of the drug control complex. It was unacceptable and dangerous to expand cultivation so the bureaucrats turned their attention to the synthetic solution.

By mid-1978, we were aware of the shortfalls in marijuana production and the pressure this situation would apply to the agencies. The only question was which option the government would choose.

We had first learned about government efforts to provide a synthetic solution through the Interagency Committee on New Therapies for Pain and Discomfort and this increasingly dysfunctional mega-committee would provide a window through which we could chart how intense the bureaucratic scrambling had become. Numerous companies, including Abbott Laboratories, Pfizer, and Eli Lilly, were investigating marijuana-like agents. The most promising of these, Nabilone, was a patented THC-analogue developed by Eli Lilly. As federal agencies continued to lose the political struggle in the states, the FDA accelerated Nabilone development, allowing Lilly to "double-track" experiments. In effect, the FDA permitted human testing to begin before animal toxicology studies were completed.

Double-tracking seemed reasonable. Marijuana and THC were safe. FDA assumed Nabilone, a close chemical cousin to THC, would have a similar safety profile.

On May 9, 1978, as the rebellion in the States was picking up steam, the Interagency Committee heard from a Lilly representative who spoke enthusiastically about Nabilone trials involving more than 100 patients. The minutes of that meeting note, "They [Lilly] anticipate being able to file for an NDA (New Drug Application) in the first quarter of 1979."

Throughout 1978 there was a general feeling the situation was under control. This was evident in the relaxed manner of the Perry Committee, the friendly banter, the knowing smiles. True, the bureaucrats had to endure some rough verbal abuse from "those folks" in New Mexico. But, all in all, things were well contained. Preliminary Nabilone results were encouraging and there was a surprising amount of pre-release press coverage for the drug. Eli Lilly was anticipating prompt approval, brisk sales, and expanded applications well beyond cancer chemotherapy. The drug was being touted as "the new Valium." One article heralded the synthetic as "The Tranquilizer for the New Age." Scientists at Lilly were even working on an eyedrop formulation.

While Lilly was licking its chops at the prospect of a profitable new drug, the bureaucrats believed Nabilone would extinguish medical marijuana's political fire, dampen public demands, and save the medical prohibition.

But then the dogs died.

Beagle dogs to be exact, caged at the University of Arizona and part of Lilly's "long term use" studies. Some of the animals, given Nabilone regularly for close to one year, began to experience "unacceptable neurological toxicity." A little more digging on our part revealed that "unacceptable neurological toxicity" consisted of numerous dogs that seemed perfectly normal until they developed profound spasticity. After hours of uncontrollable shaking the dogs collapsed, then expired.

Eli Lilly informed the FDA and promptly halted all the studies. It was January 1979. Nabilone's nearly instantaneous evaporation occurred as a dozen states were preparing hearings on marijuana-as-medicine bills. Federal agencies panicked.

With Nabilone returned to the drawing board*, drug warriors frantically renewed their search for a synthetic substitute for marijuana. Suddenly the Perry Committee hearings were decidedly more tense. Instead of relaxed banter there were terse comments. There was a palpable strain to the

---

*Nabilone would eventually be approved by the FDA in 1985 although it would not be marketed until 2006. It is commonly known at Cesamet and, ironically, is recommended for some chronic diseases including Parkinson's disease and multiple sclerosis.

meetings and a marked increase in participation by DEA representatives. Knowing smiles were replaced by furtive looks.

The only other possible substitute was THC. But there were problems with THC. The bureaucratic notion that THC and marijuana are precisely alike was, of course, deeply flawed. Marijuana is a mild euphoriant. Pure THC is a major hallucinogen. But federal bureaucrats, fixated on marijuana's "high," simply assumed that what got you high got you well. This assumption persisted even after it became obvious that the two drugs were dramatically different.

Robert knew this first-hand from his THC experiences in North Carolina, UCLA, and Howard. THC did not lower his eye pressures. The same was true for Jim Ripple or the score of patients studied by Dr. Merritt. It wasn't much better for cancer patients, as Anne Guttentag and others had learned.

The problems had first emerged in very early cancer studies at the Sydney Farber Cancer Institute conducted by Drs. Stephen Sallan and Norman Zinberg of Harvard University. Federal agencies refused to provide marijuana, insisting on synthetic THC instead. The Harvard researchers found THC could reduce vomiting in some patients but there were complaints about the erratic absorption and performance of the synthetic. The investigators determined the 'high' was essential to attaining the proper therapeutic outcome, i.e. no vomiting. But oral THC absorbed so slowly and at such a different rate among patients it was difficult to arrive at a proper dose. This could easily lead to over-dosing.

In follow-up evaluations, Zinberg learned 25% of the cancer patients in his study obtained marijuana off the streets. Why? Patients said marijuana worked better, faster, and with fewer side effects than THC. This research was published in *The New England Journal of Medicine* in 1975. Sallan and Zinberg noted,

> Theoretically, smoking might be the preferable route [of administration] since it may result in less variability of absorption...Moreover, smoking provides greater opportunity for individual patient control by

permitting the patient to regulate and maintain the 'high.'

Three years later, in May 1978, when Nabilone's approval seemed assured, NCI researchers candidly discussed the merits of marijuana and THC in much the same way as Drs. Sallan and Zinberg had in the *NEJM*. Minutes from the May 9th meeting of the Perry Committee concluded,

> The oral absorption of THC is erratic, and the current formulation of THC was felt... to not be acceptable.' The report went on to note, '[A]ll in all smoking the [marijuana] cigarette may be the best means of administering the drug.

Nevertheless, research with THC continued, most notably in an NCI-sponsored study conducted at the NIH campus in Bethesda, by a young researcher, Dr. Alfred Chang. Ultimately, his research yielded the same erratic, unstable results with THC.

In January 1980, the Lynn Pierson Therapeutic Research & Treatment Program issued its first report. Significantly, New Mexico's findings mirrored the findings of Sallan and Zinberg as well as the NCI/Chang study. New Mexican cancer patients who were given THC reported high anxiety and uncertain benefits. Ninety percent of cancer patients smoking marijuana, however, experienced reliable relief from vomiting. This astonishing result was repeatable and predictable. Little wonder New Mexico cancer patients preferred marijuana over THC.

The bureaucrats knew all this but it didn't matter. From their perspective they had no choice. Large population states were rushing to adopt the New Mexico model. In rapid order Texas, California, Michigan, and Georgia joined in the chorus for the limited federal supplies of marijuana. A month after the Neal Hearings, New York would enact marijuana-as-medicine legislation, another populous state that would need enormous supplies of federal marijuana.

The decision was made to divert THC into the NCI Group C program and while NCI wasn't particularly happy about it, in the end they caved to the intense bureaucratic pressure to "stay with the policy." The FDA could not admit a mere weed was more effective than modern synthetic chemicals. The DEA would not allow medical marijuana to erode its enforcement powers. To help their sister agencies maintain the medical prohibition NCI officials would condemn a generation of cancer patients to debilitating vomiting, uncertain relief and unnecessary suffering.

We countered the bureaucratic moves with a series of press releases outlining the federal shortage of marijuana and summarizing the problems with the synthetic. Robert expanded the attack in a full-length article that was submitted to *The Washington Post*.

On June 23, 1980, just three days before the FDA Oncologic Advisory Committee meeting that was scheduled to approve the Group C program for THC, we issued another press release, accusing the FDA of pushing "phony pot pills" to disguise a marijuana shortage.

By the time the Advisory Committee met, our news was picked up by the wires and reprinted in hundreds of newspapers, sparking a rush of radio talk as a thousand stations across America repeated the alarm. In states where patients were awaiting promised federal supplies the reaction was intense and sustained.

The FDA watched tensely as the Oncologic Advisory Committee narrowly approved the Group C program by a vote of 5-4 on June 26. There were strong objections raised by Dr. Edmund O'Brien of California's Research Advisory Panel who asked that the release of THC "be delayed until data is accumulated determining a generally recognized safe and effective dose and characterized effect." O'Brien's comments were underscored by Dr. Charles Moertel of the Mayo Clinic who said "it is premature to release THC to the cancer patient population."

But, in the end, the FDA got what it needed.

Just three days later *The Washington Post* published Robert's article in the Sunday op-ed section. "Medical Substitute for Marijuana Won't Work" read the headline. The article pulled together the various bits of information we had collected in the intervening two years—quotes from the NCI memo praising the marijuana cigarette and condemning THC, a review of the Chang study and New Mexico reports, and a sobering analysis of the number of patients who would be denied relief by the refusal of the government to increase marijuana production. Robert concluded by accusing federal drug bureaucrats of sacrificing seriously ill Americans on the altar of the drug war. *The Post* article was picked up by other press outlets around the country and helped educate the public about the pending "shell game" that the federal government was about to play.

The bureaucratic efforts to foist THC upon the states re-awakened the energies of a young activist in Georgia named Mona Taft.

Mona was not a patient but her late husband, Harrison, had died from Hodgkin's disease in June 1979. He had successfully used marijuana to treat the symptoms of his disease and following his death Mona began her grief work by becoming a fierce, and very attractive, advocate for a Georgia marijuana-as-medicine bill.

Mona Taft had raven hair, an engaging style, and an absolute sense of righteousness. She had little trouble in swaying the political consensus of Georgia to accept marijuana's medical usefulness. She was careful and methodical in her approach, first lining up the support of her parents, then calling me at the Medical Reclassification Project for information. She read and studied the data, then approached her late husband's doctors. Having won their support she set her sights on the Capitol Building in Atlanta.

Mona quickly found her legislative champions. Representative Virlyn Smith was a kindly, conservative Republican and a cancer survivor. Virlyn was a legend in the Statehouse and his support on any piece of legislation gave it great weight.

On the "other side of the aisle," Mona enlisted the powerful Democrat Senator Paul Broun. Senator Broun's wife was battling cancer and he openly embraced the proposals for a marijuana-as-medicine bill.

Throughout the fall of 1979, Mona would work through Smith and Broun's offices to prepare a bill for the 1980 legislative session. It was introduced immediately in the New Year and barreled through the Georgia legislature faster than Sherman's march to the sea. In the House it passed 158-6; in the Senate 50-0.

On February 22, 1980, Governor George Busby signed the bill into law. It was the nation's twentieth medical marijuana bill.

For Mona, who was invited to attend the bill signing ceremony, it was a bitter-sweet moment. It was the anniversary of Harrison Taft's birthday. He had been dead for eight months.

Mona Taft had attended the Neal hearings in May 1980 and returned to Georgia with a sense of unease. She wasn't quite sure what all that talk about Group C meant and the dire warnings in Robert's *Washington Post* article about "subversion of the intent of the states" had seemed a bit too strident for her taste. She was confident the state of Georgia would prevail. Besides, she was weary and needed a break.

By midsummer Mona was revived enough to re-engage and contacted the various officials in Georgia who had been assigned to implement Georgia's state law. She was dismayed at what she heard and she started to understand just what those dire warnings from Robert were all about.

The FDA attempted to force the THC solution on the Georgia Patient Review Board, the group established to implement the Georgia law. To their credit, the group refused to be intimidated. But the FDA was relentless and it was quickly wearing down the Board, all of whom had other full-time jobs. A full-time, paid employee was needed to help keep things on track and, in early August, the State of Georgia asked Mona Taft to accept the job.

It did not take Mona long to comprehend that federal officials had no intention of providing Georgia—or any other state, for that matter—with legal supplies of marijuana, despite the assurances she had heard at the Neal Hearings. She realized she would need political help in Washington if she were to secure Georgia's fair share of the limited marijuana supplies.

She returned to her original source of support, Representative Virlyn Smith, and asked if he knew of any members of Congress from Georgia who might be able to help. Representative Smith suggested she meet with his young friend, U.S. Representative Newt Gingrich.

Newt Gingrich, serving his first term in Congress, was considered by many a conservative bomb thrower. He was already making waves. Many members of Congress felt he was immature and too aggressive; even reckless.

On September 10, 1980, the federal government formally announced the inclusion of THC in the Group C program. It was hoped the announcement would begin to dampen the clamor for medical supplies of marijuana. It was far too late. Our efforts had worked and across the country there was a highly sophisticated understanding of the difference between natural marijuana and synthetic THC. *The Atlanta Constitution*, which strongly supported Georgia's medical marijuana law, editorially fumed over the government's phony pot pill scam.

Gingrich, who had agreed to a late September meeting with Mona and Virlyn Smith, was intrigued by the issue and eager to court favor with the Georgia press. He expanded his scheduled meeting with Mona and others to include representatives from the NCI, NIDA, and DHHS. Mona suggested that Robert Randall also attend.

On September 26th, the meeting was held in Gingrich's office. Prior to the arrival of the federal representatives, Mona and Robert outlined the facts to Gingrich. Gingrich proved to be a quick study. Locked into conservative concerns over irrational federal power, he readily understood the problem. Bureaucrats in Washington were blocking a Georgia law. Cancer patients were suffering. After an hour's discussion, the representatives from the agencies arrived.

The Deputy Chief Counsel of HHS and her two staffers entered the room with confidence. Gingrich was cordial and gracious, listened to their trite explanations, then unloaded.

The FDA had promised Georgia supplies of federal marijuana. If Georgia did not get marijuana, Gingrich would call for a congressional investigation. He was rough, direct, and demanding.

There was a sense of awe in the room. Everyone was surprised by the focus of Gingrich's assault. The Deputy Chief Counsel stammered to explain. Gingrich waved her off, returning to his demands. After an hour the meeting dissolved. Gingrich had made himself clear, he needed to get on to other items.

Shaken by the encounter the Deputy Chief Counsel collected her dumbstruck staffers and headed for the door. As they entered the hall Robert overheard one staffer mumble to another, "Oh, don't worry about him," the Deputy Chief Counsel said in a stage whisper, "Gingrich is only a Republican. Republicans don't matter."

Five weeks later America elected Ronald Reagan president of the United States. The Republican revolution had begun.

21. GOVERNMENT IS THE PROBLEM

As the full extent of the federal government's intransigence became clear we realized that a new approach was required. One week before the meeting in Newt Gingrich's office we formally announced the establishment of the Alliance for Cannabis Therapeutics (ACT), a tax-exempt, non-profit organization, the first such organization dedicated to the medical marijuana issue.

ACT's purpose was "to promote the public interest in and work to ensure the adequacy of cannabis supplies for legitimate medical, therapeutic, scientific and research purposes." In a town that was packed with nonprofit organizations on the scale of the Tobacco Institute or the American Association of Retired Persons, ACT was an institutional microdot: an organizational illusion.

ACT was, primarily, our platform on which to approach the U.S. Congress. Increasingly it seemed the only way to escape the prohibition's power was through Congress. After all, Congress had passed the laws that prohibited marijuana and, later, the laws that would grant federal agencies the authority to impede research and block access.

It seemed to us that Congress could, like Alexander the Great, slice through the Gordian knot of federal drug regulation and free marijuana for medical access.

There were, of course, those councils of wisdom who said "impossible." There was a growing backlash against the "counterculture." We were told Congress would never consider a medical marijuana bill, never.

We understood the odds. In a Washington landscape dominated by huge lobbying firms staffed by skilled people on lush payrolls it seemed unlikely that two political neophytes could make a difference but there was, from our perspective, little choice. Besides, the two "neophytes" had already accomplished a great deal.

Financially, ACT was a disaster. While medical marijuana enjoyed broad public support, it was not a mass movement and its strongest supporters—the seriously ill—were often desperately poor. Such people would give of themselves body and soul to fight the good fight. But they had no cash. Direct mail appeals elicited few contributions. Hundreds of grant requests to major and minor philanthropies also came up empty. Medical marijuana was too controversial for many, not controversial enough for others. We did obtain a "seed grant" of $5,000 from The Playboy Foundation but we were unable to parlay it into anything meaningful. Christie Hefner made good on her promise to provide ACT with free ad space in the slick, widely read magazine. The *Playboy* ad featured a handsome, eye-catching map outlining the states with medical marijuana laws. *Playboy* was mass media. Eight million Americans read it every month. The ads increased public awareness, resulted in hundreds of requests for information but failed to increase contributions to ACT.

Yet, for all it did not have, ACT did enjoy certain advantages. By design it was non-membership; lean, easily directed, without internal strife. A very closed system and nearly immune from external distraction. We purposefully established a small Board of Directors: president, vice president, and secretary-treasurer. Robert was president, I was the secretary-treasurer, Mae Nutt agreed to serve as our vice president.

To that core we added a battle-proven board of advisors that included some old friends: Mona Taft, the Ripples, Anson Chong from Hawaii, Ara Cron from Kansas, and Vince Mustachio from West Virginia.

There were many others who agreed to join the Advisory Board of our new group: Dr. Andrew Weil, professor of medicine at Arizona State University and (at the time) a budding author; Dr. Norman Zinberg, coauthor of the first modern study on marijuana's medicinal use by cancer patients; Dr. Dorothy Whipple, a noted pediatrician who helped secure the rights of women in the medical profession when she became the first married woman admitted to Johns Hopkins Medical School in the 1920s; Antonio G. Olivieri, City Council member from New York City, who helped spearhead passage of the New York State marijuana-as-medicine bill and would later die of cancer; Representative Virlyn Smith of Georgia, mentor to Representative Newt Gingrich; Representative Miller Hudson of Colorado; Senator Jerome Hart of Michigan, and others. We were tremendously exhilarated by the willingness of others to help our cause. Ah, youth!

ACT had the advantage of a compelling argument and the benefit of broad public and press support. ACT also had the *pro bono* assistance of Steptoe and Johnson.

Our old friend at Steptoe, Tom Collier, had moved on, becoming a deputy assistant secretary at the Department of Housing and Urban Development (HUD) but he referred us to several attorneys in Steptoe & Johnson who had assisted on Robert's case in May 1978. As we outlined our plans to approach Congress the lawyers became excited about expanding on the precedent established in Robert's case and extending it to others via codified law. Once again the issue of medical marijuana was brought before Steptoe's *pro bono* committee and, to our great delight, the firm agreed to help us. Steptoe's considerable skills, vast resources and well-seasoned reputation could help give credibility to our congressional enterprise.

While America understood medical marijuana, Congress was less aware. How do you introduce an idea to 535 people, attract their attention, and get their support? Using ACT as our vehicle we devised a strategy of "info-osmosis."

As the states rebelled against FDA's synthetic solution, ACT recycled the flood of newsprint into Congress. It was pure information with no appeal for action. Robert believed information delivered at high velocity would elicit interest and act as its own persuasion. Then Congress, like the state legislatures, would respond.

ACT's information saturation campaign was made possible by technology. At a time when very few people had a computer, we struggled to master DOS, CP/M, eight-inch floppy disks and the agonizingly intricate instructions needed to merge letters with addresses. We also made use of the computer's ability to compile a database and created a list of 2,500 media outlets.

By November 1980, ACT was directing a constant flow of information into Congress. The timing was good. Congress was in recess, its members home in their districts. Staffers would read our letters, then slowly spread the news: info-osmosis.

By the time Congress returned in January 1981, ACT had blanketed Capitol Hill with information. Congressmen from states with medical marijuana laws received multiple letters. Every pertinent newspaper article was reproduced and forwarded to the appropriate Senators and Representatives. Pure information—no plea for help.

This info loop, while very overt, fell below the bureaucratic horizon that relies on *The Washington Post* and little more. We made no effort to excite *The Post* or *The New York Times*. Our goal was to inform the nation and Congress, not the elite liberal press. This reliance on regional press and radio talk sustained a national media bubble, maintained public support and rapidly enhanced Congressional awareness. It was, we reasoned, just a matter of time.

In April of 1981 Robert would receive the phone call we had worked so hard to provoke.

"Could you meet with Representative McKinney regarding this medical marijuana problem?"

Stewart McKinney was a middle-aged, middle class, middle-of-the-road Connecticut Republican, married, Catholic, with a large family. His private office was modest and modern. The Congressman sat at the head of a long conference table, within easy reach of a Mickey Mouse phone, surrounded by eager young staffers. No pretense. Very human. Stewart began by mentioning that his friend, Governor Ella Grasso, was battling cancer. He had also been told about a medical marijuana bill in Connecticut that was making its way through the legislature. His interest was piqued. "What's this about?" he asked.

The meeting was brief. Representative McKinney was sponsoring a bipartisan bill to allow the Amerasian children of G.I.s into America. But, that bill was "in the hopper" and about to become law. Stewart was looking for another issue. "If you develop a medical marijuana bill, I'd like to look it over," McKinney said, ending the meeting. Robert was delighted. A moderate Republican interested in medical marijuana.

Doug Herbert, our newest Steptoe attorney, was an Alabama native with an interest in drafting legislation. Doug enlisted several associates and after a few weeks they produced a federal medical marijuana bill. The draft was very straightforward. Congress would recognize marijuana's medical uses, reschedule marijuana to Schedule II so it could be prescribed, and establish a reliable system of supply and distribution. Under the bill marijuana was handled like any prescription and any licensed physician could call on the federal government for supplies.

The bill, couched in conservative concerns—state rights, doctor/patient control over medical care—was radical in intent. To provide background Robert and Doug developed a detailed supporting memo. The end result was given to Reps. McKinney, Gingrich, and Neal on June 24, 1981.

Two weeks later, on July 9th, Representative McKinney agreed to sponsor the bill. "I like the scope and style of this bill and I'm happy to sponsor it." McKinney said, "But we need a few cosponsors."

The next day Newt Gingrich called and expressed his support for the bill and agreed to cosponsor. He had sent the bill to his mentor Virlyn Smith, and the ailing Georgia legislator lost no time in making his opinions known telling Gingrich, "I would personally appreciate your support of it." He followed up with a letter to Gingrich that stated:

> Even though we have a workable program in Georgia *NOW*, thanks only to your interest and support, most of the other 32 states that have tried to help in this most humane cause have not been so fortunate. It is not reasonable to think that under the limitations of research as viewed by the FDA, NCI, and DEA, that any more than just a few of these states will ever have an effective program.
>
> This denies access to a great majority of the suffering patients, or worse yet, involves them or someone

trying to help them, in the criminal process of buying and using street marijuana.

Again, I ask your support of this. I think you will feel great satisfaction in helping a segment of our society that is doomed to much suffering. Any relief that can be given seems almost a miracle.

On September 16, 1981, Representatives McKinney and Gingrich publicly introduced ACT's federal medical marijuana bill. Two other Republicans, the moderate Millicent Fenwick of New Jersey and conservative blue blood Hamilton Fish of New York, joined as co-sponsors. McKinney and Gingrich held a press conference that sparked favorable editorials in their states. Wire services carried the news across America.

After a year of info-osmosis Representatives on both sides of the aisle were quick to respond. By the end of September, House Resolution 4498 had more than twenty cosponsors.

All previous marijuana reform measures had the spotty support of ten or fewer left-wing liberals. By ignoring the left and coming from a conservative base, the federal marijuana-as-medicine bill gained bipartisan support. Medical marijuana, driven by Republican sponsors and conservative aspirations, had appeal across the political spectrum. By the end of 1981, 90 Members of Congress —from Barney Frank on the far left to William Dannymeyer on the farthest right —were backing medical marijuana. H.R. 4498 was a roaring success. Gingrich and Robert looked forward to hearings and a successful floor vote. Stewart, more seasoned, cautioned against excessive optimism.

With hindsight we now see Stewart was right.

As we moved into 1982 there were more than 100 cosponsors on the bill and more good news was on the way. In February, the National Academy of Science (NAS) released a report on marijuana's medical uses, the result of a Court of Appeals order in the long-standing NORML suit to reschedule marijuana.

At a lavish dinner held in the NAS building near the White House, the report was released to a select group of attendees. There were, to coin a cliché, "all the usual suspects" from the FDA, NIDA, and DEA. Robert was invited; no doubt the token "citizen" and legal marijuana user. Also in the hall that night was Representative Millicent Fenwick, Republican Congresswoman from New Jersey and one of the four original sponsors of H.R. 4498.

Millicent Fenwick was a Washington legend. A strikingly handsome woman, she was wealthy and looked it. In her youth she had briefly been a Vogue model. She possessed enough quirks to get her noticed and cement her "legend" status. She smoked a corncob pipe and was reputed to eat spaghetti for dinner nearly every night. She liked the pasta, she noted, and found the process of deciding what to eat "boring." So, when she ate at home, she ate spaghetti.

These numerous quirks, coupled with her bold style and frank talk won many admirers. Many claim she was the model for Lacey Davenport in Gary Trudeau's "Doonesbury" cartoon strip.

Despite her cosponsorship of H.R. 4498, Robert had never met Mrs. Fenwick and, aside from ACT's info-osmosis campaign, we had never dealt directly with her office. Her support for H.R. 4498, like that of Representative Hamilton Fish from New York, came out of the blue.

As Robert sat through the NAS dinner he listened to various speakers discuss marijuana's medical uses not in terms of "maybe" but in absolute terms. The NAS/IOM report went far beyond any previous discussion of marijuana's medical use. It stressed the drug's important medical potential in the treatment of numerous life- and sense-threatening diseases. While it stopped short of any policy recommendations it was critical of the federal approach to marijuana's use in medicine.

It was a glad-handing evening for sure. Everyone seemed to warm to the occasion and Robert listened, in astonishment, as officials from NIDA and the FDA spoke in glowing terms of how they had "helped pave the way" with their compassion towards Robert Randall.

Robert could not be still and, when finally recognized, told the gathering that compassion towards one man was not enough. Whole states were seeking relief and where was it?

Robert would later recall:

There was some tisk-tisking from the crowd. Murmurs raced through the room. There was a sense of isolation as I realized I was alone in a mass of bureaucrats who wanted to hear none of my moaning and groaning. "There's that Randall, again," they would say. "He's never content." It was a scene all too familiar.

But on that night I would have a champion, and a beautiful one at that. In her clear, yet gravely voice, Millicent Fenwick spoke directly. "Depriving glaucoma and cancer patients of medical access to marijuana is inhumane." The room became very quiet. "My office recently received a letter from a 74-year-old man who had to purchase marijuana illegally for his wife who is undergoing chemotherapy treatments. I think that is wrong."

Federal officials rushed to assure the Congresswoman that marijuana "can be obtained legally." Fenwick listened and then leveled both barrels at the bureaucrats. "I contacted health officials in New Jersey and was bluntly told it is easier for patients to get marijuana off the streets than from their doctors because of all the federal red-tape involved in getting it legally That is an outrage."

There were no spontaneous bursts of applause to greet the good Representative's common sense observations. To say I was bolstered by this event is putting it mildly. For six years Alice and I had worked hard to instill the basic message. On February 25, 1982, like the echoes through a canyon wall, the message came back, delivered by the lovely Lady from New Jersey.

The dinner concluded and I sought out Mrs. Fenwick to thank her. She was intrigued with my case and peppered me with questions as we shared a cab back to our Capitol Hill homes—hers closer to the brilliantly lit dome than mine. We said goodbye. I would never speak to her again. Representative Fenwick retired at the end of 1982. She would live another ten years, dying on September 16, 1992, eleven years to the day after H.R. 4498 was introduced.

22. PROFILES IN PATHETIC

In 1979 *The Washington Drug Review* had noted, "Marijuana . . . has enjoyed for a short time a small amount of breathing room as a public policy issue. No more."

Drug scandals in the Carter Administration, especially allegations that several of his top aides had used cocaine, set the stage for a quiet transfer of emphasis and money. Government funds were quietly diverted to "parent groups," organizations throughout the country that were concerned about drug use by adolescents. These groups had already targeted the medical marijuana issue, echoing the public bulletins of the DEA, calling medical marijuana "a stalking horse for legalization" and printing broadsides under the banner of Families in Action. These were reinforced by a vociferous publication called "War on Drugs" purportedly funded by right-wing Lyndon LaRouche.

By the time Reagan arrived in Washington the giant bureaucratic machinery of the drug agencies was poised to engage in a radical shift of direction and in Nancy Reagan the agencies found their champion.

In the latter part of 1981, Mrs. Reagan met with representatives of the National Federation of Parents for Drug-Free Youth, an offshoot of the Georgia-based PRIDE (Parent Resources and Information for Drug Education), which had been receiving government grants for a number of years, some of it funneled through the anti-poverty agency ACTION.

The First Lady had been severely criticized for her spendthrift ways at the White House and the Administration was anxious to find a "cause" in which she could engage. Staffers wanted something less political than drugs but Mrs. Reagan insisted that this was the area in which she wanted to concentrate her energies. The collaboration began and would come to full flower five months later when the First Lady spoke to the Ad Council—a private, nonprofit organization, founded in 1942 to rally support for the war effort—at a carefully arranged luncheon at the State Department.

Mrs. Reagan encouraged the group to take up the campaign against the use of drugs by children. She derided the numerous subtle ways in which "drug acceptance is everywhere" in the culture. She criticized music, movies, television, advertising, and, obliquely, the news media. At one point Mrs. Reagan said, "I wonder if anyone stops to think what perceptions kids are picking up from some of the stories about the therapeutic effects of a chemical found in pot." She went on to tell the story of a fifth grader in Atlanta who believed, "if you smoke pot you won't get cancer or have to wear glasses. Now how do you suppose a fifth grader gets ideas like these?" The inference was clear. The media was expected to censor such stories, to save the kids, of course.

From this luncheon was born the "Say No to Drugs" advertising campaign. A short while later Mrs. Reagan modified the slogan into the battle cry of the 1980s—"Just Say No!"

Initially we were not particularly worried by these efforts. Concern about drug use among kids is appropriate and besides, the medical issue was separate. We naively thought that 34 state laws and close to 100 cosponsors on a federal marijuana-as-medicine bill in Congress would delineate the two issues—drug abuse *vs.* controlled medical use. It seemed simple and clear cut to us, as different as black and white.

But as more and more money was pumped into so-called "parent groups" the bureaucrats used these groups to counter patient demands for care. Rather than spend their federal grants to prevent child and adolescent drug use, these parent groups targeted medical marijuana. The broadsides issued by Families in Action specifically took aim at H.R. 4498, filling half a dozen pages with misinformation and outright lies about the bill, marijuana's effects, research, and the struggling state programs such as the one in Georgia.

"It sends the wrong message," blared the party line from a dozen newsletters. As Nancy Reagan's "Just Say No" crusade gained momentum, attacks on medical marijuana became routine. In Dekalb, Georgia the local Families in Action sent an attack memo to Representative Gingrich.

The press in Georgia picked up on the brewing feud, but still backed Gingrich and his federal medical marijuana bill.

Enraged "parents" then started disrupting Newt's District meetings. The anti-med/anti-pot parents were loud, mildly abusive. Having won reelection by a slender margin, Newt began to sweat. He became concerned that medical marijuana might injure his budding career as a conservative revolutionary.

While government-funded "parent groups" chipped away at Newt, Washington drug warriors found a liberal ally in Representative Henry Waxman of California who was chairman of the Subcommittee on Health, part of the Energy & Commerce Committee. It was this committee that would hold hearings and forward H.R. 4498 to the House floor for a vote. Without hearings before Waxman's committee there would be no marijuana-as-medicine bill.

Intuition would suggest that a liberal representative from the state of California would be an ally for medical marijuana. But in the perverse way that Washington operates just the opposite was true. The initial four cosponsors of H.R. 4498 were all Republicans and this triggered an odd alarm among senior Democrats who feared medical marijuana might make Republicans look compassionate. Further complicating the matter was Mr. Waxman's deep connection to pharmaceutical PAC money.

Robert met several times with Waxman aides trying to understand why the Congressman would not support McKinney's bill. By summer it was clear Waxman would block medical marijuana hearings until after the 1982 election.

Without the prospect of prompt hearings and a rapid floor vote, Gingrich realized medical marijuana would not be quickly resolved. He grew increasingly nervous as 1982 slid along and the Just-Say-No crowd increased the pressure on him. His old mentor, Virlyn Smith, had died of cancer in March 1982. Without Virlyn's common sense approach and courageous articulation of "do the right thing," Newt abandoned H.R. 4498 at the start of 1983.

Gingrich withdrew his support from H.R. 4498 in a letter to Robert and Representative McKinney. He wrote:

> The medical case for the use of marijuana is sustainable, but the cultural case isn't. There are

millions in this country who are terrified of the drug problem.... At a time when our efforts should be toward crushing the illegal drug culture, and destroying the illegal dealers, it's simply unwise to confuse the message with a bill which is not understandable to our own allies—people who are with us on the effort to destroy the illegal drug culture.

The politically charged and pathetic actions of Gingrich and Waxman condemned Americans to needless suffering for decades to come. The pendulum had shifted. Through the release of THC and by skillful use of the parent groups, the government had regained its footing. The seriously ill could no longer count on the facts to win the day, at least not in Congress.

In 1983 and 1985 Stewart McKinney's federal marijuana-as-medicine bill was reintroduced into the 98th and 99th Congresses with broad bipartisan support. At the peak of its support McKinney's marijuana-as-medicine legislation had 110 cosponsors.

The proposed legislation also gained powerful endorsements. Nearly every major legal organization in the country including the American Bar Association, American Civil Liberties Union, National Association of Criminal Defense Lawyers and the National Association of Attorneys General passed resolutions supporting McKinney's bill.

But without the necessary hearings in Congress all this support was for naught. Congress, in its own way, was as intransigent as the bureaucracies.

23. CHANGING GEARS

As we entered the mid-1980s we found ourselves in a new landscape. The issue of marijuana's use in medicine had changed dramatically. Across the nation the political enthusiasm which had fueled the enactment of 34 state laws in five years began to cool, partly because of THC's release and partly because our focus shifted to Congress. Mostly the point had been made and for the first time since our arrest the river of energy, which carried us forward, slackened.

Six states managed to apply enough political pressure to receive federal supplies of marijuana: California, Georgia, Michigan, New Mexico, New York, and Tennessee.

The criteria for inclusion in the marijuana studies varied from state to state but, in the final analysis, hundreds of cancer patients legally received medical supplies of marijuana under the aegis of these short-lived, state-sponsored marijuana research programs. Every state study found marijuana safe and highly effective in reducing chemotherapy-induced vomiting. In the first half of the 1980s the states routinely reported these favorable findings to the FDA, which just as routinely ignored the facts.

Federal drug agencies continued to consolidate the gains they had secured through the Group C release of THC and sought to "privatize" the distribution of the drug. The FDA offered a sweet deal—an absolute marketing monopoly for a ready-to-go drug. No expensive research needed. No long reviews before FDA committees. Here was a drug, developed entirely at the taxpayers' expense, which would absolutely clear the hurdles of the New Drug Application process with a 100% guarantee. Yet every major pharmaceutical company in America reviewed the data and rejected the deal. It was clear THC was not a remarkable drug and the pharmaceutical companies had serious doubts about its formulation. An erratic drug with little profit margin is hardly what major pharmaceutical companies are looking for in the cutthroat world of drug marketing.

The FDA finally convinced a small New Jersey company to take THC. Unimed was developing anti-cancer drugs but had never reached the final approval stage nor marketed a drug in the United States. The small firm undoubtedly felt that THC would swiftly clear the barriers of approval and, by comparison, it did. Nevertheless it required four years for Unimed to negotiate the final hurdles of FDA-regulatory procedure. In an Orwellian twist, THC was renamed dronabinol and would be marketed under the trade name Marinol. It was officially approved in June 1985.

The Compassionate IND model developed in response to *Randall v. U.S.* expanded, although, ironically, not necessarily for patients needing marijuana. In 1984, responding to the pressure of the expanding AIDS crisis, the FDA created "treatment INDs" which permitted people with AIDS to legally obtain medical products before they received full FDA marketing approval. The Treatment IND approach was modeled on the Compassionate IND and it pleased us to see that Steptoe & Johnson's *pro bono* work really was extended for the "public good."

In 1985 federal agencies, anxious to complete the regulatory procedures necessary to market the newly dubbed "dronabinol," offered NORML a deal. If NORML did not oppose the rescheduling of dronabinol/THC, the DEA would hold hearings on marijuana's medical utility.

It was a slightly disingenuous offer. The U.S. Court of Appeals had ordered the DEA, on several occasions, to conduct public hearings on marijuana's proper classification. The delays had been infuriating to NORML, which had initially filed the legal suit in 1972. Now, years later, DEA was trying to cut a deal in order to secure the final piece of regulatory paper before Marinol could hit the market.

From our own perspective, as articulated via ACT, we had no objections to the release of Marinol if the DEA guaranteed public hearings on natural marijuana. We could see no reason to block Marinol; while inferior to marijuana it might help someone. Some drug reformers, however, wanted to delay the synthetic's marketing, arguing the drug had been developed at taxpayer expense and should not be handed over to a private pharmaceutical company. Still others just objected to "giving in" to the DEA. The prospect of "sticking it" to the agencies was appealing. Hearings would take several years and could gum up the works royally. Besides, these reformers argued, the U.S. Court of Appeals had already ordered the DEA to hold hearings on marijuana.

Eventually NORML agreed to permit THC's prescriptive use and, in April 1986, the DEA ordered public hearings on marijuana's medical value.

The legal trail that led to the proposed hearings had been long and arduous. To recapitulate briefly, in 1972, NORML, together with the American Public Health Association, petitioned the Bureau of Narcotics and Dangerous Drugs (soon to become the Drug Enforcement Administration) to recognize marijuana's medical value and remove the drug from Schedule I of the Controlled Substances Act. Five years later, in 1977, Robert and I delivered a similar petition to the DEA, this one signed by thirteen seriously ill patients. In both instances the petitions were summarily dismissed by the agency without a hearing—a violation of the law.

These petitions—ours and NORML's—were eventually merged. Several trips to the U.S. Court of Appeals reinforced the petitioners' right to be heard but the DEA, and later the Department of Health, Education and Welfare, imposed severe delays on the proceedings. In October 1980 the agencies were again ordered to hold public hearings but the DEA continued to delay the process until 1986 when it traded THC's medical release for hearings, which would formally be known as *In The Matter Of Marijuana Rescheduling*.

We believed the DEA hearings offered a tremendous opportunity—to create the most complete record of marijuana's medical use in the 20th century. Working once again with the lawyers at Steptoe & Johnson, we suggested that ACT become a lead party in the hearings. Steptoe's *pro bono* committee agreed and authorized resources for the effort. Our plan was proposed to NORML, now under the leadership of Kevin Zeese, and the organization agreed to allow ACT to join the case and take the lead. Steptoe & Johnson's vast resources gave the case a fighting chance. It would be a monumental and expensive task. It would occupy our efforts for the next two years.

24. IN THE MATTER OF ...

In the summer of 1986 Robert once again returned to Steptoe & Johnson where he met ACT's new lawyer, Frank Stilwell.

Frank sat at the head of a conference table, his eyes hidden behind super-black wraparound sunglasses. Frank's suit was half a size too large, his shirt cuffs spotted by stains he could not see. Frank Stilwell was blind and had been so since the age of seven.

In terms of appearance this man was not a typical Steptoe associate but Frank, despite the lack of vision, had graduated at the top of his law school class. Good minds are hard enough to find, but we reasoned Frank must also have a great will and strong spirit.

It was a curious pairing—the man who would be blind but for marijuana and an attorney blinded so young. But we had grown accustomed to odd pairings. Politics makes for strange bedfellows and the medical marijuana issue was definitely a political exercise.

The DEA hearings revolved around one elemental question: does marijuana have a "currently accepted medical use in treatment in the United States?" The law, as embodied in the Controlled Substances Act, contended the answer was no. ACT and NORML argued the law was incorrect. This single point, accepted medical use, was the difference between Schedule I drugs—totally prohibited, like marijuana—and Schedule II drugs—tightly restricted but available by prescription, such as morphine and even cocaine.

The hearings were conducted by the DEA's chief administrative law judge, Francis L. Young, a kindly looking 60-year-old man who spoke with a light Louisiana lilt, had wispy gray hair and exercised firm control over his courtroom. Initial planning sessions began in the autumn of 1986. There were three principle parties—ACT, NORML and the DEA.

As always, Steptoe was uneasy about working with NORML. Frank seemed especially reluctant to become entangled with a "pro-drug" organization. We appreciated, even shared these concerns, but felt they could be overcome. Better to know what NORML was doing then be blindsided.

Kevin Zeese, a young lawyer, was now in charge of NORML. We had known Kevin for almost a decade. He arrived at NORML as an intern, about the same time that I established the Medical Reclassification Project. He played a role in the litigation involving Paraquat spraying of marijuana and knew the legal issues. By the time Kevin became NORML's director the once proud organization was struggling to pay the rent. Kevin was working to put things back on track.

A New Yorker, Kevin talked fast, smiled easily, was playfully cynical and easy to like. He was less overtly complicated, more grounded than most reformers.

After several meetings it was decided ACT and NORML would develop independent, but parallel cases. By default the burden of case development fell on ACT.

To facilitate such a large case, Judge Young decided legal testimony would be taken by affidavit. Frank and Robert settled on a division of labor. Robert would collect testimony and write affidavits. My job was to coordinate the accumulation of research reports, medical studies, political facts and supporting materials. Frank would edit the affidavits, but his primary concentration would be on legal arguments and the development of briefs and motions.

For more than a month Robert conducted detailed interviews with witnesses via speakerphone in a windowless conference room at Steptoe. He would then prepare affidavits for each individual.

A few witnesses were new, their names culled from newspaper articles and public statements. Many were physicians and pharmacists who approached their testimony with clinical detachment. Others were dear friends, veterans of the struggle to enact state laws. Robert's goal was to blend each separate account into a larger story.

Dr. George Goldstein, New Mexico's Secretary of Health, outlined bureaucratic problems. Dr. Daniel Dansak clarified the results of New Mexico's landmark medical research on cancer and marijuana. Katy Brazis, an oncologic nurse, spoke in human terms of how cancer patients in New Mexico benefited from the state's medical marijuana program.

Other witnesses spoke to broader concerns. Andrew Weil, M.D., an ethnopharmacologist trained at Harvard, and John Morgan, M.D., Director of Pharmacology at the City College of New York, helped define marijuana's pharmacologic profile, medical benefits and potential harms.

Robert Stephan, the conservative Attorney General of Kansas—and a cancer patient—testified to the need for prescriptive marijuana. Stephan explained his own situation, then outlined the reasoning behind the National Association of Attorneys General support for marijuana's medical availability. Several other politicians spoke to the intent of their state laws recognizing marijuana's medical value.

The pivotal point of the hearings was whether marijuana was medically "accepted." But the law fails to elaborate just who it is that must "accept" marijuana. The law states "in treatment" so Robert sought out oncologists, ophthalmologists and neurologists with treatment experience to testify on behalf of marijuana's use as a therapeutic agent. These physicians from throughout the United States described how smoking marijuana eased the suffering of their patients and favorably altered medical outcomes without adverse effects. Many of these physicians, including Robert's doctor, Richard North, had never publicly discussed their opinions and findings.

It was exhausting work. He would later write about the toll it took:

Interviews conducted with patients or, in many cases, the surviving relations of patients were emotionally taxing. Over the speakerphone, Mae Nutt painstakingly described her son Keith's battle with cancer and, as I scribbled furiously, I was astonished to see tears falling on the yellow legal pad. With trembling voice Mona Taft, so strong and controlled throughout the passage of Georgia's marijuana-as-medicine law, sadly recounted her husband Harrison's protracted death and wistfully recalled her efforts to help Georgia cancer patients.

Not all outcomes were sad. Janet Andrews, an Idaho mother, testified about giving her five year old son marijuana cookies to get him through chemo. Josh, a cancer survivor then turning ten, had won his battle with cancer. What difference did marijuana make? "Josh would eat a marijuana cookie, get chemo and ride his tricycle down the hall while other kids were bedridden and vomiting," Janet said with bracing honesty. "We still have Josh. Most of those other children are dead. Marijuana cookies saved Josh's life."

> *Day after day I listened to the many voices of medical marijuana. Each witness offered personal insights, but told the same story. It was like passing through many rooms and looking out the windows onto the same landscape, each window affording a particular point of view, but the scene was always the same. In the quiet after midnight, I tried to capture these voices with their different cadences and tonalities intact -- to turn each witness' private journey into cogent testimony which, when combined with other voices, would tell the larger story.*

ACT presented testimony from 37 witnesses. NORML produced less detailed testimony from 5 witnesses. The DEA responded with nearly 30 affidavits. Many DEA witnesses were federal bureaucrats. Lacking factual evidence they advanced a looping argument: marijuana has no medical value because the law says marijuana has no medical value.

One DEA witness was surprising, Dr. Robert Hepler. Representing the American Academy of Ophthalmology. Hepler's affidavit had an odd flavor about it. It noted the obvious—marijuana's ability to reduce intraocular pressure. But the Academy had developed a peculiar side step to the question of marijuana's effectiveness in the treatment of glaucoma. Their official statement read:

> Effective treatment of glaucoma involves the use of pharmaceutical agents or surgical procedures that prevent progressive nerve damage. To date, the only clinically effective method of accomplishing this is by lowering intra-ocular pressure. However, merely reducing intra-ocular pressure is not necessarily beneficial to the eye, and pressure reduction does not necessarily prevent glaucomatous optic nerve pressure.

The American Academy of Ophthalmology stressed the need for a drug or surgical procedure to be safe and not cause "unacceptable damage to the eye or to other parts of the body and reduce the pressure sufficiently to prevent optic nerve damage."

Marijuana, the ophthalmologists concluded, had not been proven safe to "other parts of the body" so it could not be accepted as safe for medical use in treatment. There was, of course, no mention of the side effects of currently available glaucoma medications. Ironically it was at about this same time that the press began to report some disturbing side effects from Timolol, primarily an adverse impact on cardiac rhythms. And, of course, all the existing medications that were available had some adverse systemic impact: cataracts, kidney stones, itchy eyes, blurred vision.

In short, marijuana was being held to a higher standard. Of course the Academy generously acknowledged that marijuana should be investigated further.

Hepler, it seemed, was caught in a squeeze play. The American Academy of Ophthalmology had asked him to join the Ad Hoc Committee on Marijuana Legislation to draft a response to McKinney's bill. No doubt Hepler was pleased just to have the Academy's endorsement of further research and acknowledge the drug's ability to reduce IOP. But then the DEA hearings came along and the Academy tapped him to be the spokesperson.

Robert was mentioned in Hepler's DEA affidavit.

> Several years ago . . . Robert Randall was one of my first test patients. As a result of some of the earlier testing, I concluded that marijuana was effective in lowering his intraocular pressure when combined with traditional glaucoma medications. With the subsequently developed information about glaucoma and marijuana, I fully support the Academy's position on this issue.

Whoosh! Without realizing it Hepler was caught in the vortex of The Memory Hole.

ACT and NORML challenged the relevance of testimony from nearly a dozen DEA witnesses. Largely law enforcement officers with no medical knowledge, these witnesses offered boilerplate prattle of marijuana's link to lurid violence, insanity and other fictions. Judge Young struck the testimony of a third of DEA's witnesses.

Once the witness list was finalized any party could require any other party to physically produce a witness for cross-examination. There were differing views about the strategy to be employed. The ACT/NORML testimony was richer, more varied and much stronger than DEA's stale case. Robert argued there was no need to call any DEA witness. Kevin disagreed. Frank was uncertain. Eventually, only one DEA witness, Dr. Keith Green, the clinical researcher who developed a failed THC eyedrop, would be cross-examined.

DEA attorneys took a precisely different tack, demanding to cross-examine nearly every witness who testified in favor of ending the medical prohibition. Robert and Frank were delighted by the DEA's decision. The resulting record would give oral weight to the written testimony. To accommodate the DEA's demand to cross-examine nearly all ACT and NORML witnesses, Judge Young scheduled multiple hearings to be held in New Orleans, San Francisco and Washington, D.C.

The hearings in New Orleans and San Francisco lasted a total of four days. The Washington hearings, held in a federal courtroom on Lafayette Park by the White House, stretched over a month with almost eleven days of testimony.

By the end of the hearings the record included 15 volumes of oral testimony, 60 lengthy affidavits and more than 5,000 pages of exhibits, evidence and other supporting materials. Now it was time to write the briefs.

Unlike Tom Collier, whose great talent was in reaching out to tap the talent of others, building a team and fully exploiting Steptoe's vast resources, Frank relied primarily on himself. He did recruit one associate, Roberto Laver, an Argentine attorney working at Steptoe. Robert was the third member of the team. They divided the case into chunks. Frank and Roberto researched legal questions. Robert and I began pulling the factual case together.

It was, in the end, an immense case. Thousands of pages of testimony and evidence, with mountains of supporting materials that were footnoted, referenced and cross-referenced.

All was neatly bundled and delivered to the Office of the Chief Administrative Law Judge.

Five months later, on September 6, 1988, DEA chief administrative law judge Francis L. Young ruled marijuana had "an accepted medical use in treatment in the United States." Young called the medical prohibition "unreasonable, arbitrary and capricious," and recommended marijuana be reclassified to permit its prescriptive medical use.

It was a smashing victory, all the sweeter because so many doubted the possibility of winning. Judge Young was "their guy," the top DEA law judge. No one expected him to rule in our favor. We knew the facts supported our cause but we had learned, especially from Newt Gingrich, that facts did not always prevail. This time would be different. Judge Young would not ignore the facts. It was a courageous decision.

The DEA still had the upper hand. Young's decision could be accepted or rejected by the DEA administrator. Two weeks after Judge Young's decision *Time Magazine* reported that a cable was sent from DEA headquarters to all field offices. "DEA counsel will be filing vigorous exception to the findings." Administrative law decisions are not ordinarily overturned but this was not your ordinary decision. We began the waiting game again, this time waiting for the DEA administrator, John Lawn. Realistically we did not expect an embracing of Young's decision.

In the meanwhile, the press coverage of Young's "unprecedented" decision was overwhelming. Once again the medical marijuana issue claimed the public's imagination. Headlines screamed the news. "Judge OKs Medicinal Use of Pot" was the banner in *USA Today*.

Ironically Judge Young's decision did not extend to glaucoma. He determined there was accepted medical use for marijuana in treatment for cancer, multiple sclerosis, and a variety of rare disorders but not glaucoma. It was a disappointment but the overall decision was so monumental that the glaucoma exclusion was lost in the merrymaking. Robert would later write:

> *I can't be certain why Young ruled in this way. From my perspective the evidence was solid. Perhaps it was Hepler's defection that swayed the Judge's thinking. Perhaps it was an attempt to placate the hard-*

liners at DEA. "Well, at least he stuck it to Randall," they could say. Who knows?

An even greater irony was the date of the decision—September 6, 1988, precisely sixteen years to the day I had been diagnosed with glaucoma. On that day in 1972, Dr. Fine had looked across his desk and, with some sadness, predicted I had "3 to 5 years of remaining sight." Marijuana had undeniably altered that dire prognosis. I could still see. Well enough to read Judge Young's decision, well enough to enjoy the beauty of Washington as I walked back to our apartment from Steptoe and Johnson on that historic day.

Section IV:

New Allies

25. THE NECESSITY OF NECESSITY

BY 1988, the medical use of marijuana was widespread and well-known but legal access to the drug was virtually impossible. Using marijuana medically still carried the risk of arrest but Robert's case in 1976 had given medical marijuana users a defense—medical necessity. Judge Washington's ruling was tightly drawn and could not be used in a cavalier fashion. A patient must have exhausted all legally available medications and the illness had to pose a great danger to the patient. In other words, medical marijuana use for hangnails would not pass the test.

Since Judge Washington's ruling there had been only one additional successful argument of medical necessity. It involved a multiple sclerosis patient in Washington state, Sam Diana, who successfully raised the medical necessity defense on appeal after he was convicted of marijuana possession in 1977.

But in the late 1980s, as efforts to reform federal laws prohibiting medical access to marijuana stalled in Congress, state programs shut down and the war on drugs simultaneously heated up, it was just a matter of time before patients who were medically using illegal marijuana became trapped in the cross-fire.

Elvy Musikka, in her late 40s, was a woman of South American and Norwegian extraction. She had two grown children and lived a quiet life under the palms in Hollywood, Florida. In March 1988 she contacted ACT after she was arrested for growing six marijuana plants in her backyard.

Elvy Musikka's medical history was an ophthalmologic horror story. Elvy was born with congenital cataracts and developed secondary glaucoma. Efforts to control her glaucoma with drugs failed. She had undergone more than twenty surgical procedures—for both cataracts and glaucoma. These surgeries failed to control her ocular pressures and repeated operations had weakened and mutilated the shape of her eyes. During her last operation a blood vessel ruptured, immediately blinding that eye. Her remaining eye was badly damaged by unrelieved pressure and surgery. There seemed to be no hope. Then, Elvy found marijuana.

That was in 1976, the year Judge Washington established the medical necessity defense. "I read everything about your case," Elvy told Robert. "Funny. I knew one day we would meet."

In addition to reading about Robert's case Elvy also learned about marijuana's use in glaucoma treatment from one of her doctors. He encouraged her to try marijuana brownies. They worked. For more than a decade Elvy Musikka had quietly smoked or consumed marijuana, kept her ocular pressures under control and avoided additional surgery. While legally blind, her condition was stable and she was still able to get around with modest help. Things were going well until policemen raided her home, seized her small marijuana crop and hauled Elvy off to jail. It was the next morning, after being released on bail, that she called ACT.

The case came together with surprising ease. Elvy's current doctor, Paul Palmberg of the Bascom-Palmer Eye Institute at the University of Miami, had treated her for many years. He was aware of her marijuana use and, while not overtly approving, encouraged her to keep doing "whatever works." Robert spoke with Dr. Palmberg and he was frank. "She's my only patient where it's quite clear-cut this is the only thing that will help her." After some consideration he agreed to testify on Elvy's behalf. More importantly he agreed to help Elvy apply for Compassionate IND access to marijuana.

Elvy's attorney, Norman Kent, agreed to *pro bono* representation. Robert guided him in developing the legal case and wrote detailed affidavits for Elvy and her physician. At the same time he provided Dr. Palmberg with a draft IND. Palmberg submitted the IND application without hesitation.

In August, after months of telephone chatter, Robert flew to Florida for the trial. Elvy was a handsome woman, lively and loving. She had befriended Irvin Rosenfeld, who received FDA-approved marijuana under a Compassionate IND for a rare disease that caused painful bone spurs and tumors. We had started assisting Irvin in the late 1970s. After nearly five years of effort, Irvin's IND was approved in September 1982 and he began receiving supplies of government marijuana two months later. For several years, following the closure of the state marijuana-as-medicine programs, Robert and Irvin were the only two individuals receiving legal supplies of marijuana in the U.S. Irvin, who lived in North Lauderdale and worked as a stockbroker, liked to remain in the background, but he agreed to testify in Elvy's case, if necessary.

The August 15, 1988 trial was a carbon copy of Robert's own case. A policeman testified regarding Elvy's arrest. A chemist declared the seized substance was marijuana. The state rested, case closed.

Elvy's attorney admitted the crime and raised a defense of "medical necessity." Robert was the first to testify on Elvy's behalf—a glaucoma patient legally smoking U.S. government marijuana to save his sight. He was followed by Dr. Palmberg who reviewed Elvy's extensive medical history. Palmberg concluded, as Robert Hepler had a dozen years before, that, if legal, "he would prescribe marijuana for this patient for her medical use." He was a convincing witness who acknowledged his discomfort in the role. "I'm a Presbyterian elder, and I've had to be dragged kicking and screaming to say this."

Elvy's testimony was heartfelt. "Marijuana," she said, "saved my sight. I don't think the law has the right to demand blindness from a citizen."

The press was there and they were wowed by the story. So was the judge. Unlike Robert's case, Elvy's decision came on the spot. Judge Mark E. Polen ruled from the bench that Elvy was not guilty by reason of medical necessity. "I don't see where a better case could ever be made for medical necessity. In this case, Miss Musikka is trying to preserve herself from serious bodily injury." Promising a full written decision in short order, Judge Polen warned against others thinking this decision "was a green light" for widespread marijuana use in South Florida. "That's not the message that I want to convey," he said. "The ruling of this court is limited to the precise facts of this case."

Elvy would win the first part of her battle with a speedy trial and rapid justice. Her Compassionate IND would take longer.

There were two other medical necessity cases that summer but the results were not as happy. Ironically both took place in Kentucky.

James Burton was a 39-year-old glaucoma patient living on a ninety-acre farm near Bowling Green. He made no secret of his use of marijuana to treat his glaucoma nor did he particularly try to hide the marijuana he was growing to treat his illness. But he was growing a lot of marijuana, more than 100 plants.

Kentucky was not one of the 34 states recognizing marijuana's medical utility but Burton, foolishly, was certain he was safe. When the Kentucky State Police raided his farm Burton told them of his medical use. They didn't care.

Jim Burton found himself in a dirty little skirmish that would have a brutal ending. Because of the large number of plants involved he was tried on federal rather than state charges. The jury believed his claim of medical necessity enough to mitigate the charges against him—manufacturing and intent to sell. But it found him guilty of simple possession and he was sentenced to one year in prison without parole. Worse yet, a new weapon in the war on drugs had been hatched by the U.S. Congress. It was called forfeiture and, simply put, it meant the government could seize the property of individuals charged with drug possession. Jim and Linda Burton would lose their home of eighteen years and be given ten days to vacate the 90-acre property. The seized "drug property" would then be auctioned to the highest bidder. When Burton was finally released from jail he and his wife would flee the U.S. and settle in Holland, which was more sympathetic to his medical needs.

Rick Morris was a 31-year-old cancer patient in Paintsville, Kentucky. He was arrested in November 1987 with more than seven ounces of marijuana. He could plead guilty to a misdemeanor charge and pay the $250 fine but instead Morris decided to fight on medical necessity grounds. In late July Robert flew to Kentucky to testify on Morris' behalf.

Morris' case had fewer complications than Burton's, not the least of which was his being charged by the state rather than the feds. There was no question of forfeiture. Rick Morris had little in the way of possessions. His cancer, ostensibly, was cured but he continued to experience severe nausea and vomiting. At one point his weight dropped from 200 pounds to 130 pounds.

Dr. Daniel Dansak, a psychiatrist who worked with New Mexico's Lynn Pierson Therapeutic Research Program, testified that this was not unusual for cancer patients. The lingering effects of radiation and chemotherapeutic treatments could last for years.

The prosecutor, clearly swayed by Morris' predicament, urged the jury to convict the Kentuckian but also asked for leniency. The jury convicted Rick Morris and sentenced him to a $1 fine.

The prosecutors in both cases would argue that medical necessity should not be considered because "the court was not the place for this argument." Instead, they contended, "proponents should take their case to the legislature." Elvy Musikka lived in a state that had enacted legislation and she successfully argued her case of medical necessity. Perhaps, if Kentucky had enacted a marijuana-as-medicine bill Jim Burton and Rick Morris would have been found not guilty. We'll never know.

After nearly six months of waiting Elvy would finally receive legal supplies of marijuana. In October 1988 she became the third individual in the U.S. receiving legal supplies through the Compassionate IND process. She would be the second woman to acquire such a unique status—Anne Guttentag had been the first.

Elvy's case began to rekindle interest in the Compassionate IND process. In the coming year Robert would assist another individual into the exclusive lifeboat. Corrine Millet, a 60-something Nebraska grandmother with glaucoma, doggedly pursued legal access and began receiving federal marijuana in October 1989.

There would be one more Compassionate IND approved in that year. It would go to an AIDS patient in Texas and it would spark a firestorm of interest that would force the issue of medical marijuana back into the public spotlight. This time the light would shine bright enough to strip away the mask of "compassion" and reveal the federal government's absolute denial of marijuana's medical utility.

26. PRIZES, PAWNS AND PATRONS

At the dawn of the Reagan era a mysterious affliction came to America. Gay men in the prime of life were dying of rare cancers and pneumonia. A small ripple of death moved through an outcast community. There was silence. Then, with frightening speed, the unnamed disease leap-frogged from homosexuals to Haitians to hemophiliacs and then to heterosexuals. Near-panic gripped epidemiologists as outbreaks of this demon disease doubled and redoubled. Scientific alarm slammed into political indifference.

AIDS.

By 1983, the mystery disease had a name—Acquired Immune Deficiency Syndrome—and a profile. A virus carried in blood-based body fluids destroyed the immune system. Once the immune system collapsed infected individuals were prey to all manner of microbes. Death was inevitable.

"Marijuana helps with my AIDS," an unidentified caller told Robert in 1983. Robert pressed for details. "It just helps me eat," the man said.

As the incidents of AIDS multiplied, calls to ACT became more frequent. "Would you like to apply to get marijuana legally?" we would ask. Every man—all the callers were men—declined. With frail voices they would say, "I'm dying. I don't have time for cops and courts and bureaucrats. I just want you to know pot helps."

In retrospect it is hard to fathom the political silence and bloated hatreds that welcomed AIDS into the 1980s. There was good reason for fear. A society suckled on medical marvels could find no defense. Science was stymied. There was no cure, no effective treatment. In these early days of the crisis AIDS was nearly 100% fatal: a fearsome epidemic loose on the land. Uncertainty over how AIDS spread intensified social anxieties. Christian fanatics attributed the accelerating slaughter to divine retribution. Sinners were dying. Who cares? Then, sinless children infected by transfusion were cast from schools. Mobs formed. Homes burned.

In 1986, AIDS touched us personally for the first time when we learned our college friend, Bobby Evans and his lover, Walter, had AIDS. Walter died the following year. "Horrible," Bobby said, his voice conveying a concern for his own future. "Just horrible." Not yet 40, Bobby moved to San Francisco to prepare for his own demise.

In 1988, the AIDS Quilt came to Washington and we walked among the brilliantly colored panels spread on the Ellipse, just across the street from the White House. We wept over the deaths of so many so young. Among the panels we would find a tribute to Representative Stewart McKinney. Our former Congressional friend and sponsor had been the first U.S. Congressman to die of AIDS. Another marked the death of our neighbor Rusty. It was an awesome display that called out for acknowledgment but in an act of supreme neglect President Reagan did not bother to visit the Quilt.

"I have AIDS," Steve said choking on the stigma. "And I want your help." In early October 1989, Steve L. called for help from his bed at the Audie. L. Murphy Memorial Veterans Hospital in San Antonio, Texas. He was dying.

"I told 'em if I kept looking I'd find you," Steve told Robert, sad as a sick puppy. "I told 'em I'd find you."

Steve L. was a backwoods Texas boy. Reared in poverty he quit school in the seventh grade and worked odd jobs doing lawn care, chopping firewood, etc. By the time he reached thirty Steve was just another aimless, angry alcoholic, addicted to methamphetamine and selling blood to make ends meet. A dark bedeviled life of hard scrabble and hard luck.

Steve's life got much harder when, unable to breathe, he ended up at Audie Murphy diagnosed with AIDS from a dirty needle. He lapsed into coma, then awoke to slow recovery and transformation.

"What happened in your coma?" Robert asked.

"I remember walking down this path," Steve began. "Trees, like a tent overhead. Dark, but there was people, shadow people, standing off to both sides. But I paid 'em no mind, just kept walking 'til I come over a rise and saw this wide, black river, flat as glass. So I walked on by the river awhile 'til I come upon this small boat. I was getting in to go to the other side when a man with no face stopped me. 'Not yet,' he said. 'Not yet.' Then I woke up. And now I've found you."

"Were you looking for me?" Robert asked, trapped by the imagery.

"Oh, yeah. Looking hard," Steve said with gravity. "Looking a year or more."

Steve's pneumonia-induced coma was followed by ineffective, highly toxic medical treatments and rapid weight loss. Constantly nauseated by disease and drugs, his weight collapsed. "I'm not a big man," Steve explained, "but I lost half my weight; down to 80 pounds. Skin and bones. Then I discovered marijuana."

Following his comatose journey to the River Styx, Steve emerged spiritually transfigured. "No booze. No drugs. No anger. No fear. Like I woke from a bad dream. Happy," he said.

Happy, but terribly thin. A friend, alarmed by Steve's bone-bruising thinness, urged Steve to take a toke of marijuana. "He said it might help me eat. I thought, 'What the hell?' And it worked. I could eat. Once pot took my nausea away I couldn't stop eating. Gained back my weight, mostly, started chopping firewood again. It's like I come back to life. My doctors, everyone are real amazed. I'm telling you true; without pot I'd have died last year. That's when I started looking for you."

"How did you find me?" Robert asked gently.

"Weren't easy. I knew you existed 'cause I saw you on TV. So I started looking, making calls. I asked my doctors, the people at V.A., local police, the Texas Rangers, FDA, even the DEA. I kept telling people there was this man who legally smokes pot. But they all told me you didn't exist. That got me real confused so as I didn't know what to do. Then I got arrested."

"You've been arrested!?"

"Yep. Six months ago: March 1989. The police they come storming in 'n took my pot. That was real bad. Without pot I ended up back in the hospital. That's when I started looking for you again."

"So how did you find me?" Robert needed to know who guided this messenger from the edge of death to our door.

"Well, I called all over again. And everybody kept saying no one gets legal pot. Then I called the DEA and this real nice guy, he listens to what I'm saying. Then he told me all about you. Even gave me your phone number. That's how I found you," Steve said with the pride of a hunter who has finally cornered his quarry.

"So. You've found me. How can I help you?"

"I want you to get me legal pot," Steve said.

"Why?" Robert probed for motive.

"Because people with AIDS are dying—starving to death. That's not right. They should know marijuana helps. So I want you to get me legal pot. Then people with AIDS will know, right? That's what I want you to do."

Steve L., returned from death, was on a mission. He had, after a long, frustrating search, delivered his message inviting Robert to be his guide. "It's why I came back," Steve said with sweet certainty. "So you could help me."

Steve spoke with Fate's voice and issued a summons Robert could not—dared not—refuse. He approached Robert with a certainty that Robert was his guide to a new place, a new level. But it was Steve who would be the guide. Until Steve L. medical marijuana was about cancer and glaucoma and, ever so slightly, spasms and chronic pain. Steve's case would stretch the Compassionate IND to include the use of marijuana in treating AIDS.

Steve L. had good friends, chief among them Papa Bear (a.k.a. Robert C. Edwards), a big, burly, bearded man in his mid-fifties. Papa Bear founded and ran the San Antonio AIDS Foundation (SAAF), a charity that cared for AIDS patients in southeastern Texas. The SAAF, fueled by Papa Bear's energy, provided dying men medical care, operated food pantries, prepared a hot potluck dinner every night and delivered meals to men too weak to leave home. A human response to the spreading plague. Edwards—the father of a gay son—could not deny Steve's plea for help. "A lot of my guys smoke pot and say it helps," Bear told Robert. "Steve kept telling us you existed but we thought he was imagining things. Maybe he's on to something. How can I help?"

Papa Bear helped a great deal. He encouraged the SAAF doctor to apply for a Compassionate IND. We altered a cancer protocol and wondered how the FDA would react to a marijuana IND for AIDS. "Then there's Steve's arrest," Bear reminded us.

Steve was set up; busted after buying 13 ounces of marijuana from a vice cop. "I was getting enough marijuana to last me the rest of my life," Steve explained. Instead, Steve ended up several thousand dollars poorer, out on bail, dying of AIDS while facing criminal charges and prison.

"We told the court about Steve's condition," Bear said. "So the judge just keeps postponing the trial. No reason to drag a dying man to court."

But Steve L. wanted his day in court. "Hell, I wanna fight 'em. They oughtn't be doing this to sick people," Steve said.

Kevin Zeese would help us locate a lawyer for Steve. Within days Gerry Goldstein, a San Antonio attorney and one of the nation's finest criminal defense lawyers, agreed to represent Steve L. *pro bono*.

Within a week of calling, Steve L. had a doctor willing to apply to the FDA, and his criminal case was in capable hands. Within two weeks Robert had drafted the nation's first Compassionate IND for marijuana/AIDS. Steve's doctor submitted the IND and we began tracking its progress through the FDA. Time was short. Steve was very sick.

Aware of the stress that comes from waiting, Robert made a point of speaking with Steve nearly every night. Despite his lack of formal education Steve was an intelligent, articulate fellow who wrote hauntingly beautiful poetry. Steve often spoke of his dog, Cool Breeze—C.B.—and frequently reflected on his return from death; the path and the ferryman. Robert listened for hours as Steve pondered the meaning of the mythic imagery he was living.

"Why wouldn't the ferryman let you in the boat?" Robert asked one night.

"Unfinished business," Steve replied with simple certainty.

As Robert listened to Steve night after night he found himself far removed from congresses and courtrooms, plunged into a more ethereal, less material realm governed by only vaguely apprehended energies. Ghosts of fallen allies would manifest themselves in Steve's simply articulated goals. But there were also ghosts of future allies yet to come, a vague sensation of destinies that we could not deny.

As our years in "the issue" dragged on there were often moments of despair, particularly in the late 1980s. Financially we lived a precarious existence. I worked full-time to support the household, Robert collected the occasional speaker fee or honorarium. We weren't, as they say, getting any younger and like any normal middle-aged couple we questioned our path.

In 1988, when Mae Nutt came to Washington, D.C. to testify before Judge Young, she and I encountered each other in the hallway and shared an emotional moment. Wondering together at the final outcome of the long battle in which we had engaged, Mae looked me square in the eye and said, "There's no need to worry, Alice. We've got angels on our shoulders." In the fall of 1989, as Steve L.'s IND bounced around FDA, those angels manifested themselves with a dramatic, unanticipated event.

Our friend Kevin Zeese had left NORML and, together with American University professor Arnold Trebach, established a new group called the Drug Policy Foundation (DPF), a Washington "think-tank" established to develop alternative public policies in the war on drugs. Among the activities of the DPF was the annual presentation of awards named for various individuals who had made significant contributions to the reform of drug laws. In 1989, Kevin and Arnold informed us that DPF would establish the Robert C. Randall Award for Achievement in the Field of Citizen Activism. Robert would be the first recipient of the award. Along with a nice plaque, the DPF award came with a check for $10,000! It was a bolt out of the blue and it would mark a turning point in our lives.

The award and prize were presented during DPF's annual banquet in early November, part of a three-day conference. Robert arrived at the opening reception ahead of me and found Kevin who steered Robert towards a quiet corner. These events were always difficult for Robert. Half-blind, in a strange room crowded with people who expressed familiarity but whose faces he could not really see, Robert invariably gravitated towards a corner where he would remain as people came by, extended congratulations, made small talk and moved on. Kevin, who had been a long-time friend, knew the drill and after settling Robert in a well-lit corner he headed off to the bar to get some drinks.

"Didn't I see you smoking marijuana on Larry King?" someone asked.

Robert's eyes moved in the direction of the voice and worked hard to focus on the large, friendly man smiling down at him. "That was me, all right."

"Good job," the large man said. "Good job," he repeated, then shyly retreated as Kevin returned.

"You know who that was?" Kevin asked.

"Haven't a clue," Robert replied.

"Rich Dennis," Kevin said with pride.

Richard J. Dennis. Robert, in fact, did know something about the man who had just congratulated him. He had first encountered the name in a newspaper article several years earlier. Richard J. Dennis, the article read, made a cool $80 million in 1986 to become the fourth highest earner on Wall Street. Not much more than 40 years of age, Richard J. Dennis was a very wealthy man who helped bankroll DPF's start and the awards that would be presented during the conference. Kevin revealed the philanthropist was looking for other good works to support.

The next evening the banquet and award presentation was held. Robert later wrote of the event:

For fifteen years I had held press conferences, handled reporters, given thousands of interviews. But only rarely did I give a formal speech. I found the process intriguing. Rhetoric is more than mere words.

The speech was well-received and I was much relieved. I shook hands, made small talk without really connecting to any of the individuals. On autopilot I reached for the next extended hand. "That was a very fine speech," Richard J. Dennis said. "Give me a call. Maybe I can help."

"*Seriously?*"

"*Seriously,*" *Richard J. replied with a smile.*

Robert and I had long ago given up chasing the money dream. We had purposely designed ACT to be a small organization dependent upon ourselves and one or two other trusted individuals. Initially we made a stab at obtaining grant money but got nowhere. For years ACT had been bankrolled by small donations from individuals and by my full-time work as the administrative officer of a non-profit publishing organization, the Society for Scholarly Publishing.

Now we were confronted with the unexpected, a very wealthy individual who actually came to us and expressed interest in our work. Days later someone from Chicago phoned. "Could you outline what you would like? That will give Rich a chance to review things before you talk." Seriously.

Robert was still highly skeptical but:

With zero expectations I wrote Richard J. a long, sometimes clever, sometimes rambling overview of drug reform and medical marijuana. I made it painfully clear we had no interest in empire building. There would be no organization to support, no fund-raising effort, no direct mail campaign, no outreach to activists nor seminars nor membership drives nor bake sales. I didn't give a damn about such frivolous distractions. Given a choice between creating a big organization or a vital issue I would build an issue. All I really wanted was to pursue medical marijuana. No strings.

It was a brutally honest, utterly unorthodox "non-proposal": heartfelt, but hardly politic. Without pausing to consider the consequences, I dropped the missive in the overnight mail bin. Chicago called the next day to give me Richard J.'s L.A. number. "Call any time," Chicago said.

Robert made the call on Sunday, December 7, 1989. Richard J. answered, a football game blaring in the background. "I could call back," Robert suggested. "No need," Richard J. replied. "And call me Rich. So, how would you win medical marijuana?"

"That's an unfair question; a bit like me asking you how to win in the stock market. There's no easy answer. The point is I know how to win."

"What's important to you?" Rich asked.

"Aesthetics," it tumbled out. "Ethics, style and an ability to communicate. That's the problem with drug reform—all argument, no aesthetics."

"So, what are you working on now?" Rich asked.

"I'm working with some people in Texas. We're trying to make medical marijuana available to people with AIDS …"

It became a long, elliptical conversation. Rich asked unusual questions and Robert responded with unusual answers. "Would you like me to support ACT or you?" Rich asked.

"ACT is an illusion," Robert replied. "I'm very real."

"In your proposal—I guess that was a proposal—you mention $100,000?"

"Yes. But I've decided it will take more," an honest, too-candid response.

"How much more?"

"$150,000 total."

"Would you like that in a lump sum or installments?"

Robert finished the conversation and made his way downstairs. He found me in the kitchen and there was a peculiar look on his face.

"So, how'd it go?" I asked.

"Swell," Robert replied in a daze, "just swell."

In the span of a phone call, football blaring in the background, we found a patron and gained economic freedom.

There was some additional back and forth with Rich's aides. Formalities. After that Rich's checks arrived in quarterly allotments, the first appearing in the mail on Robert's 42nd birthday. "That's more than I make in a year," I observed, staring at the numbers. Robert giggled a bit and said, "And we get three more just like it this year!"

With angels on our shoulders we faced a new beginning for medical marijuana. Fate was arming us for the struggle ahead.

On December 13, a week after Rich's fateful phone call, the FDA approved Steve L.'s Compassionate IND request for medical marijuana. Steve's goal was to let others know about marijuana's medical use so Robert lost little time in preparing a press release. Wire services around the world carried the news: "FDA approves marijuana in AIDS care." Rich saw the story in the *L.A. Times* and told Kevin, "That's what I call a fast return on an investment."

Steve had often told Robert he wanted to inform the world about marijuana's usefulness to people battling AIDS. Fax machines had arrived on the scene and we embraced this new technology to spread the word about Steve. Several weeks later Robert obtained a copy of the UPI story from a Tokyo newspaper and forwarded it to Steve with a note, "You wanted everyone to know, Steve. Now, even the Japanese know marijuana can help people with AIDS."

The FDA's approval of Steve's IND, under anxious prompting from Robert, Papa Bear, and Steve's doctor, was unexpectedly fast, less than six weeks. But when would Steve L. actually receive his promised supplies of legal pot? We had seen how long this could take. The decade-old memory of Lynn Pierson was still fresh in our minds.

Christmas came and went. In Texas Steve L. waited anxiously for his marijuana supplies. Even though his IND was approved the DEA was delaying the first shipment of medical marijuana. It was not unusual for the DEA to drag its feet in approving shipments but this particular delay seemed especially cruel and premeditated.

These delays made no sense until Friday, December 29, 1989. On the last business day of the decade, with reporters home for New Year's Eve weekend, DEA Administrator John Lawn formally rejected Judge Francis Young's recommendation that marijuana be rescheduled for medical use. In Administrator Lawn's skewed view marijuana had no accepted medical use in the United States.

Rejecting the testimony of ACT's witnesses as "pro-drug" and ignoring the factual record, DEA argued that ending the medical prohibition would unleash sin upon the land and, of course, "send the wrong message." It was a deeply stupid statement. ACT and NORML would appeal.

But the timing of the release made it clear why Steve had not received his promised supplies of marijuana. How very awkward it would be to release marijuana to an AIDS patient while denying marijuana's medical value. Officials at the DEA knew such hypocrisy would not go unnoticed by the press. So they simply ignored the approved IND until after the Administrator's decision was released. To hell with Steve. A national policy was at stake. The AIDS patient could wait.

Steve L. was a pawn, caught in the dreadful cross fire of the war on drugs.

For several weeks, as Steve's condition worsened, Robert tried to find a remedy. Instead, he got the red tape run around. DEA Washington blamed DEA San Antonio. DEA San Antonio blamed the Audie L. Murphy V.A. pharmacy. Steve, the subject of all this finger pointing, remained moot. From the beginning of our association Steve had insisted on remaining anonymous. Ashamed of his illness, Steve was adamant about staying out of the public spotlight. Robert respected this and in press releases designed to build public pressure on the DEA Robert referred to him only as a "Texas AIDS patient named Steve."

"If you don't become real I'm not sure I can help you," Robert warned.

"I told you I don't want no one to know about my AIDS," Steve and his stigma said.

"Look. We're headed for criminal court. That's public. Everyone will know who you are and what disease you have. But without your help right now I won't be able to force the DEA into action." Robert explained to the frightened young man.

"Alright. What should I do?" Steve said, the will to complete his mission finally overtaking his fear of exposure.

As soon as Steve relented, Robert arranged for a San Antonio television station to carry the story. It was the second week in January. Steve, still in the hospital, appeared in the report wearing a surgical smock and mask—still anxious to conceal his identity. Robert was interviewed by an affiliate station in Washington, smoking his legal joints, demanding to know why the DEA was depriving Steve of FDA-approved access to similar care.

The separate video clips were merged into a single report. At the conclusion the reporter explained that the DEA had, that very day, decided to comply with Steve's request. Problem solved? Hardly. Having deflected a minor media hit, the DEA returned to delaying tactics and refused to release Steve's shipments. It was New Mexico all over again. Apply a little public pressure and the agencies would say what the public wanted to hear. Once the video lights turned off the feds returned to the trenches.

And, like New Mexico, the federal bureaucrats were hoping Steve would die before they were compelled to make good on their promise of legal access to marijuana. The stakes were just as high. Lynn Pierson spoke to thousands of cancer patients and unleashed a tremendous demand for medical marijuana. Steve L. could do the same for AIDS.

Flush with cash thanks to our new patron, Robert flew to San Antonio the next week, walked into the Audie L. Murphy Memorial Veterans Hospital and asked to see the director. Working his way through the hierarchy he tried to ascertain if there were any remaining problems that could prevent DEA from releasing supplies. Everyone swore the V.A. was not to blame. Robert met the hospital pharmacist who told him, "We're ready to go; just waiting for supplies."

After these brief encounters, he finally met Steve. Gaunt and tired-looking, Steve had the look of a man near death. On his arm were medication patches. His hair was thin and wispy. Only 34 years old, he had the slow mannerisms of an elderly man.

"I'm sure glad you came. I get no straight answers. Do you think I'll ever get my pot?"

"Yes," Robert said without promise. "I think so."

The next day Robert increased the media pressure, working the phone and speaking to several local reporters who then called the DEA. Struggling to not look purely evil, the DEA relented, assuring reporters that Steve would receive his first shipment of marijuana the following day. The news blanketed Texas and moved out into America.

The following day Steve L. smoked his first legal joint. The logjam had finally been broken. The phone rang in Robert's hotel room and the soft twang of Steve's voice immediately conveyed the good news. "Guess what I'm doing, Robert?" he asked from his hospital bed. "I'm smoking a fat, juicy joint, and eating lunch." The joy was unmistakable as was the renewed resolve. "So, when can we talk to more reporters?" he asked.

The next morning Steve L., released from Audie Murphy, arrived at the AIDS foundation as reporters from San Antonio and Dallas were setting up their equipment. Steve L. was a touch scruffy; thin moustache, old baseball cap, heavy flannel shirt, dark sunglasses: just another Texas good ole boy. Now "legal" Steve's fear of exposure quickly faded as he and Robert sat under quartz lights, answering questions. "I think we should smoke a joint," Steve suggested. Matches flared. Cameras rolled.

"Half the state of Texas is drooling right about now," Steve told Robert through a haze of smoke.

"And the other half wants to arrest us," Robert replied.

An odd pairing. The nearly blind Washington man in a blue wool suit and a thin, scruffy Texas redneck dying from AIDS. Steve got his legal pot and sent his message. Mission accomplished. After so much excitement Steve was anxious to retreat, get home and see C.B. "I'm making my coffin," Steve explained without sadness. "But I'll be here if you need me."

In his battered pick-up truck Steve drove Robert to the airport and the two men said goodbye. "Thanks for everything, Mr. Randall," he said, giving Robert an unexpected hug. Beneath his thick work shirt, Steve was bone thin.

A few days after smoking his first legal joint Steve was back in the hospital. Doctors said his spleen was failing. No one knew why. When Robert phoned the hospital a kindly woman answered.

"Are you the nice man who came to Texas to help my baby?" Ollie, Steve's mother, asked. "Steve's asleep right now."

"How is he?"

"It's bad, real bad. Mind, they don't tell me much. But a mother knows. He's in a lot of pain."

"Your son is a remarkable man."

"Thanks. Maybe I shouldn't say this. But AIDS gave me back my baby." The confession was bittersweet. "Before Steve got AIDS he was just plain mean. Don't know why. Always was." Ollie's voice was filled with emotion. "But then, after he near died, he came back so kind. I just wish my baby had longer to live."

On February 12, 1990, Steve L. died.

The press release about Steve's death reached around the globe, educating people about marijuana's potential use in treating AIDS. Out of the blue an editor at *High Times Magazine* called. "We got this press release about the Texas AIDS patient," the editor explained. "We were thinking maybe you'd like to write his obit?"

"I think I'd like that very much." Robert replied.

It was mid-February and *High Times* wanted to include the obit in their next issue, scheduled to hit the stands in mid-March. Robert quickly set to work and contemplated the potential energy of this emerging therapeutic use. There would need to be new torch carriers to complete the job Steve had begun. Were those angels still on our shoulders or had they fled with Steve's spirit?

27. MESSAGE IN A BOTTLE

You never know where Fate will take you. Steve wanted to send a message. So we helped Steve send his message and then Steve died. On April 2, 1990, a phone call would bring the fading echo of a dead man's desire to be heard and, if you listened very carefully, you might have heard the quiet flutter of angels' wings.

"Hello? This is Kenny. Kenny Jenks. Hello? Is this ... Is anyone? Hey, Hop, it's a answer machine."

"So? Tell 'em why we're calling."

Robert listened with some amusement. These two were young, very young.

"Oh. Yeah ... Hello," the voice continued. "This is Kenny Jenks. Me and my wife—Barb and me—we just been arrested—eh, 2 plants—that's all. We just got out of jail 'n ..."

"Tell 'em about Steve, Kenny. Tell 'em about Steve ..." It was a woman's voice in the background.

"Oh, yeah. We got this *High Times* and there's this story—about Steve. Steve L. It says here you helped Steve. Well, Barb 'n me, we're like Steve. Ah ... we got what Steve has—had. My wife and me, we ... Barb and me we ... we're just like Steve..."

"Can he help us Kenny? Can he ... ?"

"Shush, Hop. I done told you it's just a mach ..." click.

Young, in love, so very alive, so utterly alone, Kenny and Barbra Jenks were dying of AIDS in Panama City Beach, Florida. Blood crimes had mortally wounded a man and his mate; disease condemned them to terrible afflictions and death. Into this sea of sorrow a pitiless agent of the State was now seeking to convict this dying young couple for the crime of growing medicinal weeds.

Kenny and Barbra were a Walmart couple wearing hand-me down clothes, easily overlooked. Exceedingly ordinary people who were about to engage in an extraordinary experience. Fate led us to guide them and, before we were done, everything would change—everything but the outcome.

After that first call from Kenny and Barbra Jenks we immediately set about acquiring the necessary components to assist the young couple. With Kevin's help we found a local attorney, John Daniel, to represent the young couple *pro bono*. Working with an AIDS group in Pensacola, Robert located a doctor willing to explore marijuana as an AIDS treatment. Having gained these commitments, he flew to Florida to meet the principal players and prepare for the upcoming criminal trial.

Robert arrived at the Pensacola Regional Airport on May 7th. Dazed by sunlight, disoriented in the crowded terminal, he felt lost.

"Mr. Randall? You Mr. Randall, sir?"

"You're Kenny?"

"Yes sir," said the tanned young man wearing dark glasses, a pink baseball cap and dirty white T-shirt. "And this here's my wife, Barb," he said, squeezing her small shoulders. "I call her Hop."

"It's Barbra," Kenny's short wife said. "Barbra. Like in Streisand."

Barbra, 23, was transiting between eighteen and infinity. Once plump, she had a large, English face framed by raven black hair. She was born in Enid, Oklahoma into an abusive family where loutish parents raised criminal sons and paid no mind to "the girl." Her smile was generous, her laugh warm. But Barbra was deeply suspicious of a world that had seldom been kind. She occasionally flared with anger.

Kenny was five years older, but hardly more mature. Tall, thin, with angular features, bony arms and knobby knees. His sharp tan face was shielded by badly scratched photosensitive lenses. A baseball cap covered brown, close-cropped hair. He was often loud, always opinionated. A military brat, he grew up in pain from the hemophilia that would eventually lead to his infection with HIV.

As they ate their lunch Robert learned the story of their "courtship." They met in Tucson when Barbra was 15. "Love at first sight," she sighed. "Kenny'd sneak over 'n spend the night. 'Til we near got caught," Barbra relished relating the tale of her seduction.

"One night I told Barb's parent we was going to eat at the Red Lobster," Kenny continued the story. "But we didn't go to no Red Lobster. Not in Tucson anyway. I just kept driving 'til we got all the way to here."

The couple reminded Robert of the Dorothea Lange photographs of the Great Depression—stark, compelling and very real. They had only the most basic education. Kenny did not know where New York was, Barbra didn't care. Most Americans would simply dismiss Kenny and Barbra as poor white trash. Kenny would bristle at such a suggestion. He and Barbra held a mortgage, paid their bills. But they had never not been poor. They had few skills, but worked very hard. As a song lyric once said they were, "Two American kids doing the best they can."

Over the next two days Robert would collect the facts about Kenny and Barbra's life. He started with Kenny.

Kenny was a hemophiliac—a bleeder. At 30, he was an old hemophiliac: a product of miracle medicine and wonder science. Paradoxically he was both surviving and dying because of Factor VIII—an infused clotting factor refined from the blood of thousands of donors. Kenny got AIDS from HIV-tainted blood products.

"Them blood companies and hemophilia people just plain decided to kill us," Kenny said with bitterness. "They didn't give a damn about people, just profits."

A harsh indictment: mass murder for money. But it was true. The philanthropic fellows at the Hemophilia Foundation, a creature of the companies that trade in blood, made the cold and fiendish decision to sell HIV-infected blood to hemophiliacs. The FDA did nothing. Nor was this a uniquely American decision. The same logic dominated blood boardrooms in Paris, Tokyo and elsewhere. Now those craven decisions made by powerful men were killing Kenny. He was not alone. Nearly every hemophiliac in the industrial world was infected and dying.

"Them men decided to kill me," Kenny repeats. "And kill my wife, too."

Kenny got AIDS from a tainted Factor VIII injection. Barbra was infected by love. Alone and together they were doomed beings pursuing inevitable outcomes.

Hemophilia is a lifelong affliction. Kenny had been in and out of hospitals all his life. He bled nearly every week. A major bleed could send him to the hospital for weeks, even months. If the hemorrhage was severe, blood collected under his skin. The resulting pressure on joints and nerves could cause temporary or even permanent paralysis. Like most hemophiliacs, Kenny walked with a slight limp.

"Things got a lot better when Factor VIII came along," Kenny would tell Robert. "It's real expensive; $800 an injection. But it's better than weeks in the hospital or being a cripple."

When Kenny first asked his doctors about AIDS in the mid-1980s they laughed at his concerns. "One chance in a million," they assured him. "One in a million," Kenny scoffed. "Hell, Mr. Randall, every hemophiliac I know has AIDS."

It was Barbra who became sick first. Unable to breathe, hospitalized, and tested, she lapsed into a coma just before Christmas, 1988. While watching Barbra struggle for life, Kenny learned they both had AIDS. "Like getting a death sentence," he said.

After Barbra's hospitalization she was too weak to work. Kenny, despite his diagnosis, continued to work 8-hour days. "It was the only way we could make ends meet."

Barbra and Kenny began intensive AIDS treatments: massive doses of highly toxic AZT to slow the virus and megadoses of antibiotics to stop infections. "Just look at all them drugs," Kenny would say, pointing to nearly 50 brown bottles containing dozens of potions and hundreds of pills.

"It's kinda hard just remembering what to take when," Barbra interjected.

"Them pills, they was killing Barb," Kenny noted. "We was taking all these drugs and we just couldn't eat. Barb couldn't stand the smell of food. She really started losing weight, nearly 50 lbs. Ain't that right, Hop?"

"At least 50," Barbra affirmed, dryly.

"She was wasting away. Dying in front of me. Then we started going to this AIDS group at County Health." One young man in the group approached Kenny after a meeting. "Your wife," he said, "needs to gain some weight. Why don't you smoke some pot?" The young man handed Kenny two joints.

Barbra—a Reagan baby—Just Said No. She had never smoked marijuana and was terrified to try, unwilling to break the law. Kenny, slightly older, was less reluctant. When they got home, and over Barbra's stern objections, he took a couple of hits.

"It was amazing, Mr. Randall. Amazing. First, my nausea just vanished. And I got real talkative. Me and Barb, we had kinda stopped talking. But that night I told Hop how sorry I was she got infected cause of me."

"That was real nice," Barbra added. "AIDS was pushing us apart. We couldn't even say the word, AIDS. But talking brought us back together."

"And then I got hungry. Real hungry." Kenny continued. "I started going through the kitchen, eating anything I could find. Amazing."

"I hadn't seen him eat nothing for 6 weeks. But he just ate the rest of that night. Eating and talking."

The next evening Barbra asked Kenny if she could smoke some marijuana with him. Together, they smoked half a joint, talked some more, fell into a laughing fit, then sat down to eat together for the first time since Barbra had gone to the hospital three months before.

"It was like we was husband and wife again," Kenny said. "And Barb, she really started gaining weight." When the couple discovered marijuana Barbra weighed 102 lbs. With marijuana's help she regained over 25 lbs.

Over the next year Kenny and Barbra hid their AIDS, smoked pot and stayed out of the hospital. Kenny went to work. Barbra stayed home and fixed dinner. Their only problem was finding and affording enough marijuana. "My wife would die without pot," Kenny said with certainty. "That's why we decided to grow some."

They grew two small marijuana plants in their bedroom. Then, an informant turned them in. On March 29, 1990, they were sitting down to dinner when nearly a dozen heavily armed policemen stormed their small trailer in the piney woods. They were taken away in cuffs and chains, charged with felony cultivation.

When Kenny finished his story Barbra was not certain she had anything to add nor was she accustomed to being asked her views. But with Robert's gentle prodding, Barbra haltingly began to tell her story.

She began to get ill in July 1988, just before her 21st birthday, when she developed a massive yeast infection.

"My tongue got all white. I brushed 'n brushed, but it wouldn't go away. It got so bad I went 'n seen the doctor. He gave me some pills and told me to get tested." She paused. "But I didn't."

Kenny interrupted to explain. "It's like we told you, Robert. We was scared. There was these stories on TV. People find you got AIDS they go crazy; run you outta town, set fire to your home." Barbra nodded her agreement and continued her story.

"The yeast cleared up ... sorta. Then I got a bad cold that wouldn't go away. By Thanksgiving I was real tired. Then one day I couldn't barely breathe. So I went to the doctor and told 'em it was an emergency. But them nurses made me wait 'n wait. So I come home. I was gonna go back, but I barely made it inside the trailer before I passed out."

"Flat out," Kenny energetically picked up the story. "I come home 'n Barb's on the floor. Burning up, Robert! Just on fire! So I took her to the hospital." He paused and became more subdued. Looking at his wife he continued, "By the time I got Hop to the hospital she was hardly breathing. So the docs put her on oxygen 'n IVs 'n all. But we was too late. Barb went into this coma ..."

For the second time in less than six months Robert was listening to an AIDS patient speak about a pneumonia-induced coma. He immediately thought of Steve. "You remember any of this?" he asked the suddenly quiet woman.

"Naw, I was good as gone." It was almost a whisper.

"Yeah, Robert. Hop stayed in that coma three weeks. The docs told me she was done for. Wouldn't make it."

"Did you have a near death experience?"

Barbra, visibly jolted by Robert's question, was slow and awkward in reply. "Maybe .. . yeah."

He had come upon a deep and secret memory. Kenny, with a trace of hurt, said, "Hey, Hop. You never told me."

"Course not, silly. Cause I didn't want you thinking I'd gone nuts or something."

Barbra was reticent but Robert sensed she wanted, very much wanted, to talk about her experience. "Steve also had a near-death experience," Robert said. "Would you like to talk about yours? What did you see?"

"A light." The response was without hesitation. "A bright, white light." She was bolder now, remembering something she could not forget. Kenny, uneasy, hummed the "Twilight Zone" theme. "Quit that, Kenny." Her tone was abrupt and she slapped him hard on the leg. To Barbra this was very serious stuff.

"Did you know you were dying?" Robert prompted, trying to regain the moment.

"Oh yea! I was a goner." Barbra gratefully returned to the dialogue. "But it didn't upset me none. The light was so nice, really beautiful. I was in this dark place and I was moving, floating, to this wonderful light. I was trying to get to that light, floating closer 'n closer."

"Did you know if you went into the light you would die?"

"Uh huh. But that didn't matter none. It was so peaceful 'n all. I'd have been happy to die."

"So, why didn't you go?"

She hesitated, unsure again, but continued on, "You'll think I'm crazy. ... Well, I was being surrounded, swallowed up like by this light, getting sucked right into it. .. but I suddenly wondered who was gonna fix Kenny's dinner. As soon as I thought about Kenny things changed. The light got further away so's I couldn't reach it no more. And then it just disappeared 'n everything got dark 'n suddenly I was in all this pain. That's when I woke up 'n come out of my coma."

"So it wasn't your time?"

"Yeah. Cause Kenny needed me'n..." she paused. "Oh, I dunno, Robert. It's like I wasn't done; like there's something I still need to do—gotta do—before I can go."

"That's what Steve said," Robert remembered.

"So, why didn't Steve go, Robert?" It was more of a demand than a question. Barbra was beginning to sense something.

"Same reason. Steve says—said—he came to a river, but couldn't go across because he still had things to do."

"Yeah!" Barbra was excited, beginning to see things in a different light. "We're all here to do something. We're supposed to help each other. That's what I think."

There was a moment of silence. "You liked Steve, didn't you Robert?"

"Yes I did. Steve wanted to help people; people like you. He thought people with AIDS should know marijuana helps. So I helped Steve do that. He was the first person with AIDS to speak out. That took guts."

Kenny had been listening intently and begun to realize where the conversation was heading. "That was so strange, Robert. After Barb 'n me got out of jail, that same morning, I got this magazine 'n opened it up and there's this whole big story all about Steve 'n AIDS 'n marijuana. It was like I was reading about Barb 'n me."

"You write that story, Robert?" Barbra wanted answers.

"Yes, I wrote that..."

"So me 'n Kenny, we found you because of Steve. That's what I think. That story you wrote 'n all. It's like Steve was reaching to us. Like a message in a bottle. You know, Robert?"

"Yes, Barbra. I know."

Robert had known since the previous day when he entered the pine filled lot that held their trailer, saw the pound pups lazing under a rusting pick-up truck on blocks in the front yard. Kenny and Barbra Jenks were people Steve L. would have known and liked. Simple folk. "Spooky, huh?" Barbra suddenly shivered with a chill.

"Yeah. Spooky," Kenny admitted. Once again he hummed the "Twilight Zone" theme.

"Quit that, Kenny," Barbra reached across to give Kenny a slap but this time it was more playful and relaxed.

For the rest of the afternoon they would talk about Steve, AIDS, and marijuana. Barbra's recollections of her near-death experience had led the trio to an unexpected understanding of their purpose together. After a room-service dinner Barbra decided it was her turn to find out about Robert.

"So, can me 'n Kenny ask you questions, Robert?"

"Sure. Only seems fair. What do you want to know?"

"You get pot from the government, right? Legal pot?" Kenny wanted to know how that worked.

Robert patiently explained about his glaucoma and the long road that led to legal access.

"So was you the first American to get medical marijuana?"

"Uh huh. Nearly fifteen years ago." As he spoke he realized Barbra was only six when he smoked his first legal joint.

"Are you famous, Robert?" Barbra's question was so innocent and paradoxical Robert began to laugh.

"Some people probably think I'm famous. But I'm not famous. Being famous takes too much work."

Kenny, wondering about his future, asked "How many people get legal marijuana, Robert?"

"Five."

"Five people! In the whole United States?" Kenny wasn't sure those were good odds.

"And Steve," Barbra was trying to keep things straight, "he was the first AIDS patient to get legal marijuana?" Robert nodded. "So, me 'n Kenny, we'd be the second and third people with AIDS to get legal marijuana?" The words trailed off. Barbra was putting the pieces together.

"So you just fly around 'n help people?" Kenny was trying to figure out who Robert was. Before Robert could answer Barbra spoke up again. "So, Robert, you think me 'n Kenny can really get legal pot?"

"Uh huh. I think we can do that. It won't be easy. There are no guarantees."

"But do we have to go to court?" Kenny feared exposure.

"Yes. Unless you admit you're guilty and hope the judge gives you a reduced sentence. In your case—first arrest—they'd give you probation and send you home."

Kenny, looking for an easy out, says, "So then we wouldn't have to tell nobody we got AIDS?" I nodded.

"But we'd be guilty? Me 'n Kenny we'd have criminal records 'n stuff?" Barbra was wary of easy outs.

"Yes. You'd have a criminal record," Robert replied.

"So we'd be criminals," Barbra concluded, "and them policemen, they could come arrest us again?" She was coming to grips with her jeopardy.

"If you're out on probation and keep smoking pot the police can arrest you anytime they want."

Barbra had heard enough. "No way! I ain't no criminal. I ain't gonna let anyone make me no criminal. I ain't gonna die with no criminal record."

"Then, you've got to go to court and convince the judge you're innocent. We will argue there's no crime in growing marijuana to save your life." Robert outlined the defense.

"So, would this all be in the newspapers 'n stuff?"

"If we do it right your story will be in every newspaper in America. TV, too." Robert paused and considered the two silent individuals before him. "Scared?" he asked.

"Yeah. It's real scary," Kenny said. Barbra amended his fear, "Kinda. Sorta."

"Good," Robert advised. "It's good to be scared. Life's scary."

"What if crazy people, nuts 'n stuff start calling us on the phone?" Kenny remained unconvinced. Barbra, bored with being frightened, had a different question, "Robert, you think me 'n Kenny going to court 'n all would help other people? Other people with AIDS?"

"Barbra, I'm here because you and Kenny got Steve's message. Now, you and Kenny need to decide if you want to send that message to others. Win or lose in court, if you speak out other people with AIDS will learn marijuana can help."

"But we could lose?" Barbra wanted assurances. Robert declined her hope. "You could lose, go to jail, die in prison. I don't think that will happen. But there are no guarantees."

Robert spoke carefully, aware of the responsibility that had been bestowed on him and the potential outcome. He would later write:

> *It was a dialogue of destiny. Fear was the barrier. I knew things I could not say. I had been summoned to assist, not to play a tempting serpent. I could provide insight, allies, instruction. But alone together Kenny and Barbra had to elect the path. If they clung to fear there was little that could be done. The State would condemn them as criminals; their fast-ebbing lives would be consumed in isolation and despair, grim beyond bearing.*
>
> *Arrest, paradoxically, had opened an alternative path. If Kenny and Barbra ignored their fears to accept the path Fate now offered they would enter a universe beyond their imaginings. I knew these things but dared not speak them. After all, there were no guarantees. And the decision was not mine to make.*
>
> *It was Barbra who made the decision. "I ain't no criminal 'n I ain't gonna die with no criminal record."*
>
> *Fate smiled.*

28. HEARTS AND MINDS

We were entering a vortex of events that would irrevocably alter the dialogue. It was the night before the trial. For Kenny and Barbra these were the last isolated moments of their lives. And the most terrifying. There had been a small amount of local press, orchestrated by Robert, and CNN had arrived on the scene the day before the trial to film some background footage on Kenny and Barbra. It had all been overwhelming but was nothing compared to what was coming.

On July 26, 1990, the Jenks' appeared at the Bay County courthouse. The case of *Florida v. Jenks* was to be argued in the second floor courtroom with Judge Clinton Foster, a grandfatherly fellow, presiding. There was no jury.

The courtroom was without adornment or grandeur. Usually, marijuana cases are quickly, quietly dispatched absent public notice. Attorneys wheel and deal: clients pay a fine, go to jail or get paroled. Panama City is a law and order town. Unless there is violence—a murder, say—the local press is blasé about pot cases down at the courthouse.

Today was different. An historic case had come to town. By design, Florida had TV-friendly courtrooms. CNN and the local stations were already set up: their harsh quartz lights further flattened an already stark scene. Kenny and Barbra, wearing second-hand clothes, were captured on video as they entered the arena of their fears. Poor, dying, they evoked sympathy and compassion in the brittle light.

The prosecutor, having been confronted with CNN the day before, had fled town, leaving the case to his assistant prosecutor. The state's case was basic. Police raided a trailer and seized two pot plants. A vice cop testified regarding the arrests. A chemist verified "Cannabis." Case closed. For Robert, sitting in the courtroom, it was all too reminiscent of a Washington, D.C. courtroom in 1976.

John Daniel informed the Court he would argue Kenny and Barbra Jenks broke the law to save their lives; that any sane person would make the same decision. He would prove that marijuana's ability to enhance the appetite of people with AIDS created a "medical necessity."

The prosecutor objected, claiming there was no precedent. The Musikka case was mentioned and citations intoned for the record. Judge Foster, aware of the watching lenses, agreed to take testimony on "necessity" before ruling on the merits of such a novel defense. John Daniel called his first witness—Robert.

He provided background, explained his unusual status, and reviewed the FDA's approval of Steve L.'s marijuana/AIDS IND. He concluded by telling the court Kenny and Barbra's doctor had already asked the FDA for legal permission to provide the couple with medical marijuana.

Kenny and Barbra's doctor did not appear but he provided a written statement for the judge, stipulating that he had been unable to effectively treat their nausea with legal drugs and if he could legally prescribe marijuana he would.

Kenny, then Barbra entered the dock. These were gripping minutes of testimony as each explained their sad circumstances.

Kenny's testimony was reasoned and steady. "We were growing the plants because we couldn't get the marijuana we needed and if it was available we didn't have the money to buy it." No one doubted the young man's story. "I really didn't have a choice," he continued, "Anybody in my position would do anything they could to have a decent life. I fully believe without marijuana my quality of life will deteriorate and I will die. And my wife will die too. Your honor, my wife would not be alive without marijuana."

As Robert listened to Kenny testify he realized how quickly the young man had absorbed the concepts of medical necessity and the righteousness of his action. Despite his "motormouth," Kenny did listen.

Barbra's testimony, while similar, was more pointed and dramatic. "I don't feel I was doing any harm at all. I was doing it to survive, so that I could eat. I've got to smoke marijuana. I've got to or I'm gonna die. I'm gonna die anyway but I would like to have my life a little better."

It was an electric moment. Throughout the courtroom the simple words invoked a heartache of understanding. It was a sad madness that people already so wretched would be called to trial for growing weeds.

The final witness was Dr. Daniel Dansak, the former director of New Mexico's pioneering marijuana/cancer study. As Dansak approached the witness chair Robert couldn't help but think of Lynn Pierson and how the ripples of his long ago acts had washed across the years.

Currently at the University of Alabama in Mobile, Dr. Dansak continued to work with terminal patients and was aware of marijuana's spreading use among people with AIDS. He was a superb witness; engaging and friendly. Judge Foster, skeptical throughout, listened as the doctor carefully outlined how marijuana helps people with AIDS survive.

Closing arguments were spirited. The state argued crime is crime. John Daniel argued it is not a crime to save your life. Staring into the quartz lights Judge Foster promised a decision "next week."

With the courtroom testimony skillfully edited into the story the CNN reporter compiled a brilliant report that played and replayed on Headline News for nearly 18 hours. While satellites beamed the news worldwide, the local impact was of more immediate concern. Kenny and Barbra's case was all over the local newspapers. Clips of their haunting testimony were featured on local news shows. In the course of a single day they had catapulted out of anonymity and into the hearts and minds of 40 million people.

The morning after the trial, Kenny and Barbra were walking out of a drugstore when an excited middle-aged woman stopped them. "Ain't you that nice young couple in the newspapers?" Reflexively "the nice young couple" began to recoil as the woman rushed on, "I sure hope you win your case. I'll be praying for you."

Kenny's greatest fears were phantoms. The people of Panama City Beach did not assault them with pitchforks and torches. Three days after the trial, before the decision was rendered, the local *News Herald* editorially declared "Trial Unwarranted in Marijuana Case" and instructed the local citizenry on tolerance and the need for compassion. It was a thoughtful, but unnecessary sentiment. In the space of a few days Kenny and Barbra had become hometown celebrities.

The judge had promised a decision in a few days but it was more than two weeks before the verdict was rendered. Robert and I were in Juneau, Alaska when CNN reported Judge Clinton Foster had found Kenny and Barbra Jenks "guilty." To temper his verdict the judge sentenced them to "500 hours of community service to be defined as loving and caring for one another."

A cream puff conviction that left them guilty of a crime but extracted no punishment. In the short CNN clip Kenny and Barbra appeared agitated. "I ain't no criminal," Barbra protested. John Daniel also appeared. "This isn't justice. We will appeal."

Later in the day CNN expanded the clip slightly, borrowing from footage shot two weeks before. Once again the story would replay for hours, assuring maximum, global coverage.

Morley Safer, correspondent for "60 Minutes," saw the story while on assignment in France. It piqued his interest and he made a note to speak with the show's producers about it. Perhaps it would make a good segment.

The story of Kenny and Barbra Jenks was a media producer's dream. No matter the medium—television, radio, print—the story resonated with a vibrancy that few stories can match. The genuine quality of their nature and the compelling fight they were forced to endure—both in terms of their disease and also the arrest—created an allure that was, oddly, captivating.

In late August they were invited to New Jersey to appear on the morning television show, "9 in the Morning," broadcast by WWOR. While I stayed in Washington to field the rapidly increasing phone calls and information requests, Robert met Kenny and Barbra in Newark.

"9 in the Morning" is broadcast in New York and fed to scores of cable systems throughout the U.S. Robert had done this type of show dozens of times but for Kenny and Barbra it was all new and surreal.

In the guest waiting room Robert chuckled when Kenny returned from makeup. "Never been through a thing like that," Kenny sputtered, brushing powder from his upper lip. Barbra appeared with lipstick and rouge. The producer came to collect them. "Ain't you coming, Robert?"

"No. The first segment is you and Kenny."

As he watched from the waiting room, Robert was apprehensive as the stage manager counted away the seconds. The couple was dazzled by the lights, distracted by the commotion of camera crews, aware of the raucous studio audience in the dark beyond their sight. They were ON AIR: unedited, live.

The host introduced them and asked his first question. Kenny, after briefest hesitation, settled into conversation. Barbra, nervous answering direct questions, was shining as she interrupted Kenny to finish his thoughts. They were a likable, familiar couple.

A New Jersey trooper and Robert were introduced into the second segment. The trooper was "the balance," there to present the other side. He was law and order: lock 'em up. He quickly offended the studio audience which rushed to Kenny and Barbra's defense. "What," one angry audience member demanded of the trooper, "would you do if Barbra was your daughter and had AIDS and marijuana helped?"

Looking Barbra in the eyes the trooper honestly replied, "I'd probably go buy her some marijuana." Cheers. "But it's still against the law." Boos.

It was a rout. At the end of the show the studio audience was polled. For medical marijuana—sustained, standing applause. Against medical marijuana—four hands, including two people who arrived with the trooper, clapping into a vast silence.

After the show Robert took the couple on a tour of New York City. He would later write:

> *It was one of the sweetest days I can remember. Everything was new to them. The flight, the limo, the TV studio, the ferryboat, the huge buildings and crowded streets. "What's that smell?" Barbra asked as we descended into the subway. "New York," I replied.*

After dinner and a hot fudge sundae, Kenny was anxious to discover more of New York. But Barbra was deeply fatigued. "I wanna go to the motel," she said.

In the incandescent glare of Times Square—Kenny and Barbra in tow—Robert approached three cops to ask directions. "Excuse me, officer? Could you tell me where . . .."

"It's you guys!" the large cop in the middle shouted. Robert was thrown. Kenny looked as if he was about to bolt. "You three," the cop repeated, wagging his thick finger.

"I was just telling my buddies here about this couple with AIDS who was smoking marijuana. That was you guys, right?"

"Yeah," Kenny nodded with uncertain relief. "That was us. Sir."

"Well, let me shake your hand," the cop said extending his big paw. "You kids like New York?"

"Oh, it's excellent, sir. Excellent," Kenny gushed. Handshakes all round. Robert got directions. "Best of luck," the big cop said, retreating with his buddies into the Manhattan night.

"How'd he know us?" Kenny worried.

"Well, they may be following us," Robert teased, "or maybe he was just one of the four or five million people who saw you on television this morning."

"That many?" Barbra marveled. "Millions?"

Offers of additional news coverage developed without any effort. In September Robert met Kenny and Barbra in Philadelphia and did more media, then traveled by train to Washington where I finally met the two in person. They stayed in a nearby hotel and we showed them Washington, D.C. The travel was new, the cities were new, the train was new. Even as they were dying, Barbra and Kenny's universe expanded with each day.

In October, Kenny and Barbra asked Florida Governor Bob Martinez for a pardon. It was Robert's idea and could be easily executed with John Daniel's help. It was just before the election and he felt there was a chance of succeeding. The Governor responded with silence but the exercise did generate even more press. Martinez would lose the election. President Bush would appoint him Drug Czar.

Behind the escalating media screen much was happening that was hidden from public view. Calls to ACT were up dramatically, and many patients were willing to invest the time and effort needed to secure legal marijuana from the federal government. While Robert was the public face of medical marijuana I was spending most of my time preparing dozens of IND requests for a variety of disorders—glaucoma, cancer, multiple sclerosis, and paralysis. But AIDS had dramatically altered the dynamic and I quickly recognized the danger. If ACT attempted to craft patient-specific Compassionate INDs for each new AIDS request we would be swamped; our energies sapped. It was a trap of paper that could easily bury us.

Since 1978, we had prepared about half a dozen marijuana INDs for individual patients. Now it was time to re-conceptualize the Compassionate IND. Each IND prepared before 1990 contained volumes of personal medical data. If the FDA refused to respond in the appropriate time the resulting document could easily serve as the basis for legal action. Constructing one of these ironclad and cumbersome applications often required weeks. In 1979, Anne Guttentag suffered needlessly while the FDA insisted on miniscule changes to her IND request. In 1988, Elvy Musikka's physician, Dr. Paul Palmberg, estimated he spent more than 50 hours responding to often frivolous FDA demands. It was not unusual for doctors to withdraw from the process after initially agreeing to help. It was an intensely intimidating regulatory procedure. It was never meant for the private individual.

This unresponsive, paper-heavy system, if wrongly engaged, could consume us utterly without seriously threatening any aspect of the medical prohibition. It was time to define an alternative approach that shifted the stress from patients and physicians back into federal agencies. We soon realized that with AIDS there was a uniformity of disease progression that offered a means of accomplishing our goal. Our objective was to translate the abstract, highly skilled craft of IND construction into a simple formulation any patient or physician could easily follow.

Our goal was mass production.

In the early fall of 1990 Robert met our patron at the Four Seasons Hotel in Washington for drinks. Rich was impressed by media reaction to the Jenks case and listened with interest as Robert outlined our emerging plan of mass produced INDs. "Sounds good," Rich said. "Send a budget."

They met again before the Drug Policy Foundation conference in November. The Robert Randall Award for Citizen Achievement for 1990 was being presented to old allies, Mae and Arnold Nutt. The presence of the Nutts, coupled with the media coverage of the Jenks case, was creating a buzz in the drug reform community that would begin to manifest itself in the coming months.

At that moment, however, Robert's focus was on momentum. Without funding it was foolish to continue. Rich agreed, increasing our base funding to $200,000. An additional $30,000 was targeted to support two ACT projects. One would generate Compassionate INDs for people with AIDS. A second, less advanced project, would do the same for people with spinal cord injuries resulting in paralysis.

"What are we going to call these projects?" Rich wanted to know.

"Don't know about the spinal cord project," Robert replied. "For the other I'm thinking of Marijuana/AIDS Research Service or MARS."

Richard J. smiled.

In December we received an unexpected call from the FDA. They wanted to meet with Robert. The agency had noticed an increase in Compassionate IND applications—we had, at that point, managed to complete about a dozen requests for varying disorders—and FDA wanted to discuss matters. It was the first time in 15 years the FDA had indicated a desire to talk.

Sensing danger, Robert invited me and an attorney from Steptoe & Johnson. Robert's arrival—with two witnesses—caused a commotion. The agency had clearly planned a very intimidating and conspiratorial meeting; just Robert and one or two FDA staffers.

With witnesses present, however, the small, private meeting became a major production. Government attorneys were called and the entire New Drug Therapies Unit staff assembled. More than a dozen anxious bureaucrats crammed into an airless room, glancing furtively at one another. With witnesses present—with everyone present—how to deliver the message?

Curtis Wright, M.D., an oafishly rumpled man with unkempt hair and dirty fingernails was the spokesman. It was an unfortunate choice. Wright was not in charge of the Unit, merely an IND review officer recently imported into the FDA from the DEA. He was a man of mingled motives and no authority.

With so many eyes watching, Dr. Wright was slow getting to his point. The FDA wanted to turn Compassionate INDs into "N-of-1 studies." It was a bureaucratic desire to adjust semantics. N-of-1 is virtually the same model as a single patient Compassionate IND, but by eliminating the word "compassion," the FDA hoped to escape the trap of public condemnation that was sure to accompany refusal of some requests.

"If you accept our N-of-1 approach," Wright suggested, "you might be able to claim a proprietary interest in medical marijuana."

"Are you saying I could own medical marijuana?" Robert asked. That was precisely what FDA IND Review Officer Curtis Wright, M.D., was suggesting. A dozen bureaucrats leaned forward for the answer. "We could be of great help," another voice said.

"I'm not interested in owning medical marijuana," Robert replied. "I want to solve this problem."

"With Compassionate INDs?" Wright scoffed.

"If necessary," Robert replied. "That's for the FDA to decide."

"Compassionate INDs are a lot of work," Dr. Wright responded. "What if the FDA decides to stop Compassionate INDs? Where would you be then?"

Threat delivered—fail to cooperate and everything will shut down . . . including Robert.

I had been here before. At least Wright was smart enough not to put it in writing.

I realized the enticement I rejected would be offered to others. The threat, however, was for me alone.

I also realized that "proprietary interest" in marijuana would render me mute. New drug developers, i.e. pharmaceutical companies, are prohibited from publicly "advancing" a drug not yet approved for marketing. Such "minor" regulatory concerns could be overlooked in some cases. I doubted I would qualify for such an oversight.

It was an odd, inconclusive meeting fraught with sinister overtones. The Steptoe attorney was virtually speechless upon our exit. "They were threatening you," she exclaimed.

Perhaps in a vain attempt to seduce Robert into acceptance the FDA demonstrated "good faith." On December 20, 1990, the FDA signed off on seven Compassionate INDs, including the Jenks'. In a relatively short period of time we had tripled the number of approved INDs. As 1990 drew to a close there were approximately fifteen approved INDS with five patients, including Robert, receiving supplies.

After months of retooling and prototype testing we were poised to engage the drug control system in a way bureaucrats could not imagine. MARS, the poetically potent acronym that invoked the mythical god of war, was coming together piece by piece. This time the battle was not for the heavens, it was a battle for hearts and minds.

Kenny and Barbra were the key. Before we could advance they had to get legal marijuana. Approval of their Compassionate IND triggered another round of media. "Marijuana Approved for Couple with AIDS" headlined the local paper on December 23 and wire stories carried the announcement across the country.

Kenny and Barbra briefly celebrated. But the DEA, as usual, snarled the marijuana shipment in red tape. Christmas came and went. No marijuana. The regional DEA office refused to authorize a shipment without first printing up formal, official, special DEA marijuana order forms. It was all too reminiscent of Steve's experience.

January became February. More press salvos were fired. Despite a terrible pounding in the Florida media, the DEA continued to obstruct the shipment. It looked as if the DEA would let Kenny and Barbra Jenks die before allowing marijuana to flow into the hands of another AIDS patient. Then, against a backdrop of growing public antagonism the DEA finally relented.

"We got our pot today," Kenny happily shouted into the phone. It was February 19, 1991, nearly nine months after their application was filed and two months after it was approved.

Three days later Robert joined them in Panama City, along with John Daniel, to publicly celebrate the arrival of their legal, FDA-approved pot. Cameras rolled. Shutters snapped. "AIDS Couple Receives Govt Pot." The story managed to poke through the media haze of the imminent Gulf War.

The Marijuana AIDS Research Service (MARS) was slated to be launched in less than a week in Rich's home town, Chicago. Kenny and Barbra were the Honorary Co-chairpersons of MARS and would be a part of the official announcement on February 28. The final countdown had begun.

On Monday, February 25, John Daniel drove the couple to Tallahassee where he argued for the reversal of their conviction before the Florida Court of Appeals. The argument before the Court hinged on the defense of medical necessity and with the recent arrival of FDA-approved marijuana the Court couldn't help but draw the obvious conclusion: If the FDA was giving them legal marijuana perhaps marijuana was a "medical necessity." The DEA's idiot delays afforded a sweet conjunction.

The next morning Kenny and Barbra were on a plane to Chicago. The window to MARS was opening.

29. MARS

"We are here to announce the formation of MARS—the Marijuana/AIDS Research Service," Rich told the packed room on February 28, 1991. The press was out in force. In Chicago, Richard J. Dennis is a draw.

"Kenny and Barbra Jenks legally smoke marijuana. Jim Barnes, our first man from MARS, won FDA approval using the MARS model IND," Rich explained. "These individuals are living proof that people with AIDS can apply to the FDA and legally obtain marijuana. MARS allows any AIDS patient in America to petition the FDA for legal access to medical marijuana. I'm honored to back such a worthy enterprise."

The MARS launch was flawless. Wire services carried the news out of Chicago. WGN beamed the MARS news across the continent. NBC transmitted the story for optional play on local news screens. In Washington, I added to the density of coverage by faxing MARS announcements to New York, D.C. and San Francisco media plugs. Before the Chicago press conference was over people with AIDS were phoning ACT for MARS packets.

MARS was an act of faith and aggression: a double-edged sword designed to pierce the prohibition to its heart or unmask the menace at its core.

For more than a decade federal agencies had evaded medical marijuana by mumbling a trite mantra: Marijuana has no medical value, and anyone who medically needs marijuana can legally obtain it. A doctor need only ask.

The first contention, the DEA's official line, was a widely recognized lie. Even the DEA's administrative law judge had called it a lie.

The second contention, the FDA's "compassion posture," emphasized the fraud of the first. If the FDA provided marijuana to people with legitimate medical needs then obviously marijuana has medical value. The FDA conveniently deflected this logic by calling such access "research."

This distorted good-cop/bad-cop routine confused the public mind and, by 1991, confusion was deep. Medical marijuana had been news for fifteen years. Everyone had read the headlines. The courts and thirty-five states recognized marijuana's medical value. Some people, like Kenny and Barbra, legally received marijuana.

"So," the public asked, "what's the problem?"

If federal agencies kept their promise—anyone who medically needed marijuana could legally obtain it—there was no problem. But, as this narrative suggests, legal access to marijuana was altogether rare.

MARS was designed to clarify the public mind and, like a touchstone, test the value of the government's tender.

MARS embraced the government's promise of care by providing AIDS patients with the tools they needed to easily apply for legal access to marijuana. By bundling IND forms with clear instructions, MARS altered the dynamics of the Compassionate IND system. Prior to MARS, physicians who requested IND forms from the FDA could wait for weeks, even months for the forms. When the papers did arrive there was often no explanation about how to complete the 31 questions. Some were relatively routine but others were head-scratchers. For example:

> List numbers of all investigational new drug applications (21 CFR Part 312), new drug or antibiotic applications (21 CFR Part 314), drug master files (21 CFR 314.420), and product license applications (21 CFR part 601) referred to in this application.

This intimidating question can be answered simply with "Reference NIDA master files 1631 and 366." But no one in FDA would ever tell a doctor that little bit of information. Private physicians were forced to play the same shell games as New Mexico and the other states had in the late 1970s, stabbing in the dark to find the right answer, trying to find the little bit of correctness that would inspire an FDA official to say, "you're getting warmer."

Our MARS IND forms were approximately 90% completed. Only personal information about the doctor and patient was required and we developed a series of checklists to simplify this aspect of the form's completion. Physicians who once struggled for hours to complete the forms, could sit with an AIDS patient, open a MARS packet, go through a checklist and put an application in the mail in under an hour.

MARS made applying for a Compassionate IND easy and accessible. We theorized, correctly, that such a MARS-induced collapse of application time would trigger intense interest in the AIDS community. Even before Kenny and Barbra, word was already spreading in the AIDS community that marijuana seemed to help people with AIDS live longer. Kenny and Barbra coalesced the thought and MARS harnessed energy behind it.

MARS unlocked a landscape of intentions. Positively engaged, MARS would rapidly increase the number of AIDS patients receiving marijuana. This, in turn, would cause an explosion of knowledge as treating physicians evaluated marijuana's medical utility. MARS was an extremely robust, highly accelerated research model. If the government wanted to know if marijuana could help people with AIDS, MARS could quickly and inexpensively provide the answer.

We had been down this road before when New Mexico and the other states attempted to bring a happy ending to their efforts to provide legal, medical marijuana to their citizens. We hoped this time would be different but we knew there was a darker, alternative path.

It is possible the federal government does not want to know if marijuana can help people with AIDS—or any disease for that matter. It is possible the prohibition is more important than people, in which case bureaucratic efforts to maintain the medical prohibition—to resist MARS—would put federal agencies on a collision course with public opinion.

In the starkest of terms MARS was a game of cosmic chicken played with human lives. There are only two possible outcomes.

If the FDA responded to MARS with optimism the needs of many sorely afflicted people would be eased and the medical prohibition would melt into antiquity. This would happen only if the government could be trusted to keep a publicly made promise to provide medical care to dying people.

If federal agencies failed to deliver on their promise "that anyone with a legitimate medical need can legally obtain marijuana," and if bureaucrats blocked MARS, the feedback would disrupt the control system and irrevocably tear up the institutional illusion of compassion.

Two possible outcomes; MARS favored the former, but either would serve our interests in advancing the issue.

MARS was barely off the launch pad when there was a disruption in Robert's access to marijuana. On March 4, 1991, just five days after the Chicago announcement of MARS, his pharmacy in the Washington Hospital Center couldn't fill Dr. North's script. Just a coincidence?

Explanations were immediately requested. The National Institute on Drug Abuse (NIDA) reported the FDA failed to process the pharmacy's supply request in a timely fashion. The order had arrived at the FDA shortly after the December 1990 meeting at which Curtis Wright asked, "What if the FDA decides to stop Compassionate INDs?"

The order sat in the FDA for so long—more than six weeks—that it became invalid. A glitch. Just a glitch they said. NIDA cooperated fully and the pharmacy received supplies within 48 hours.

On that same day, March 4, a hearing was held in the U.S. Court of Appeals where ACT appealed the DEA's refusal to accept Judge Young's decision *In The Matter Of Marijuana Rescheduling.*

Our old friend Tom Collier, now a senior partner at Steptoe & Johnson, returned in a cameo appearance to argue ACTs case. He strongly stated ACT's basic argument: Marijuana clearly has an "accepted medical use in treatment in the United States." Any other conclusion is, as Judge Young said, "unreasonable, arbitrary and capricious."

Department of Justice attorneys argued that only the DEA Administrator can decide if marijuana is medically useful and they cited regulations which allowed the administrator to ignore the recommendations of the agency's chief judge.

The three-judge panel asked several inconsequential questions. Then one judge wondered why a law enforcement agency like DEA should decide if a drug is medically useful. Shouldn't doctors, patients and health care professionals make such a decision?

Another judge wondered what "accepted" might mean. "Accepted" by whom, under what conditions? For example, if FDA was approving marijuana for medical uses like cancer, glaucoma and AIDS then how can DEA claim marijuana is medically useless? Seemed like a contradiction.

The Department of Justice attorneys stammered. The judges called for additional briefs. The once slight divide between the FDA and DEA's publicly uttered mantras was suddenly a legal chasm. Each approved IND for marijuana eroded the DEA's legal argument before the U.S. Court of Appeals.

Two weeks after the Court of Appeals hearings "60 Minutes" came to call on Kenny and Barbra Jenks. Morley Safer had followed through with his interest in the Jenks story after seeing the CNN report on their trial and asked "60 Minutes" producer Gail Isen to look into it. Every newspaper and television station in Florida covered "60 Minutes" covering Kenny and Barbra. The biggest of big media had arrived.

Kenny and Barbra were only vaguely familiar with the show. Robert resisted the urge to fly to Florida and monitor the taping. When he started giving instructions Barbra told him "We can handle it, don't worry."

It had been less than a year since their arrest. Eight months previously, they had agonized about friends in Panama City Beach learning about their AIDS. Now they were about to meet Morley Safer and appear on America's most popular news show. Barbra's nonchalance was charming and wonderful.

Gail was "delighted" with the Jenks, John Daniel, even the vice cops; a colorful collection of improbable characters living through unusual circumstances with national implications. A great story.

"What those poor kids are living through," Gail said of Kenny and Barbra, "is so very moving."

The spring of 1991 would prove to be a dazzling time for the medical marijuana movement. While America celebrated victory in the Gulf War, news of MARS flashed through the AIDS community, ricocheted into the gay community, and then slowly settled into the national mind. The response was stunning.

In December 1990, Robert had written to the Steptoe lawyers and explained the MARS strategy. "The target," he wrote, "is to get 1,500 IND application forms in the hands of AIDS patients/physicians, with 200 completions into formal IND applications from physicians to FDA for access by the end of 1991. It is difficult to know if these targets are wildly off the mark."

By the end of March 1991 we realized these estimates were, in fact, far too low. AIDS groups in San Francisco and Miami requested permission to copy the MARS packet. Soon AIDS groups in New York, Los Angeles, Atlanta, Dallas, Minneapolis and Chicago were also photocopying MARS. We quickly began to lose track of how many MARS IND applications were "out there." In many ways it wasn't important. Our goal had been to enable others to apply on their own behalf. Goal accomplished.

On March 15, FDA approved the first IND request for marijuana use by a paralyzed individual. For years we had heard from paraplegics and quadriplegics who used marijuana to quiet involuntary muscle spasms but few were willing to publicly acknowledge the use. In the rapidly escalating war for medical marijuana Chris Woderiski, a paraplegic from Tampa, Florida, agreed to test our prototype IND for paralysis. In April Robert joined Chris in Florida to announce his success. He would join the growing list of individuals waiting for supplies from the federal government. As MARS was barreling along we began planning the launch of a second program— PALM—Paralyzed Americans for Legal Medical Marijuana. Chris would be our point man and he was already busy lining up recruits.

For 15 years the FDA had used complexity and paperwork to deflect physician interest in medical marijuana. MARS and

PALM radically adjusted the balance by removing the mystery of IND preparation. Physicians treating people with AIDS or paralysis were quick to respond.

On March 24th an article entitled "U.S. Provides Marijuana for Some AIDS Patients," written by Michael Isikoff, appeared on page A3 of *The Washington Post*. The article was unbelievably bland, deftly managing to minimize the plight of patients while constantly relooping to "pro-pot" activists. Isikoff had spoken with Kenny and Barbra ten days before. "Didn't like him much," said Kenny. "He didn't seem to understand."

Nevertheless the article correctly captured the FDA mantra when it stated "most seriously ill applicants who meet the agency's criteria—a note from their doctor and a signed consent form acknowledging the risks—would likely be favorably considered for legal access."

Associate FDA commissioner for public affairs, Jeffrey A. Nesbit, echoed a long departed Ed Tocus. "I suppose you can say the agency acted compassionately" in supplying the Jenks with legal marijuana.

On April 19th the Florida Court of Appeals upheld the defense of "medical necessity" in the treatment of AIDS and in a landmark decision the Court overturned the conviction of Kenny and Barbra Jenks, declaring them "not guilty." It was the nation's first successful "medical necessity" defense involving marijuana's use in AIDS care.

"It's a great relief," Kenny Jenks told the news reporter. "I was worried it wouldn't be resolved before something happened to my wife and me." Barbra received the news in a hospital bed in Pensacola. She was admitted on April 10 with severe bleeding and borderline pneumonia. The news made her very happy.

"I couldn't believe it at first, but it did happen. I feel we made a little bit of history," she said. "If something was to happen to me I didn't want to go feeling like I was a criminal."

Eight days later there was another Court of Appeals victory, this one in Washington, D.C. "DEA Told to

Reevaluate Marijuana's Medical Value" headlined *The Washington Post.*

> A three-judge panel of the federal appeals court here ordered the Drug Enforcement Administration to reconsider its 1989 decision that marijuana has no medical value, saying the agency acted unreasonably in evaluating the drug's possible effectiveness for cancer victims and other seriously ill patients.

It was a jubilant moment but a careful reading of the 10-page decision gave the Steptoe lawyers some concern. The judges had not quarreled with the DEA's rejection of the facts. It seems the case could hinge, ultimately, on a careful interpretation of the administrator's authority.

This case was not yet over.

Nor was the Jenks case over. During the first part of May the state of Florida began the process of appealing the Florida Court of Appeals ruling. It was unbelievable that the state would pursue this matter any further and there was a strong feeling those in charge were reacting to advice from outside.

In early May, we took MARS on the road. Kenny and Barbra joined us at the 4th Annual AIDS Up-Date Conference in San Francisco. Now well-clad and no longer criminal, they were official MARS spokespersons. Our MARS table, in the entry area of the conference, was swamped by patients and physicians interested in marijuana, AIDS, and asking "How do I apply?" It was beyond our wildest dreams. San Francisco exceeded all expectations. The human reaction to MARS was so warm, thankful, urgent, grateful, intense, and personal.

Kenny was in his element. His notorious "motormouth" was an asset at these events. Like a barker in a carnival crowd, Kenny enticed scores of passing strangers asking, "Wanna see how marijuana looks when it's legal?" He was animated and tireless. Barbra was far less involved. Out of the hospital just a few weeks, we worried if we'd done the right thing in bringing her so far.

She slipped away from the exhibit to wander the inner hall that was filled with tables offering support, services, and medications to the AIDS-afflicted and their caregivers. Lining the walls were panels from The Names Project Quilt, the simple and glorious memorial to those who have been claimed by this 20th century scourge.

Barbra exited the hall looking shaken and tired.

"You feeling alright?" Robert asked.

"Naw, I'm okay," she said.

"You'll tell me if you want to stop?" Robert asked.

"I don't ever want to stop, Robert." Her reply to a simple inquiry said far more than the status of her energy level. She was on a different plane. Robert waited, knowing there was more.

"I had a dream, Robert."

"What about?"

"A tree. Just a big, old tree," Barbra replied. "When I was in the hospital."

"Any water nearby?"

"Yeah!" she looked at him, a bit surprised. "A nice little stream."

"What do you think it means, Barbra?"

"Oh. I'm gonna die in the spring, Robert," she was certain and calm.

"Why? What about the tree tells you that?"

"The leaves—they was all fresh 'n new. Like in spring. I'm gonna die in the spring ... some spring."

Barbra and Kenny's appearance at the AIDS Update Conference generated a massive media release on the West Coast and then reverberated nationally when "CBS Morning News" included the couple as part of their AIDS conference report. As the news flooded out into the country INDs flooded into the FDA.

By June 1991, federal agencies were facing stark decisions. If the FDA kept the government's promise to provide marijuana to people with legitimate medical needs, NIDA had to increase marijuana production. If NIDA increased marijuana production to meet accelerating patient needs, the DEA would lose control over both supply and demand. Once engaged, this cycle of expanding supply and spiraling demand would rip the medical prohibition to shreds.

Bureaucrats were once again meeting in airless rooms to discuss "this medical marijuana thing." But the meetings were no longer public. No special committees were formed to give the sense of "doing something." There was no time for that. These meetings were of the upper echelon and the decision they reached would be a dramatic one.

Compassion or closure? MARS had reached critical mass.

30. THE COLLAPSE OF COMPASSION

In mid-June the government began to flex its muscle and started a systematic disruption of supplies to the existing IND patients. The first call came from the most remote and vulnerable.

"They've stopped sending my marijuana," Corrine's voice was tinged with alarm. "The FDA won't tell my doctor what's going on. Can you help me?"

Corrine Millet, a 58-year old Nebraskan grandmother with glaucoma, had legally smoked the government's marijuana for over a year with excellent results. In early May, however, she went to the pharmacy to pick up her monthly supply. It wasn't there. She had waited for more than a month to call us. Now it was a Friday night in mid-June. There was little we could do on the weekend.

Calls to the FDA on Monday, the 17th, were not returned.

On June 18th Robert traveled to his pharmacy and discovered Corrine's disruption was not unique. For the second time in three months his pharmacy could not honor Dr. North's prescription. The pharmacist explained that the FDA had placed a "hold" on supplies. He had no further explanation.

Robert's attorney at Steptoe & Johnson, Steve Davidson, immediately phoned the agencies but discovered all the responsible bureaucrats were meeting at the posh Breakers Resort in Palm Beach, Florida.

Robert was unable to make any sense of this news. Why were federal officials involved in medical marijuana meeting in such plush and pampered surroundings?

On a hunch he called the hotel and asked for the representative from Unimed. "Which one?" the desk clerk replied.

It was 1981 all over again. MARS had sent the agencies scrambling for synthetic solutions. The FDA was at the Breakers, selling AIDS patients to Unimed, the manufacturer of delta-9 THC, a.k.a dronabinol, a.k.a. Marinol,.

Stern messages were delivered to the beach-bound bureaucrats and by early evening Robert's pharmacy was sending a new order directly to FDA officials in Palm Beach via overnight mail. Just a glitch, the bureaucrats assured. The marijuana would arrive at the pharmacy by Friday.

The next day brought another call.

"Um, Robert?" It was Kenny's voice and it seemed unsteady. "We went to our pharmacy but they don't have no pot for us."

Robert explained that he and Corrine were having the same problem. "How can anyone be this mean?" Kenny wondered.

Barbra took the phone from Kenny. There was defiance in her voice. "They ain't gonna get away with this." Then, a bit frightened, "Are they Robert?"

It was a profound provocation. These multiplying supply disruptions were obviously premeditated and intentional. But to what end? Were the bureaucrats testing the circuits? Corrine had been cut off weeks ago and nothing happened. Did the bureaucrats think they could, one by one, remove the "legal smokers" from the medical marijuana landscape while plotting to release Marinol to appease AIDS patients?

It was time to return fire. It wasn't 1978 or even 1981. Medical marijuana was not an embryonic issue begging to be heard. Robert lifted the receiver and called "60 Minutes" producer Gail Isen.

The "60 Minutes" medical marijuana segment was "in the can" and waiting for a time slot in the fall season. Gail knew the story had power and she had grown fond of "the kids" in Florida. She was, as Robert anticipated, enraged at Kenny and Barbra's supply disruption.

She by-passed the mid-level bureaucrats sunning in Florida and placed a call to the FDA administrator. She reached an assistant administrator. It must have been a heart-stopping moment for the man. Gail demanded to know why the government was "trying to kill those kids." Excuses were made and blame was focused on NIDA. But the shell game wouldn't work with Isen who responded by giving him the names of specific FDA employees blocking the Jenks' shipment. The assistant administrator started to crumble. Then Isen put Morley Safer on the line. It was every bureaucrat's ultimate nightmare.

As darkness fell phone lines between Parklawn and the Breakers lit up. Fingers, no doubt, were pointed. Careers threatened. Amid the chaos one crystal clear order was given: Restore Kenny and Barbra Jenks' access to marijuana.

Immediately!

If there was any doubt that "something was up" it was dispelled on two days later on June 20 with a phone call from Michael Isikoff of *The Washington Post*.

Robert listened as Isikoff repeated rumors and searched for an angle. He "demanded" to know what was going on. *The Post*, he says, believed the FDA was planning to close the Compassionate IND system. FDA and DEA were blaming NIDA for lack of supply. But was there another "reason"? Were the pro-pot groups just using this to get legalization?

Isikoff did not seem to grasp the significance of the news he was relating. For more than 15 years the feds had promised medical marijuana, on a compassionate basis, to anyone with a "legitimate" need. Now, as people have finally been given the means to ask for this promised compassion the government threatened to close the program down. Why?

What the DEA hoped would become the official government line—pro-pot groups were just using medical marijuana to get legalization—had been leaked to *The Post* and they found a willing conduit in the person of Michael Isikoff.

Despite the reporter's inability to focus on the real story at hand, Isikoff's call made it clear that the medical marijuana control system was in crisis. Compassion was killing the medical prohibition, MARS was pulling interagency arrangements apart.

The FDA was approving new INDs while, at the same time, disrupting supplies to existing INDs. It was like some bizarre Ponzi scheme. NIDA was being drained of supply while being threatened with extinction in the next budget cycle. The control system was fragmenting.

Isikoff revealed that interagency frictions were so intense the White House was becoming involved. The bureaucratic plan to kill the Compassionate IND program apparently came as a surprise to the administration that wanted "a kinder, gentler nation." Herbert Kleber, assistant director for the Office of National Drug Control Policy, had appeared on "The Today Show" just six weeks before and proclaimed that anyone could access medical marijuana with "a note from your doctor." The waiting period, he declared, was "less than a month." Now Dr. Kleber was about to be made a fool.

The Isikoff article appeared on June 22nd. The headline said it all. "Health and Human Services to Phase Out Marijuana Program." The subhead—"Officials Fear Sending 'Bad Signal' by Giving Drug to Seriously Ill"— more aptly told the tale.

The U.S. Public Health Service had decided to kill the Compassionate IND program. Isikoff wrote:

> A federal program that has provided free marijuana to the seriously ill is being phased out by Health & Human Services officials who have concluded it undercuts official Bush administration policy against the use of illegal drugs, according to HHS officials.
>
> While a small number of patients already receiving marijuana will continue to do so, new applicants will be encouraged to try synthetic forms of delta-9 THC . .. rather than the weed itself, according to a new policy directive due to be signed by James 0. Mason, Chief of the Public Health Service.
>
> Mason said yesterday he was concerned about a surge in new applications in recent months, especially from AIDS patients, and the message it would send if HHS were to approve them.
>
> "If it is perceived that the Public Health Service is going around giving marijuana to folks there would be a perception that this stuff can't be so bad. It gives a bad signal."

The article was clear, the directive had not yet been signed. Was this a trial balloon?

The following day *The New York Times* would weigh in with an AP report on the proposed program closing. The AP gauged the situation more accurately than Isikoff when it reported,

> The government's action seems certain to add fuel to a long standing debate about the restrictive nature of its policy on marijuana as a medical tool. ...
>
> In its announcement on Friday, the Public Health Service said recent publicity that marijuana might curb AIDS patients' loss of appetite had brought a rapid increase in applications to use government supplied marijuana.
>
> The agency said it would not cut off the supply of marijuana to the 34 people who now have government permission to use the drug to cope with the illnesses that include cancer, glaucoma and AIDS.

The government, it seems, was prepared to provide medical marijuana to the seriously ill— as long as no one asked.

The gauntlet was cast down and the immediate future was clear. We needed to counterattack in order to clarify the record. The media was confused by a not-yet-signed order to kill compassion. So, while the bureaucrats scrambled for the "right" message, Robert traveled to the Midwest, moving fast and leaving media blisters in his wake. The feds could try and kill compassion if they wished but they would know their victims.

On June 26th in a Minneapolis hotel, Robert and AIDS patient Tim Braun were seated in a small conference that was packed with TV crews and print reporters. The halogen lights made Tim Braun claustrophobic and he squinted hard into the bright light. He was uncomfortable with notoriety but mad enough to endure it.

FDA had approved Tim's request for marijuana nearly seven months ago, at about the same time as Kenny and Barbra, but Tim still did not have legal pot. According to the news accounts Tim Braun, because he was FDA-approved, would eventually receive care.

But when? Tim asked at a press conference.

A second AIDS patient, sitting next to Tim, had used MARS to apply for access but his request had not yet been acted upon. He was not one of the FDA's "magic 34." He would be denied care. Is this fair, he asked?

The next day Robert was in Des Moines in another small conference room, facing another collection of lights and cameras. Joining him at the front of the room was George McMahon, a legal smoker approved in late 1989, who suffers from a rare neurologic condition. George had benefited greatly from regular access to controlled quantities of marijuana. His doctor was astonished by George's improvement. His family was delighted. Government threats made George want to publicly tell his story.

Also at the table was. Ladd Huffman, wheelchair-bound from multiple sclerosis whose IND application was in limbo.

The three men waited for the nation's first MS patient approved for legal access to marijuana. Barbara Douglass made a dramatic entrance, walking into the room on India rubber legs. Armed with two canes, supported by her husband and another man, it had taken nearly 5 minutes for her to make the 50-foot trek from the elevator to the meeting room. "I wanted you to see how bad MS can get," Barbara told the press.

Barbara Douglass, Republican, well-dressed and well-connected, received FDA approval to legally use marijuana three months ago. Would Ms. Douglass ever receive her FDA-promised supplies? The second MS patient, Ladd Huffman, applied to FDA at the same time as Douglass. But Ladd was still waiting for a response from the FDA. Would these patients receive equal care?

The conference was excellent. The message clear.

On the next day Robert would be in Nebraska, sitting in the tidy living room of Corrine Millet. "Marijuana is such a godsend," she told the Associated Press reporter who scribbled furiously. Robert watched quietly from across the room.

Corrine, a surgeon's widow, was shy and didn't want to make a fuss. But she was also going blind and was angry at her supply disruption. Robert arranged for one-on-one interviews. Corrine, clearly worried about losing her vision, was plainspoken and direct. "I can't believe my government would do this to me."

The AP reporter called Washington for comment. By late afternoon an emergency order was sent from the FDA to NIDA. Corrine's marijuana would arrive within 24 hours.

The total elapsed time of Robert's Midwest swing was 60 hours. Local media coverage was heavy and national wires picked up the MS story. Each stop triggered a cascade of inquiries as reporters from Minnesota, Iowa, Wisconsin and Nebraska phoned the bureaucrats back in Washington. The questions were the same: Why was the government depriving such fine people access to needed medical care? Didn't the government promise to provide compassionate care to patients in need?

We were defining the battle: grinding down bureaucratic credibility. *The Pilot-Tribune*, Barbara Douglass' hometown paper, succinctly stated it. "Let us continue to wage the war against drugs, but let not the first victim be human compassion."

It's difficult to know what the bureaucracies were attempting to accomplish in that fateful month of June 1991. There seemed to be little, if any, coordination among the agencies. Clearly there was growing concern about the influx of INDs and there was, most certainly, a desire to shut things down.

What the agencies did not anticipate was the onslaught of public anger. Hundreds of enraged patients felt betrayed and discriminated against. They let the bureaucrats know it. Many of these patients made it past the switchboard, and tapped deep into the reaches of the bureaucracy. The effect was devastating.

The bureaucrats—operating behind screens of forms and physicians—were insulated from direct human contact. Few of the people administering the medical prohibition had ever encountered actual patients. The sudden flood of incoming anger struck like a riptide. "Why are you killing me?" one AIDS patient demanded of a woman at NIDA. "Why?" By the time he was done she was in tears, sobbing at the craven cruelty of her agency's policy. "I'm sorry," she said. "Very sorry."

This aggressive telephonic battering had a profoundly corrosive effect on institutional morale. There was more to come. While Robert worked the press in the Midwest, I spent the week fielding calls from the National Association of People with AIDS, Cure AIDS Now, and ACT-UP. Mad. Madder. Maddest. These and similar groups were deeply agitated by the Public Health Service (PHS) announcement. They wanted to vent and federal bureaucrats felt their anger. ACT provided patients with telephone numbers into the FDA, NIDA and the White House.

On June 27, 1991, the nation experienced its first "medical marijuana protest" when representatives of ACT-UP and a drug activist group called the Green Panthers closed Health and Human Services headquarters for an hour by staging a "die-in."

By moving to kill compassion the feds had given the drug reformers and activists a bully pulpit. They wasted little time in clambering on.

There would be two bright spots in that summer of 1991. On July 20, Barbra's 25th birthday, Robert delivered the good news that she and Kenny had won the Robert Randall Award for Citizen Achievement from the Drug Policy Foundation.

"An award for us, Robert? You don't have to give us no award." Kenny was confused by the award's name. Robert explained the award's history and what DPF was. "There'll be a banquet here in Washington in November. We'll fly you up."

The young couple was thrilled. "There's more," Robert said. "The award comes with a check for $10,000."

Now they were stunned. Kenny was actually speechless. When the news finally sunk in he let go a hoot and the couple started to laugh and giggle. "Hey Robert," Barbra poignantly joked, "Do you think we can buy me a new body with $10,000?"

The second bit of good news came one month later on August 30, when Iowa MS patient Barbara Douglass received her first supplies of marijuana cigarettes, seven months after her Compassionate IND was approved. Barbara had turned to her Republican friends in Congress—Senator Charles Grassley and Representative Fred Grandy. They had finally shaken her medicine free.

Ladd Huffman, the similarly afflicted but less politically attached Iowan, did not receive his supplies. Barbara was outraged and told the press, "The DEA is playing God," Douglass said with disgust.

"My next job is to get Laddie's okayed. It's too bad that it comes down to who you know."

In September the issue took an interesting and unanticipated turn when activists in San Francisco managed to place an initiative on the city ballot that would legalize medical use of marijuana. An editorial in the archly conservative, California *Orange County Register* must have given the White House pause.

> San Francisco voters will have an opportunity in November to tell state and federal authorities that a more compassionate and rational approach is in order regarding the medical use of marijuana."

Proposition P, a ballot initiative, would mark the first time the American public could vote directly on the issue of medical marijuana.

At any other time the politicians could blithely dismiss the "zanies in San Francisco" but by threatening to kill compassion the feds had created some strange bedfellows. Driving the *Orange County Register* to support a voter initiative for medical marijuana in San Francisco seemed a clear and unequivocal sign that the proposed policy to eliminate Compassionate INDs had badly backfired.

In October we traveled to California to drum up support for Proposition P. Despite the unceasing media coverage of the medical marijuana problem interest in the ballot measure was curiously unfocused.

We took Kenny and Barbra with us and, as usual, they shined. Just a few days before the trip the Florida Supreme Court had upheld the Florida Appeals Court ruling squashing the state's attempt to reinstate the guilty verdict. Barbra was particularly relieved at the outcome. "I told you I ain't no criminal!' she said. Barbra was losing ground to AIDS. She seemed to be battling a growing list of ailments which, if taken singularly, were not too serious. Collectively, however, they were wearing her down. So were the high doses of medicine she took to counteract the diseases.

At a press conference organized by Proposition P proponents, just a week before the election, we met Jo Daly, San Francisco's first lesbian Police Commissioner. Once called "the wonderful Jo Daly" by columnist Herb Caen, Daly was highly respected and well liked in the City by the Bay. When we met her she was retired, battling cancer and an ardent supporter of medical marijuana. She was a powerful spokesperson and captivated the press with her straightforward, no-nonsense talk.

The compelling comments of Jo, Kenny, and Barbra, together with the presence of nearly a dozen other patients who medically needed marijuana, made for a powerful media presentation. On November 5, 1991, Proposition P passed with 79% of the vote. The lopsided victory only added to the Bush Administration's confusion over how to handle Compassionate INDs.

31. BITTER BLOWS

The overwhelming acceptance of Proposition P was astonishing, even by San Francisco standards, and it intensified intra-agency conflicts over what to do about the compassionate IND program. The firestorm of public criticism that accompanied announcement of the program closure had subsided, but patients and caregivers continued to make their feelings known. "We've had a lot of dying people calling and asking us for help. It's sad." said the chief of staff for the White House Office of National Drug Control Policy (ONDCP).

On November 12th, in *The Washington Post,* the strained relations among the various federal agencies became very public in an article by Michael Isikoff that starkly portrayed a power struggle, citing "a four-month interagency battle between Health and Human Services and the Office of National Drug Control Policy." Isikoff wrote of "alarm among senior officials at the Department of Health and Human Services" at the prospect of marijuana's medical use by a "new population"—AIDS patients.

James O. Mason, director of the Public Health Service (PHS), was identified as the chief administration official pushing for the program's closure. AIDS patients who medically use marijuana, he said, "might be less likely to practice safe behavior whether it's sharing needles or sexual behavior."

Mason's comment infuriated AIDS and medical marijuana activists. Some of these activists had known Mason since his days as Director of the Center for Disease Control (CDC), and the comment reminded them of Mason's difficulties in dealing with AIDS and the homosexual community. In his first days at CDC the Utah native was unable to even utter the word "gay" while meeting with gay delegations.*

The article noted that Mason seemed to be winning the debate inside the Administration. ONDCP chief Bob Martinez was reportedly in agreement with the HHS decision to deny all new applications for marijuana, directing patients instead to Marinol. The sticking point was the existing 16 patients receiving marijuana and the applications approved but not yet supplied. The article stated that Mason wanted to cut them off but Martinez's aides disagreed, arguing such a move would be unfair.

"We said it would not be compassionate to cut off people who have gone through this process in good faith," said an ONDCP aide. "We didn't think it would be moral or just."

In mid-November Barbra and Kenny traveled to Washington for the Drug Policy Foundation (DPF) annual meeting and banquet.

On the night of the banquet the recipients of the Robert Randall Award for Citizen Achievement sat at a table in the middle of the room and nervously picked at their food. "Do you have a speech ready, Barbra?" I asked.

"Uh-uh, I don't do speeches. That's motormouth's job," Barbra replied with a poke at Kenny's ribs. "Whatcha gonna say, Kenny?" Barbra teased.

Kenny, uncharacteristically, had no retort. He grinned nervously and took his wife's hand for a moment.

Robert led them up to the dais and gave a short introduction. The audience applauded warmly as he presented the Jenks with an engraved plaque and an envelope containing the check. Then he stepped aside for Kenny to move to the microphone.

In the audience I watched as Kenny's eloquence spilled from him. He always amazed me. He and Barbra could be so chatty, so unfocused and scattered but at moments like these

---

*After Mason's departure from the federal government he would go on to become a member of the board of trustees of Evergreen International, a Utah-based non-profit organization that seeks to assist Latter-day Saints and other Christians who wish to "diminish" same-sex attraction and homosexual behavior.

he seemed to draw from a deep well of expression and style that would simply captivate those listening with its simplicity and unwavering focus. Barbra would inevitably underscore his remarks with her own form of comment—short, rougher-edged, and very to the point. Tonight was no exception. As Kenny clutched the plaque and promised it would always be important to him, Barbra snatched the check away, moved to the microphone and said, "He can keep the plaque. I'm happy to receive the check."

The audience was charmed and immediately rose to their feet in laughter, applause, and admiration. As they made their way back to the table people reached out to shake their hand or pat them affectionately on the back. The applause was continuing even as they sat down at the table. As the applause finally began to die, Kenny leaned over to me. "Did we do okay? What did I say?"

I took his hand and squeezed it warmly. "Fine, Kenny. You did just fine." If I said any more I was sure to cry.

Two weeks later, on December 1st, Morley Safer introduced the long-awaited "60 Minutes" segment, "Smoking to Live."

"Marijuana is not good for you. It's an axiom. But for some people, marijuana could be the difference between life and death. That's what they and their doctors say. The doctors prescribe it and the patients smoke it to live."

The broadcast came at a perfect time—World AIDS Day.

Barbra and Kenny were at their best, focused and appealing. Safer also interviewed Harvard professor Lester Grinspoon, Robert, Dr. Ivan Silverberg from San Francisco, a doctor who tried to give the "government angle," and the Jenks' lawyer John Daniel who was remarkably effective when Safer asked him why he took the case *pro bono*. "Because it was the right thing to do," he said. The DEA refused to be interviewed for the segment, thereby underscoring their refusal to play fair.

In Pensacola, Barbra and Kenny watched the segment in Barb's hospital room. The young woman had taken a turn for the worse following their trip to the DPF conference in

Washington. When we spoke to them after the broadcast their pride was evident. Barbra termed the show "beautiful."

Across America the story beamed into millions of homes just a few days after Thanksgiving. It was the largest single audience yet for the medical marijuana issue.

With the December 1st airing of "Smoking to Live" the medical marijuana question in America went from an "issue" to "a problem." There is a world of difference between the two. The penetration of the "60 Minutes" piece can perhaps best be expressed by comments from a friend's 80 plus year-old aunt, who watched the show. "I had no idea," she said. "This is terribly wrong. Something should be done about this problem."

On January 31, 1992, *The Los Angeles Times* published the contents of a letter to Public Health Service chief James 0. Mason from Ingrid A. C. Kolb, acting deputy director for demand reduction at the White House Office of National Drug Control Policy (ONDCP).

Kolb took Mason and the Department of Health and Human Services (HHS) to task for delaying so long in reaching the decision about whether or not to supply the 30 previously approved patients with medical marijuana. "For HHS to treat this matter as just another bureaucratic decision is unconscionable and, to me, shows an intolerable lack of compassion," Kolb wrote.

In addition to the previously approved patients, Kolb said dozens of patients who would have been eligible for the drug "are suffering from great pain—many are dying."

It was a brutal letter, demonstrating just how deep the split was between the White House and the agencies. At the time we took the letter as a sign that compassion was still possible. But it was, in retrospect, a final gasp from the White House.

Mason would not comment on the letter but his spokesman did say the chief of public health would not be drawn into a public dispute with "an employee" of the drug control office. Clearly Mr. Mason had forgotten that he, too, was an employee.

Significantly the spokesman went on to note the concern of HHS "that harm may result from smoked marijuana for immune-suppressed people." The government had begun to back away from the homophobic notion of medical marijuana inducing unsafe sex but little else had changed.

Ms. Kolb's letter generated a quick blast of news coverage, and we used this as a springboard to call, once again, for Mason's resignation. On February 4, 1992, ten of the twelve legal marijuana recipients sent a letter to the PHS chief demanding that he step down. "You are engaged in a calculated campaign of medical terrorism directed against desperately ill people," we wrote. "Your actions are not merely illegal, they are immoral and have caused much unnecessary human suffering."

Mason again refused to comment. A spokesman said the final decision regarding the Compassionate IND program was with HHS Secretary Louis Sullivan. The Secretary's office had nothing to say. For six more weeks bureaucrats in Washington would drag their feet.

And in Panama City Beach, Florida, Barbra Jenks was dying.

On the first anniversary of MARS, Barbra and Robert sat on the deck of the Jenks' trailer. The air was warm and sweet in the early Florida spring and there was a heavy, earthy smell from the slash pines that graced Barbra and Kenny's yard. Officially spring was still a month away but in the Sunshine State the first blushes of change had already begun.

The last time Robert had seen Barbra was in late December. She had been hospitalized for nearly the entire month, battling numerous infections. She had lost a great deal of weight. The hospital had refused to allow her to smoke her legal marijuana, insisting the new drug Zofran would relieve her nausea. It didn't. Kenny, in agony, had watched as Barbra vomited into a pan even as intravenous Zofran dripped into her arm. Finally he barricaded the door, stuffed towels around the bottom and lit a joint. Within minutes Barbra's vomiting subsided. The next day he took her home.

Robert arrived the following day and found a gravely emaciated and virtually incoherent Barbra. But by the end of his three-day stay Barbra was eating, bitching, and making plans.

Now, two months later, her color had returned. She was calm and talkative but no longer mentioned the future. She had despaired of caring for her hair and had most of it cut off. The effect was strangely compelling. Robert said, "There was an odd, almost ethereal, beauty about her." In 1991, Barbra had dreamed she would die in the spring but it seemed she might barely make it.

On March 9, 1992, during a routine press conference, reporters learned Secretary Sullivan had made the decision "last week" to close the compassionate IND program. The news was delivered in response to a query by the Associated Press. The Public Health Service (PHS) spokesperson would not specify exactly when the decision had been made, saying only that James 0. Mason had recommended permanent closure of the Compassionate IND program for medical marijuana and Sullivan "did not have any problem with it."

When asked for a copy of the signed order another PHS spokesperson, Raford Kytal, suggested the inquirer file a Freedom of Information request.

Public reaction was fast and furious. In Minneapolis Tim Braun told an AP reporter, "They're giving me a death sentence." Mae Nutt, whose son had worked so tirelessly to pass the Michigan state bill before dying of cancer, said she felt as though "I've been kicked in the stomach." Editorial response was also harsh. *The Chicago Tribune* was typical: "The Public Health Service's message to these people [who medically need marijuana] is: Drop dead."

Nine days later, on March 18, a second blow was delivered when the DEA responded to the April 1991 request by the U.S. Court of Appeals for clarification of the agency's rejection of Judge Young's 1988 ruling. The "clarification" was remarkably similar to the initial rejection in both tone and content. It called medical marijuana a "cruel hoax" and the DEA administrator, Robert Bonner stated, "Beyond doubt, the claims that marijuana is medicine are false, dangerous, and cruel."

The rejection contained some harsh words for advocates of medical marijuana. "A century ago, many Americans relied on stories to pick their medicines, especially from snake oil salesmen," Bonner wrote. "Thanks to scientific advances and the Federal Food Drug and Cosmetic Act, we now rely on rigorous scientific proof to assure safety and effectiveness of new drugs."

ACT quickly issued a press release claiming the DEA and PHS were "acting in concert... to force seriously ill people into hiding." It went on, "The federal agencies ... are seeking to impose a climate of fear in an effort to end the public debate over marijuana's medical use."

These were bold, harsh moves by the federal agencies. It was the final push, a desperate attempt to shut down public debate and silence the opposition. In the same week that Secretary Sullivan quietly signed the order killing the program, representatives from the National Institutes of Health (NIH) contacted each of the remaining physicians who had been granted permission to medically employ marijuana in the treatment of their patients but had not yet received supplies. The physicians were queried about their medical practices. Had they tried every possible medication? Perhaps the patient was addicted to marijuana and just thought they needed the drug medically? Was the doctor aware that marijuana could lead to unsafe sex?

It was a game of medical terrorism and, in some cases, it worked. Ten doctors withdrew their applications but the others held fast—a testament to the Hippocratic oath and the open-minds of these practicing physicians.

The bureaucrats were gambling the future of the medical prohibition on a Draconian approach and there was no backing away from it now. They were well aware that media assaults would be harsh and inflict some damage but megawatts alone would not alter the outcome. As far as the bureaucrats were concerned, the debate was over.

32. MARS ON THE MALL

It was nearly 10:00 p.m. by the time I arrived at the small trailer set back in the Florida pines. There were no streetlights and no moon. Picking my way carefully along the unfamiliar ground I walked to the trailer door and knocked. The door opened and there was Kenny, a look of surprise on his face. "Alice! How did you get by... ? Where are the dogs?"

In an instant they upon me, not menacing and ferocious but calm and friendly, as if I was a frequent guest. The two dogs angled to get close, hoping to edge into the trailer with this newly arrived visitor. As Kenny followed me in and closed the door he wondered aloud, "How did you get past the dogs?"

I looked quickly around the tiny space. The hospital bed, with Barbra's frail body, virtually consumed the room. Just inside the door was a large, overstuffed rocking chair. It held a young woman who smiled weakly.

The door shut behind me and I turned to give Kenny a hug. "Thanks for coming," he said. As we separated he introduced his sister, Penny, in the chair. She didn't get up. I began to offer my hand but then, impulsively, bent down to hug her. Penny clung to me for an instant, like a child who had found a lost parent.

There were some brief, mildly awkward exchanges about plane rides, hotel accommodations, and the unbelievable number of college students that were packed into Panama City Beach, Florida. It was March 26th; spring break and the migration of drunken, rowdy college students was in full gear. To the uninitiated it was stunning. To PCB it was economic lifeblood. To me it was a cruel and ironic counter-image to the shrunken form in the hospital bed.

"Here's Barb," Kenny said needlessly, moving towards the bed in the cramped and cluttered living space. He stroked Barbra's forehead. "Honey, you've got a visitor. Look who's come to see you." Barbra's eyes opened and looked around. As they found my face a look of puzzlement crossed her brow. I could see that Barbra was thinking hard. Was this a dream?

"Hey Barb," I said, leaning over the bed and taking Barbra's hand. "Barb, it's Alice." Barbra's eyes seemed to focus on my face and then began to open wide as she realized it wasn't a dream. It seemed to me that Barbra was absorbing my image more than seeing it. Her eyes moved beyond me, looking over my shoulder. "No honey, Bob isn't with me. He's in Washington." I took my time speaking the words and as I did Barb's eyes moved repeatedly across my face, like a scanner on a copy machine. "I was visiting my Mom in Sarasota. When I heard you were so sick I had to come. I had to come see my traveling buddy."

I stroked Barb's forehead as I spoke and Kenny softly cautioned me to avoid the sore that had formed at the hair line. "Shingles," he explained. The frail figure held my hand hard. I wondered where all that strength was coming from. Barbra had the sunken form of a concentration camp prisoner. She couldn't have weighed more than 85 pounds. Her lips were parched and dry, her breathing was labored despite the presence of an oxygen cannula.

"Oh friend," I whispered, "Look what this has done to you."

In those last 48 hours of Barbra's life I would watch a remarkable series of scenes as friends and family arrived and departed. Kenny's mother would insist upon a minister who arrived mid-afternoon on Saturday. He prayed at Barbra's bedside and then asked everyone present to hold hands and say a prayer with him. No one bothered to turn off the stereo or the TV. The elderly minister worked hard to make himself heard above the din, reciting a formal prayer about deliverance and salvation. I couldn't help but feel the real message was on the stereo as The Eagles triumphantly sang "I'm Already Gone." I could almost see Barbra's spirit starting to lift from that shattered body.

Barbra Jenks would die on March 28, 1992, just as the sun began to rise on Panama City Beach. She was 25 years old. Kenny was with her in the small hospital bed and he felt her slipping away. He got up and put their favorite song on the stereo, Stevie Nicks singing "Leather and Lace." Then he rejoined her in bed. As the song played and the sun entered the trailer through the small windows, Barbra died peacefully in Kenny's arms, in the spring.

A month after Barbra's death we took Kenny to California for some needed rest, relaxation and issue building. We met with many AIDS patients, did some media, encountered earthquakes in Los Angeles and San Francisco. Towards the end of our trip we traveled to Santa Cruz where a local activist, Scott Imler, was attempting to put a local marijuana-as-medicine initiative on the November ballot.

People in Santa Cruz were very kind to Kenny. He enjoyed walking the pier and watching the sea lions. We did local media in support of the upcoming voter initiative. One morning several good ol' boys took Kenny fishing. In the evenings Scott arranged group dinners with an abundance of eccentric but easy-to-like people who shared our concerns.

When we returned from California Robert asked Kenny if he wanted to stop. "Hell no, Robert. What those bureaucrats did was wrong. People need help and I'm the only AIDS patient in America who gets legal marijuana. That's wrong. I gotta speak out. Besides," he grinned broadly, "If I stop talking Barb would have my hide."

Indeed, despite—or perhaps because of—his faltering health Kenny developed a fervor about "speaking out" and "doing something." We accommodated his desire to remain active and, over the next six months, arranged a series of trips to AIDS conferences around the country where Kenny could speak with other PWAs (people with AIDS), promote MARS, and agitate for change.

In the summer of 1992 we learned The Names Project was coming to Washington to display its rapidly expanding AIDS Quilt—it now contained over 21,000 panels memorializing Americans who had died from the rampaging plague. When unfolded the Quilt, now the size of twelve football fields, would carpet the Mall from the Washington Monument to the Lincoln Memorial. Twelve football fields of sorrow.

Quilt organizers expected several hundred thousand people would visit their display. They also announced there would be a special area set aside for AIDS-related exhibits. We decided the Quilt provided MARS with the unique opportunity to directly involve people with AIDS in a protest against the Bush administration closure of the Compassionate IND program.

Gauging the gargantuan dimensions of the Quilt display we realized we would need help. There was no way Robert, I and our part-time helper, Linda Barefoot, could put MARS on the Mall without some outside help. It was time to recruit some Men from MARS.

Kenny, despite some incidental infections, was the first to volunteer. We also invited Jim Barnes, the man who had driven to Chicago to be part of our February 1991 MARS launch. Jim, a short, balding man with a bushy beard, lived with his lover, Gil, in near isolation, deep in the cold woods of the U.P. in Michigan. Jim's MARS application had been one of the first approved by FDA in February 1991. The bureaucrats even sent him a letter promising to provide him with medical marijuana. But then PHS closed the program and Jim Barnes never received his promised supplies. Jim immediately accepted our invitation.

Kenny and Jim were familiar friends. We also reached out to a newer acquaintance, Ezekiel Ramshur who hailed from Monroe, Louisiana. Ezekiel spoke with the slow, sweet lilt of his region and I believed him to be something of a country bumpkin, unfamiliar with big city ways. This image was reinforced when he told me he had never flown before or traveled more than 100 miles from his home. When Ezekiel asked if "a friend could accompany" him to Washington we quickly agreed. The more hands the better.

When I picked up Ezekiel and his friend at National Airport I was surprised to find two smartly dressed gay men. Ezekiel was thin, even frail looking with a discreet, pencil-thin braid of hair which hung down the nape of his neck. His lover, Robert, was younger, hyper-blond and far more flamboyant—a Louisiana drag queen fresh from being crowned Miss Monroe. "The city, not the star," he exuberantly explained.

To round out our Men from MARS brigade we called Scott Imler. By this time Scott had put Prop A on the Santa Cruz ballot and, despite the upcoming election, he jumped at the opportunity to come to Marble City to help us put MARS on the Mall.

As we began our plans for the exhibit table we thought about a petition to the Bush Administration asking it to re-open the Compassionate IND program but we quickly dismissed the idea of a petition. It was too static. People would need to stop and sign. We could lose many supporters who didn't want to wait.

We needed something that would engage the public and AIDS patients in a more dynamic, less cumbersome enterprise. After much debate we decided to hand out postcards pre-addressed to the Senate Committee on Health chaired by Senator Ted Kennedy. Individuals could sign their cards and leave them with us or take them home and send them on to Congress.

In addition to these postcards of protest we also prepared thousands of MARS brochures and dense packets of information. Finally, we printed large banners for our table and got MARS T-shirts so visitors to the Mall could quickly identify our Men from MARS.

We flew our troops in early and sent them off to Capitol Hill to meet with their respective Senators. Kenny and Robert visited Senator Kennedy's health aide and were pleased with the reception. "Maybe," the Senator's aide said, "we'll get a new president. Then he could just reopen the Compassionate IND program."

Kenny got excited but we knew better. Talk is cheap in Washington, especially political talk.

On October 9th, the opening ceremonies of the Quilt display were delayed by a steady, cold rain. But the wet day had some redeeming features. The rain forced more people into the exhibit tent, and thousands made their way through the mud and maze of tables to our booth. As the crowd increased our Men from MARS began passing out postcards by the handfuls. In exchange they began to receive the gratitude of those who had come to see the Quilt. Their spirits soared. Doctors, nurses, other PWAs flocked to our MARS exhibit, anxious to participate in our efforts. Among the clamoring hordes the most touching visitors to our booth were mothers who spoke of buying marijuana off the streets to help a dying son. There were tears of sorrow and solidarity.

By Friday afternoon the sun broke through the gloom and the number of people seeking information began to multiply. Energized by the manic demand we worked late into the evening.

Saturday dawned clear, cool, and bright: a brilliant autumn day. The trees, tinged with changing leaves, created an exquisite backdrop for the multi-colored hues of the Quilt. The crowds were massive. In the exhibit tent our Men from MARS worked non-stop, distributing information, passing out postcards, collecting signatures. The outpouring of support and encouragement was invigorating. Kenny was in his element: laughing, joking, "doing something." Ezekiel, who seemed so frail, blossomed as he and Robert worked tirelessly. Jim Barnes, less outgoing, found the flood of people disquieting, but worked hard and was clearly moved by the constant praise he received for his efforts to get legal marijuana to PWAs.

That evening we closed our booth, ate boxed dinners beneath the Washington Monument, then joined 200,000 other people on the Ellipse for a candlelight march past the White House to the Lincoln Memorial. As thousands of marchers filed past the White House they chanted "Bye bye Bush" and "Pack your pearls, Babs," a reference to Barbara Bush's trademark necklace. Watching 200,000 candles flicker down Marble City streets was an awe inspiring sight.

Once we arrived at the Lincoln Memorial people gathered around the Reflecting Pool, their candles turning the water a mellow yellow. Prayers were said. Songs sung and speeches made. The huge crowd was hushed except for the sound of quiet tears.

Sunday was no less stressful. Hundreds of thousands of people descended on the Mall. The demand for MARS materials was overwhelming. By the time we closed our booth it was clear MARS on the Mall had been a tremendous success. We collected nearly 6,000 postcards on-site and distributed another 10,000 to people who would provide their own delivery. "They was like pigeons on popcorn," Kenny said.

At the end of the day we surveyed our weary volunteers to make certain each was holding up all right. When Robert took Ezekiel aside and asked if he was okay he replied in his soft, so gentle voice, "Mr. Randall, this has been the best day of my life. I feel great."

Our Men from MARS were very happy, very tired campers.

We had barely recovered from the Quilt exhibit before we were back on the road. To Kenny's delight we returned to California to campaign for Scott Imler's Proposition A initiative. Prop A was the first county-wide ballot initiative for medical marijuana. The previous year Prop P—a city-wide initiative—had passed in San Francisco,.

Prop A would test the political strength of medical marijuana in a more conservative, politically diverse environment. The city of Santa Cruz was notoriously liberal and populated with "free spirits" who would be expected to support medical marijuana. But the rest of the county was largely rural and populated by people with strongly conservative inclinations.

Kenny's spirit was indomitable, but AIDS was beginning to get the upper hand. He arrived in Santa Cruz in a great deal of pain. Despite his legal marijuana, his appetite was failing and vomiting was becoming a serious problem.

On November 2, 1992, Prop A would win decisively, gaining 77.5% of the vote. In the post-election analysis, Scott Imler would note with pride that Prop A carried every district in the county. Medical marijuana, once again, revealed its trans-ideological appeal. Liberal or conservative, Americans believed seriously ill patients should have legal access to needed care.

Immediately following the election, Kenny and I traveled in Florida for two conferences: AIDS Manasota in Bradenton, and Association of Nurses in AIDS Care at Disney World. Kenny, now obviously unwell, was insistent upon continuing his quest to "do something." In a letter to a friend I would note, "He has changed so much since Barb's death. I watch him at these conferences, soaking up positive affirmations, bouncing around the surrealness of his life. These meetings are more therapeutic than any drug he can get but there aren't enough meetings in the world for Kenny and he knows it."

The national election saw Bill Clinton squeak by. There would be a new administration. Maybe Kennedy's aide was right, maybe the program could be re-opened. Our hopes grew even more when Clinton tapped a black woman, Dr. Joycelyn Elders, for Surgeon General. In the December 17, 1992 *Arkansas Times* Dr. Elders sent some encouraging signs. "We prescribe morphine for pain and I think doctors should be able to prescribe marijuana as well, if they feel it's medically called for."

In December 1992 we began preparing recommendations for the new administration. As we worked to outline the future it became clear Kenny's health had collapsed. An opportunistic infection of unknown type was ravaging our friend. Kenny took massive overdoses of antibiotics and was given morphine to quell the pain. By Christmas the crisis passed. Kenny would rally, regain lost weight, slowly rebound. But we all knew Kenny had seen his last New Year.

33. FALSE HOPE

In the early part of 1993 we would fly Kenny back to D.C. to hand-deliver the signed postcards from MARS on the Mall to Senator Kennedy. We had hoped to do this before the new year, but Kenny's health was beginning to fail and his strength wouldn't allow a trip.

When we finally arrived at Kennedy's office we learned that thousands of postcards had already reached the Senator independently, fulfilling our hope that people would return home and distribute the cards to others.

Kennedy's aide was encouraging and supportive but he was also wavering. Bill Clinton's election had given the Senator an excuse to "wait and see." "Things are going to change," the aide promised. We'd heard it before.

It would be Kenny's last trip and he stayed with us while in Washington. On more than one occasion I was up during the night comforting Kenny as he coped with terrible pain that brought on waves of nausea and vomiting. Pain seemed to be constantly with him. He was munching morphine like some people eat peanuts.

Kenny was slipping away.

When Robert and I were arrested in 1975 Gerald Ford was president. Now, seventeen years and four presidents later, Bill Clinton was taking the oath. Bill Clinton was our age, our generation. His oblique comments about marijuana use—tried it but didn't inhale—did not cause us any consternation. We really didn't care what Bill Clinton proposed to do for social smokers. We wanted the Compassionate IND program open again and that did not seem like too much to ask.

We prepared a 50-page booklet entitled *Marijuana as Medicine: Initial Steps: Recommendations for the Clinton Administration*. The goal was simple: to provide the incoming Clinton Administration with the history of the medical marijuana problem and suggest three avenues of action: 1) restore compassion, 2) encourage research, and 3) explore options. It was ready by the end of January, and we began mailings to every incoming member of the Clinton Administration plus all members of Congress. The Compassionate IND program had been officially closed for less than one year and we felt there was a strong possibility of succeeding with our requests. Once again, however, we underestimated the forces at work within the federal marijuana prohibition. The New Year had begun with an announcement that synthetic THC, marketed for nearly a decade as Marinol, would be approved for use by people with AIDS for appetite stimulation and treatment of nausea and vomiting.

The feds had correctly observed that the pressure for medical marijuana was primarily coming from the AIDS community, just as cancer patients had driven the first medical marijuana push in the late 1970s and early '80s. The bureaucrats hoped that by officially approving Marinol for AIDS-related symptoms they could relieve the pressure and quiet the issue once more.

But AIDS patients were not fooled by the federal gambit. Off-label use of Marinol by AIDS patients had been ongoing for several years. The synthetic didn't work for the same reason it didn't work for cancer patients: poor bioavailability, difficulty in determining the proper dose, and the practical problems of keeping down a pill when a patient is vomiting.

The federal shell game also failed because of a radically different patient population. Cancer patients seemed to have an assurance that society and the medical community was doing all that could be done for them. AIDS patients, ostracized and stigmatized by society, had just the opposite impressions. They had grown accustomed to fighting for every treatment available. There was a strong, and sadly, often correct feeling that society could care less about these terminally ill people.

And there was a political savviness. The AIDS Coalition To Unleash Power (ACT-UP) was notorious for public demonstrations, particularly at federal agencies such as the FDA. ACT-UP had also begun a service for AIDS patients called "buyers' clubs" where PWAs could purchase needed drugs at reduced prices. In 1992, as the feds moved to shutdown MARS and the Compassionate IND program, some

PWA buyer's clubs began to include marijuana as part of their inventory.

This concept of patients helping patients was not new, but in late 1992, when cannabis buyers' clubs first emerged, there was a new feeling, a new stridency. The anger and righteousness that we had counted upon was evident in the news articles, the editorials, and the public's mood. The beast had been unmasked. The decades-old federal lie—"anyone with a legitimate medical need can obtain legal access to marijuana"—was revealed. The Memory Hole was unearthed.

The feds did not care about the seriously ill. Their goal was to maintain the total and absolute prohibition regardless of what truth they trampled in the process. In 1977 Peter Bourne had written to Robert and grandly assured, "The responsible agency staffs and researchers involved…all share with me a great feeling of compassion and are pledged to pursue the question."

It was bull then and it still was in 1992. Each successive administration had boldly promised the same unerring devotion to "compassion and pursuit of the truth." Yet the federal government, which controlled medical marijuana, did not have a single research project underway that would help answer the questions first posed in the early 1970s. Billions were spent for the war on drugs but not a single cent was allocated for researching marijuana's therapeutic use.

Weary of government's lies, the people took matters into their own hands, and the cannabis buyer's clubs were born. The clubs began in San Francisco, which was struggling to implement Prop P, a citywide initiative that recognized marijuana's medical utility but did nothing to provide supplies of the drug to the seriously ill. There was talk of allowing limited cultivation but the talk droned on and no official action was taken. So citizens began to take their own action. Brownie Mary, an elderly woman who volunteered on the AIDS floors at S.F. General Hospital, began bringing marijuana brownies to the wards. There was talk of opening a "marijuana store."

In Washington, D.C., a cannabis buyer's club opened in December 1992. We were under some pressure to endorse these clubs but we resisted. We were unwilling to openly encourage illegality and place patients at legal as well as medical risk. Nor did we feel that home cultivation or contraband supplies were the answer to medical access to marijuana. Such solutions were inappropriate for the vast majority of those needing medical access. We saw no reason why marijuana should not be available by prescription. The seriously ill needed a regulated, reliable source of medicine. Lastly, we viewed the "clubs" as too loosely structured, allowing many with questionable "ailments" to obtain marijuana. This source of abuse could potentially harm the medical marijuana movement.

ACT was criticized for not embracing the buyer's club concept. We took pains to avoid the conflict but club organizers felt "snubbed." One D.C. activist accused us of "not caring about the sick." After seventeen years of battling to expand the medical use of marijuana it was an odd accusation to hear.

We continued on the path that we had long ago established—attempting to reform the legal barriers that prohibited medical access to marijuana. We placed our fate in the hands of the man from Hope, Arkansas. Across the land there was hope that Bill Clinton would do the right thing.

The year would move on slowly while Clinton settled into the job. Rumors were flying about his plans for medical marijuana. He appointed Dr. Philip Lee from San Francisco as the head of PHS, James Mason's old job. Activists from San Francisco claimed the Compassionate IND program would soon be reopened by "their good friend." It was promising but with each passing month there was a growing sense that our "friends" in the White House didn't much care about medical marijuana. Efforts to meet with administration officials and discuss the issue fell flat.

It was our least publicly active period in four years but there was plenty going on. Press interest in the issue continued to multiply and Robert seemed to be constantly engaged in talk radio or press interviews. In March 1993 we captured the unanimous endorsement of the American Medical Student Association. In a strongly worded resolution the association of aspiring doctors called on the new Attorney General, Janet Reno, to abide by the 1988 decision of Judge Young.

"President Clinton...should end the medical prohibition against marijuana by creating a rational system of prescriptive medical access to a now-prohibited drug." The group went on to note, "Seriously ill Americans are suffering because of prohibitory federal policies" and asked the Clinton Administration to reopen the Compassionate IND program.

We also spent this time preparing ACT's response to the DEA rejection of marijuana. In the process we enlisted the support of The Physicians Association for AIDS Care (PAAC) and the National Lymphoma Foundation. Both groups filed "friend of the court" briefs on behalf of medical access to marijuana.

As the mechanics of the issue churned on we watched, with heavy hearts, the decline of friends as AIDS continued to take its toll.

In April, returning to D.C. from a visit with my mother, I stopped in Panama City Beach to help Kenny contend with a film crew from The Discovery Channel. The cable network was preparing a four part documentary, "In a Time of AIDS" and had first met Kenny on the Washington Mall during the AIDS Quilt display and that wondrous weekend of the Men from MARS. Now, they were conducting more detailed interviews. Kenny was worried about having the strength to make it through the taping and I was there to act as a buffer.

The film crew, young and energetic, wanted Kenny to go with them to the beach and walk on the wharf. They had seen this on "60 Minutes" and it was good footage. Kenny, polite by nature, had initially said yes but I could see he was too ill. I quietly pulled the producer aside and explained. Even the obligatory walk through the front yard was almost more than Kenny could bear. As the interview started in earnest I could see Kenny was having a very hard time concentrating. When the producer asked him to talk about Barbra he became uncharacteristically quiet and asked for a break.

"You okay, Kenny?" I asked.

"I just didn't know what to say, Alice. What can I say about Barb?" Kenny's grief for his wife was still raw and his pain was palpable. I looked around the trailer for something of Barbra and found the photographic montage that Kenny's sisters and Barb's friends had prepared for Barbra's funeral. I pulled the producer aside and said, "Get him to talk about the pictures." With camera and lights off, Kenny and the producer reviewed the montage together. Laughing and telling tales, Kenny found his focus and finished the interview.

I would return to Panama City in the last week of June and on July 1 I would say goodbye to Kenny. "I don't think I'll see you again," Kenny said and I knew he was right. It was a deeply emotional moment.

"Well, Kenny," I said, "if we don't meet again in this life be certain you save a place for Bob and me on the other side."

"You know I will!" The old Kenny suddenly emerged from the layers of illness and grief. His eyes twinkled and he smiled broadly. "Me and Barb will be waitin' on you. I love you guys."

"And we love you, guy."

Kenny would remain in his trailer, with his dogs and memories. Federal funds, paid under the Ryan White Act, provided Kenny with housekeeping services and Fate sent him a real-life angel named Fatima, a Portuguese immigrant who grew very fond of Kenny and took good care of him.

On July 19, 1993, Kenny died in Fatima's arms in his trailer under the slash pines. It was the day before what would have been Barbra's 27th birthday. Kenny was 31 years old.

Section V:

End of the Beginning

34. BEYOND MARS

Kenny's death not only left a void in our life, it left a void in the issue. In the weeks following his death a curious question was presented to us over and over again. Some were able to deliver the question with sympathy and tact. Others were incredibly crass. "Who is Kenny's understudy?" they asked. Several AIDS patients phoned to volunteer for the "role," as if Kenny and Barbra were concocted constructions, as easily fabricated as paper mache stage props. The reformers wondered "Who's the next 'star' of medical marijuana?"

As Barbra would have said, "They just don't get it!" Those who saw Kenny and Barbra as icons set against a static backdrop believed endless reproductions would turn the trick—were the trick. But even the best story, too often and poorly told, wears thin and frays.

They did not understand it was time for Fate to weave a new story.

MARS, in final flower, had played its role brilliantly. Medical marijuana was now part of the national dialogue. The battle for hearts and minds had been won. The government's charade—anyone who medically needed marijuana could obtain it legally—was revealed for the duplicitous lie that it was.

Our support spanned the political spectrum. In May 1993, the conservative *Orange County Register*, Ronald Reagan's hometown newspaper, polled its readers and reported a whopping 93% favored making marijuana legally available for medical use. Clearly, our message resonated. The goal now was to translate this preponderance of popular support into useful power. How could this be done?

Alas, such questions were no longer our exclusive concern. MARS, as expected, had created vast reservoirs of energy. We had played Tom Sawyer well; making medical marijuana so enticing that everyone wanted to paint our fence. Many were anxious to "get in on the action." There were packs of alpha-pups aching to take a bite. The rush of so many new, discordant voices was jarring. For years we had been autonomous, able to articulate our message without competing overtones. Now, in the vast vortex of new energies, medical marijuana was beginning to lose its singular voice.

We watched these new actors with a measure of dread and delight. While the infusion of new voices was bracing, the danger of mingled motives was clear. Drug reformers wanted to turn medical marijuana into a "grow your own" issue. But the desperately ill were not looking for a unique horticultural experience. They were seeking critically needed medical care. Drug reformers seemed oblivious to such fine distinctions.

Robert reasoned our best strategy was to ignore these newly activated players and refuse to engage. In this way, he believed, we avoided being drawn into the petty politics and vicious in-fighting which dominated much of the drug-reform movement. We had no interest in debating whether patients should be legally allowed to grow 2 plants or 6 plants. Such debate trivialized the problem and diverted attention from the Federal Government's refusal to meet basic human needs.

On Oct. 1, 1993, the case of *ACT v DEA* was once again before the U.S. Court of Appeals. Among NORML and the other reform groups there was great optimism. In the ACT camp things were not quite as cocky. Steve Davidson, our attorney from Steptoe & Johnson, warned us the law was not on our side. The case hinged on a very basic question—did DEA have the right to refuse the findings of its own administrative law judge. Steve made a forceful argument before the Court that the facts demonstrated DEA's arbitrary handling of the case. But Steve was aware that administrative regulations were not on our side.

USA Today reported on the Court of Appeals case and carried a sidebar entitled "Cannabis clubs open for medicinal business." The article reported that clubs were operating in San Francisco, Washington, D.C., New York, and Little Rock, Arkansas. "Other clubs operate underground," the story reports, "but are well-organized."

The San Francisco club was run by Dennis Peron, the author of Proposition P. Peron, a gay pot grower and oft-arrested drug dealer, had moved to the forefront of medical marijuana efforts in California. It had long been Peron's ambition to run a retail pot shop, and his use of sick people to reach that goal was bound to attract attention. In exotic San Francisco a gay drug dealer openly peddling pot may be tolerated, even celebrated. But America is not so naive.

As we entered November 1993 the level of media coverage was off scale. It was "sweeps" month for television, that odd time of year when stations outdo themselves to garner the highest ratings. Medical marijuana was "hot" and it seemed every local, national, and cable network was running a story on the denial of medication to the seriously ill.

From the ridiculous to the sublime the video images seemed nonstop. NBC "Nightly News" weighed in with a piece that was borderline tabloid. The segment featured Steve Smith, an AIDS patient who had opened the Washington, D.C. Cannabis Buyer's Club. Smith was articulate and compelling but the presence of a bong—a pipe used to smoke marijuana—undercut the message. Then it was on to swinging San Francisco where large groups of people passing joints in Peron's cosmically decorated "cannabis cafe" hardly conveyed medical need. The NBC story ignored the plight of patients. It was trite, tabloid TV.

CNN weighed in with a story about a Rabbi who delivered pot to dying cancer patients. It was very powerful. In this media-frenzied month Robert seemed to be constantly on the phone with radio shows from all over America. A glut of new stories, including several wire overviews, were tumbling out of the media machine.

In that same month The Discovery Channel documentary "In the Time of AIDS" aired. Just seven months before, I had helped Kenny through the interviews for this show and we were anxious to see how our friend would be portrayed.

The show was televised on four consecutive nights. On the first night our old friend Kenny was electronically resurrected and he finally got his opportunity to publicly condemn the blood companies that conspired to murder him and Barbra. Kenny's elegant simplicity was damn good stuff.

The next night's show contained a jumbled segment on "new therapies" and the marijuana/AIDS connection popped open briefly to file footage of the Jenks trial and Kenny proudly wearing his MARS T-shirt.

The third segment had nothing about Kenny or medical marijuana. The fourth, and last, installment droned out its sad story for almost an hour without any sign of our departed friend.

We had about given up hope of seeing Kenny in the program again when, at the very end of this extensive overview of the global AIDS crisis—after tons of talking heads, endless statistics, and numbing personal stories—then came the show's final images. I gasped as we were suddenly transported back to MARS on the Mall and there was Kenny at the Quilt, warmly lit in the autumn sun, cheery in his yellow MARS T-shirt and ready smile. He was explaining why he didn't bring a panel for Barbra to the Quilt Display. "It didn't seem right to just have a panel for Barb. My wife and me, we were never separated in life. It didn't seem right to be separated in death."

As his voice-over continued the images faded to archival video of Kenny and Barbra in their trailer, happy and full of life, mugging a big kiss for the video eye. The audio shifted to Michael Callan's haunting song, "What We Don't Have Is Time," the song that had moved 200,000 marchers in the candlelight vigil for AIDS at the Quilt Display. And as the video image froze on Kenny and Barbra's kiss, the date of Kenny's death appeared on the screen.

It was sublime. Old friends, gazing back from across the River Styx. Watching the images in our living room that night I found myself choking back a sob of emotion. Tears were falling from my eyes and when I looked at Robert he too was crying. There was something unspoken between us in that brief glance, something large and foreboding in the room. It was easy to put it off to the images that had just passed. But it was something more. It was November 1993. In November 1994 we would be sobbing again but this time it would be for ourselves.

35. GOING GLOBAL

As we entered 1994 medical marijuana was the star issue of drug reform. New players filled the stage, mimicking scenes that were well-etched in the public's mind, reenacting battles already won. Robert would later say of this time, "I was like an actor who had grown accustomed to a long monologue. I was variously distressed, incensed, bemused, confused and stunned numb by the cacophony of so many abruptly babbling voices." Conspicuously absent were the patients.

But there was a more abstract view. For almost twenty years we had dominated the issue. Robert was the face of medical marijuana, well on his way to being named the uncontested "father of the medical marijuana movement." Every movement has analogies to tides and now, in the mid-1990s, we were looking at our ebb tide. Now, it seemed, we were the authors, sitting in the darkened theater, looking on from the safety of an audience seat as a spotlight revealed raw ambition on the boards: a host of hot hams hoping for center stage. In truth we had enticed these actors to our stage and each player gave our vision new inflexion.

As the year unfolded we watched as others jockeyed to be the new star, the new director, and the new writer. This was amplified in February when the U.S. Court of Appeals ruled in favor of the DEA, upholding the agency's right to reject the findings of its own administrative law judge. Predictably the activists went wild but surprisingly the decision drew little press attention. The Court's decision did, however, lob the ball straight into President Clinton's court.

The Clinton Administration was in a position to provide the solution but the growing tide of legalizers and reformers made the White House nervous. Clinton could do the right thing and come down on the side of facts and evidence, just as Judge Young had in September 1988. But Clinton had taken a lot of heat for his decision on gays in the military. There was no evidence that doing the right thing had bolstered the President's courage. More than anything Clinton wanted to be reelected and being "soft on drugs" was not a good stance for the incumbent.

We anxiously awaited the President's decision and tried to ignore the growing hiss of The Memory Hole.

As new dramas began playing out domestically our attention began to drift overseas to the medical marijuana issue in Europe. The seeds of global expansion had already been sown. Marijuana is, after all, an ancient herb, used by cultures throughout history. Despite the relentless whooshing of The Memory Hole the drug warriors had not succeeded in obliterating the memory of marijuana's medical use. They could not, for it seems we are born with a memory for marijuana. New research had revealed receptors in the human brain designed specifically for the chemicals found in cannabis.* Each of us has tiny neural receptors waiting to find its partner in the chemicals that nature provides in the cannabis plant.

On a less microscopic level, the vast social use of the drug had spawned many serendipitous medical users. None of the illnesses that marijuana could help were specific to America. It was only natural that others throughout the world would discover marijuana's therapeutic utility.

Britain was the obvious launch point for our global assault: similar language, same culture. In geopolitical terms the United Kingdom is a small country on an isolated island off the edge of Europe. In press terms, however, Britain retains Imperial reach. Some of the biggest media plugs on planet Earth are located in London.

As the year began there were promising news reports that seemed to underscore our new international strategy. In early February the British Medical Association (BMA) reported 70% of U.K. physicians supported the legalization of marijuana for medical purposes.

---

* The discovery of the endocannabinoid system was in 1988 but it was work by Raphael Mechoulam in 1992 that really gave birth to the study of the human body's receptors for cannabis.

British media interest had been well primed thanks to the work of Liz Brice (a.k.a Clare Hodges) and Dr. Anne Biezanek. Liz, an MS victim, was a polished writer who placed several articles about the medical use of marijuana in English publications. Media interest in Dr. Biezanek was piqued by her trial for marijuana possession. The doctor was found not guilty by reason of medical necessity after she explained she possessed the marijuana to treat her adult daughter, Lucy, who suffered from several mental health problems.

In February 1994 there was a video salvo on the aptly named television show "The Big Story," a kind of English "60 Minutes" but with longer segments allowing for more intense story development. We had begun working with the producers from the show in late 1993, providing background information and putting the show in touch with Liz.

"The Vicar's Desperate Remedy" brought medical marijuana into 5 million homes. A primarily British-based story with some American angles, it was engaging and cleverly done.

The first segment outlined the situation and introduced several patients, most in wheelchairs, who smoked pot. Then, an inspired producer airlifted three mature British matrons with MS to a canal-side cannabis cafe in Amsterdam. The women, clearly excited by the unfamiliar surroundings, reviewed the menu, selected several lush buds and were handed a small pipe. After a few puffs they became quite gabby and were variously affected. One loved the strong smell of burning hemp; another was repelled; the third was hungry. How was their MS? Looking quite rosy and relaxed, the women admitted they "feel better."

The second segment was "the American story." Robert was featured smoking legal U.S. government joints along with file footage of the NIDA pot plantation. There was talk of the California ballot initiatives and the focus shifted to Santa Cruz where, with Scott Imler's help, the producers met and interviewed a paraplegic named Scott Hager. As fate would have it, the camera was on when Hager was seized by violent leg spasms that nearly sent him tumbling from his wheelchair. He smoked a small amount of marijuana and, with the video camera still rolling, his violent spasms subsided within a few minutes. It was a Eureka moment, captured on video for millions to see. Hager regained enough muscle control to continue his planned workout in the swimming pool and gracefully slipped from his wheelchair into the cool, blue waters. It was graphic, gripping footage.

In the final segment we returned to England where we met a round, friendly Friar, the middle-aged vicar of a small country church. The vicar suffers from MS, drags a leg, has had little success with conventional therapies. "The Big Story" flew the Friar to Holland for an afternoon in the cannabis cafes. We watched the vicar, unsteady on his feet with cane in hand, awkwardly walking down a Dutch street. He slipped into a corner cafe, reviewed the variety of marijuana on offer, made a selection, then slowly inhaled his first puff of marijuana smoke. He took a few more puffs, mildly coughed, found it "interesting." Within minutes his stiff frame relaxed; he became animated and chatty. The reporter asked, "How do you feel, vicar?"

"Better," the vicar replied with surprise. "Less shaky." But it is the tape that tells the story. As the vicar left the cafe the change in his gait was remarkable. His walk was steady, easy, assured.

A very good piece, "The Big Story" on medical marijuana would rerun in Britain before being exported via syndication to outlets in Australia, New Zealand and other outposts of Empire.

Globalization was under way.

As the year progressed we became increasingly perplexed about what to do domestically. Pressures were constantly exerted on Robert and ACT to "do something". I could see Robert's growing frustration and anger with groups and individuals whom he harshly dismissed as "culture clowns." Inwardly I was concerned that our effective strategy of the past two decades was now inappropriate. We must reach out and form alliances, just as our organization—the Alliance for Cannabis Therapeutics—suggested.

Robert began focusing on a new idea, a Medical Marijuana Fund. Rich's support was a fortune to us and showed the value of investing in the issue. But in the grand scheme of things it was small change. To resolve the medical marijuana problem, Robert determined, would require much more. It would take millions of dollars. The Medical Marijuana Fund was envisioned as a grand philanthropic endeavor, three to four wealthy men joining together to provide the financial support needed to sponsor community-based research projects throughout the U.S.

The money was a critical element but the character of the contributor was even more critical. A consortium of the powerfully wealthy would send a signal to the politicians that it was time to resolve the problem. If there were doctors to do the science and money to support the research how could the feds deny this plan?

It was a simple plan, a kind of MARS on steroids. Robert began to sketch this idea to Rich and he listened carefully, giving Robert the encouragement he needed.

"Keep working," he said, "keep working."

Robert did. But something was wrong. He would later write:

I did keep working, endlessly going over the same ground. Writing and rewriting proposals that sat in my computer. My focus was myopic and scattered all at the same time. I felt a heaviness of mind and body. My weight had increased in odd ways; I was bloated about the face and belly. There were rashes that wouldn't clear.

Something was happening to me but I was blind to it.

Robert may have been blind to it but I was keenly aware of the changes. In all of our years together—first as friends, then as lovers, and then as husband and wife—I had always known him as the most even of companions. There was little that could rile him, with the exception of the medical marijuana prohibition. He could be critical but rarely harsh. Trained in debate and rhetoric he could easily see both sides of an argument and methodically work through which was the strongest point of view.

But throughout 1994 Robert became someone unknown to me. He seemed constantly annoyed and irritated. At first I thought he was simply over-worked. We had been going flat out with the medical marijuana issue for nearly five years. We had suffered grievous losses of friends and allies. I suggested that we take a vacation and even this simple suggestion was met with irritation.

Thinking that perhaps he needed time to himself I traveled alone to North Carolina. It would prove a tipping point of sorts.

He would later write about that time:

> *Suddenly it was a quiet time with little to do. On one gentle evening, alone and sad, I fell into a pool of dark humors which inflated, then ignited into an intense rage. Pure anger. Deep, random explosions of emotion. Shouting into the silence of my living room; screaming at nothing and everything.*
>
> *Alice phoned into the bared teeth of this emotional storm. With fury, I lashed out at her absence. Stunned by the blistering temper of my tone she tried to calm me, to find out what was wrong. Furious, I slammed down the phone, ending her inquisition. Then, like a fever abruptly broken the rage receded.*
>
> *Exhausted, stunned, I reflected on my utterly uncharacteristic behavior. I had rarely been angry before and seldom raised my voice. Certainly, I have been enraged by some unjust or vile act. But I had never before experienced such a cold, terrible rush of unchecked rage. I could not rationally isolate a particular cause. It seemed as if something deep in the heart of my universe was disturbed. My brain scrambled to logically explain and, in a moment of exhaustion, I concluded that it was just a great fatigue at the folly of the world. Anger and denial. Classic emotions of the terminally ill.*

The phone call was like a slap across the face and my reaction was very emotional. I had started to fear that Robert and I had run our course, that our relationship was ending. That phone call, with it's wild accusations and targeted insults, seemed to confirm my thinking. I was visiting an old friend in the cool Carolina mountains and I tried to explain the changes I was seeing in Robert. "There's something else happening," this dear friend would say. "This isn't like Robert."

She was right. What I didn't tell my friends, what I could barely tell myself, was the growing fear that perhaps Robert's changed behavior was organic in nature. I was concerned Robert might have AIDS.

Robert was bi-sexual and in the 70s and 80s he had been sexually active with men. I knew of this. I had known about Robert's bi-sexuality from our earliest days. In college we would have long talks about his confusion with respect to his sexual orientation. A few years after we moved in together Robert began casual liaisons with men. When I learned of this I was upset and angry, thinking, as women so often do, that there must be something wrong with me. Robert assured me that wasn't the case. He couldn't fully explain his need for these often anonymous encounters but he made it clear that his love for me was not a part of it. As the years passed our love and devotion to each other grew stronger and I came to accept that these sexual encounters were a part of who Robert was, a part I could not change.

In the 1980s, as AIDS began to move into the nation's psyche Robert and I talked again about his sexual activities. Things had changed and I was now at risk. Robert knew that and acted responsibly, curbing his behavior and adding protection. But we both knew there was a chance he had been infected. At one point in the late 80s I encouraged him to get tested but he did not. In 1990 I did get tested and it was negative. I didn't have HIV. Perhaps that gave each of us a false sense of security.

In the summer of '94 I returned to Washington and we simply got back to work. The volatile telephone explosion was ignored—another uncharacteristic behavior. Each in our own worlds we proceeded on.

On the last day of August Robert received a faxed invitation to speak at the University College of London on October 11. The prospect of international travel was invigorating and quickly pushed to the background the tension between us.

We were going to Europe! After a year of pelting Britain with medical marijuana stories, we could now ratchet up the amps through a blitz of London. Liz's fledgling ACT-UK had attracted an upper crust of support, including that of Dr. Patrick Wall, one the country's preeminent pain specialists and the source of Robert's speaking invitation. He had arranged a cozy lecture on "The Therapeutic Uses of Cannabis" that would have an eclectic audience of physicians, BBC producers, pharmaceutical company reps, Fleet Street editors and select patients.

We had been down the international road before and knew the problems Robert would encounter in attempting to travel with his marijuana. We knew that Holland offered safe haven and settled on an itinerary that would allow some R&R in Amsterdam before crossing the Channel to England. It would give us a chance to explore the cannabis cafes and speak with officials in Holland about medical marijuana use.

It was a lovely weekend at the Amsterdam Hilton and we spent the time touring, wandering museums and the neighborhood streets. It was warm and sunny. In the civil atmosphere of Amsterdam, Robert and I began to relax again with one another. The rage, which exploded in August, had continued to linger beneath the surface but in this relaxed city Robert began opening up. I spoke of my concerns about his health—the nagging cough and uncharacteristic fatigue.

Over split pea soup and sandwiches we talked calmly about the possibilities and, for the first time in many months, we became friends again. Robert couldn't deny the changes nor could he argue with the need to "get to the bottom" of his health problems. He promised to see a doctor upon our return home.

On Monday we hopped a train for Belgium. Robert had brought some of his legal marijuana and was initially planning to "challenge" the border guards by declaring it upon entry into Britain. He had alerted the British government of his plans to "import" his federal supplies of marijuana and the British government had advised him that this would not be tolerated. Robert figured the encounter would make for some good press. But, in another uncharacteristic move, he crumpled the cigarettes and threw them away as we sped across the Lowlands. We crossed the channel and entered the country without any hassle.

We arrived at our hotel in King's Cross in time to meet our British contact, Liz Brice, for dinner. Liz was an interesting woman, married with two young sons. Well-dressed, stylish and deeply sincere, Liz's focus was, understandably, on the disease that afflicted her, MS. Indeed, to our surprise, and probably because of Liz's efforts, marijuana's use in MS was the focus of most British media attention.

In October 1994 London was beautiful, warm and sunny. We had left our jet lag in Holland and our first day in England we were up early to see the obvious sights.

The University College lecture was scheduled for 5 p.m. The audience was, as promised, diverse, intrigued and attentive. There were no "hard news" reporters present, but nearly half a dozen print editors and television producers were anxious to ask questions. Follow-up interviews were scheduled for the next day. It was a lively, much enjoyed exchange of views.

Dr. Biezanek had traveled from Mersey to hear Robert's speech and after the reporters left we walked a short distance to the Student Union Hall. Liz, Dr. Wall, Dr. Biezanek, Robert and I plus one or two others cheerfully drank pints of beer and discussed our common interest.

The next day was even more interesting when we met Liz in the late afternoon at St. Stephen's entrance to Parliament. We three were ushered through a "Members Only" door, and guided down dark stone corridors to a meeting with Lord Partick Whaddon who greeted us with enthusiasm and invited us into the House of Lords' tearoom—a beautifully paneled room that seemed to ooze history. It was a bit late for traditional British high tea, but Lord Whaddon managed to obtain several pots of Chinese green tea and crumpets.

The Lord was an aging peer, highly regarded by his fellow Lords. He was keenly interested in Liz's efforts and marijuana's medical use in spasm control. There was no specific agenda. It was mostly a "get acquainted" meeting to discover if we could work together. We could.

In conversation Lord Whaddon became intrigued by the British Home Office's refusal to allow the importation of Robert's legally prescribed marijuana. He thought it a matter worthy of press attention and promised to make some calls.

Following the meeting we took Liz to catch her train to Leeds. After several days of effort and travel she looked frail as, with mild spasms, she climbed onto the train. She was intelligent, dedicated and anxious to expand marijuana's medical use in Britain. We worried if she had the physical strength to endure such a challenge.*

The London Times phoned early in the morning. Lord Whaddon had worked his magic. *The Times* rang off and another publication phoned. The story was taken and photographers were rushed to our hotel for snaps. It was Robert's last scheduled morning in London and it became somewhat frantic. Should he stay another day? No. Eye pressures were rising: it was time for him to go home.

I remained in Britain several more days, traveling to Leeds to meet quietly with Liz, then on to Liverpool/Mersey for more talks with Dr. B. and to meet Lucy.

I flew home about four days later and Robert almost immediately flew to Florida to see family and visit with a dying uncle. I reminded him of the promise to see a doctor about his cough. "When I return from Florida," he said. "Don't worry."

But I did.

---

*Liz did indeed have the stamina to continue her efforts. Her tireless efforts on behalf of MS patients led to the development of Sativex, an oral spray made from synthesizing cannabis. It is available in Europe and currently undergoing tests in the U.S. Liz died in August 2011 at the age of 54.

36. A PASSING SHADOW

On November 15, 1994 we saw the doctor.

"Mr. Randall, the blood test confirms HIV infection. Your pneumonia would suggest you are full blown AIDS but we won't be certain of that until we get the T-cell count in a couple days."

"How long?"

"Well, now that's a bit difficult to say. Let's get the pneumonia controlled and then worry about the next step."

In the blink of an eye our world was utterly altered. I spent an anxious night wondering about my own status. I was tested the next day and the results were negative. Unlike Barbra Jenks I was not infected by love.

"How can that be?" I asked the doctor.

"We don't know that yet. Some people do seem to have a natural immunity. Is it so important to know 'how'? It's a blessing."

Of course, but the question would linger. Later tests revealed that Robert was likely infected in the late 70s so my negative test was all the more a mystery. There had been ample opportunity for infection.*

On November 21, 1994, the tests returned with an awful audit of Robert's condition. Expecting a much higher number we were stunned to learn he had 22 T-cells. Normally, people have 1250 T-cells. As HIV spreads and the immune system declines AIDS usually becomes full-blown and impossible to ignore when the T-cells drop to around 250. Kenny and Barbra, at diagnoses, had 150-200 T-cells. As HIV decimates T-cells the advance of AIDS is marked by night sweats, nausea, vomiting, rapid weight loss, fatigue, mysterious aches, phantom pains, a myriad of major and minor infections and afflictions.

---

* Many years later I would learn that some people have a gene—TRIM22 or CCR5, the literature is confusing about this—that blocks HIV by preventing the assembly of the virus. Obviously I was one of them.

But Robert was an active man just returned from travel to California, Europe and Florida. He was 50 pounds overweight with mild pneumonia and 22 T-cells. He was something of a novelty. Why such an unusual progression? We were certain constant access to marijuana had made a difference. But there was little time to expand on this thought. Knowing the debilitating dynamics of AIDS, we realized Robert was already deep into dying. There was little time, but much to do.

The next five months were a roller coaster of emotions and crisis. There were the "simple" questions: Who to tell? And when? I immediately informed my sister and our assistant Linda. Another close friend was told when I collapsed in tears after she routinely asked, "How's Bob?"

Robert, however, was in no rush to disclose his "pending departure."

> *Death—one's own death—is not easily interjected into casual conversation. My mother, sister and brother were not told. It was too close to Christmas, and not the kind of news that should arrive by telephone. There would, God willing, be time to tell them in person.*

We made the decision to return to Florida—home. Having made that decision there were many more awaiting us. What of medical marijuana? Do we issue a press release about Robert's health? Do we disband ACT?

We formulated a plan that involved elusively easing away. Nothing abrupt. ACT would continue with our assistant managing the office on a part-time basis. We would set up a small office in Florida. Or not. It depended.

While Robert wobbled between weakness and worse, I moved decisively forward. I was acutely aware of Robert's fragility and realized he was susceptible to just about any infection you could name. I had seen how rapidly AIDS patients could decline. I constantly wondered if we had the time to move to Florida.

This fear was underscored on March 30, 1995. I was in Florida making preparations for the move, lining up contractors for work on a condominium we had purchased and still maintaining silence about Robert's condition. He wanted to tell his family in person.

On Wednesday I received a call from the mortgage broker in Sarasota. He had called our D.C. phone, unaware that I was in Florida. He cleared up whatever business it was that had caused him to phone and then dropped a bombshell. "Your husband," he said with a thick Jersey accent, "he don't sound so good. Is he sick?"

My heart plummeted and an awful fear consumed me. I immediately called home and from the moment Robert answered the phone I knew we were in serious trouble. He talked about waking with "a fire in my gut and terrible pain." The last part was obvious from his voice. I told him to call 911 but he stubbornly insisted that wasn't necessary. I just as stubbornly insisted it was. We compromised and he agreed to go to the doctor's office, which was not far from our home.

From 1,000 miles away I was trying to coordinate Robert's healthcare. I called a cab to get him to the doctor's office and then called our good friend Karen, explaining everything that was going on, including Robert's diagnosis, and asking her to please meet Robert at the doctor's office. She readily agreed. By the time she got to the doctor's office they were about to call an ambulance. Instead they bundled him into Karen's car and sent him on to Washington Hospital Center Emergency Ward.

The emergency team quickly moved through the basics. Blood was taken, Robert's guts were scanned, an IV was jammed into his arm; saline and morphine began to drip slowly. The pain faded. Tests revealed a seriously malfunctioning gall bladder and an inflamed pancreas. Surgery was discussed. From the muffled depths of morphine Robert asked if surgery is dangerous for someone with AIDS. "It certainly adds an element of risk," was the clinical reply.

The chaos in Washington extended to my situation in Florida. We had not told either of our mothers about Robert's condition. They thought we had decided to move back home because we wanted to return to the warmth. Now, however, the situation was greatly changed. My mother had heard me on the phone with Robert and then Karen. She had picked up the essence of the situation and I sadly filled in the gaps of her knowledge.

Robert's urgent condition compelled me to also tell his mother and sister of his desperate plight. It was a difficult conversation, the kind of discussion that forces recognition of so many things in a short period of time. Thelma, Robert's mother, absorbed the news about his AIDS, looked at me sadly and asked, "Did he get it from you?" I was startled but realized it was a logical question. "No," I said, "Robert is bi-sexual and he contracted it from an encounter with a man." She took the next logical step with little hesitation, "Are you infected?"

Blessedly I could answer no. Thelma absorbed the horrible news and then, as planned, took me shopping for carpet. Her Welsh practicality was welcome in this desperate hour. I was now scrambling to pack five days of work into two.

I returned to Washington late on Friday and Robert had surgery to remove his gallbladder on Saturday morning. I spoke briefly with the surgeon who told me, given Robert's weakened condition, there was a one in three chance he would not survive the surgery but absent an operation he would very likely be dead in days.

Five hours later the surgeon emerged. He said he had never seen a gall bladder such as Robert's; necrotic and gangrenous, it was shrouded in a sac of milky fluids. He was clearly puzzled by the appearance and, if time had allowed, we might have pursued the matter more thoroughly. But we were scheduled to leave Washington in less than three weeks and there was much to do.

Two weeks after Robert's hospital release the moving van arrived and we were off to Florida.

We had been in our new Florida home for less than a month when Robert's gut exploded with fire once again. This time the diagnosis was "acute pancreatitis."

The treatment for pancreatitis was simple: morphine for pain, no food and plenty of saline. In a few days, once the pancreas "cooled," things would be fine. That's what the doctors said.

Throughout the summer of 1995 his pancreas smoldered constantly, often erupting in paroxysms of intense pain. There was nausea and vomiting with nearly every meal. He lost more than 40 pounds and began to walk with a shuffle of the aged. Things seemed very grim.

In our 1998 book he wrote of that time in the summer of 1995. It is, perhaps, one of his finest pieces of writing.

> *My mind–unhinged from any future–began an archival dump by retrieving and reviewing a maze of memories. How had life been this time around? Not bad. Born in the heartland of a powerful empire, I had never been ill-housed, ill-clothed or ill-fed. I arrived into Eden, had loving parents and a grand passage from infancy to literacy. Well-educated, I never pursued a precise ambition, but instead followed as fate led me down an improbable path few others have traveled.*
>
> *I had lived the life of a democratic man, successfully defending my rights against a hostile and brutish state. I had made legal and medical history, enacted laws, aided the afflicted and altered global perceptions. Along the way we had encountered an endless cast of players worked with dying people and rising politicians, met medical mandarins and toiled with some of the nation's finest young attorneys.*
>
> *It seemed upon reflection that the whole of my adult life had challenged others to make difficult decisions involving ethics and self-interest.*
>
> *Good guys. Bad guys. Lots to learn. Law. Medicine. Politics. Media manipulation. In this life I learned how to cast my voice across continents. Delighted by rhetoric, I practiced ancient arts with powerful tools. An intensely private man, I played upon a grand stage.*
>
> *Beyond art and artifice have been the people who had populated my path. Lynn, Mona, Steve, Kenny and Barbra. Who guided whom? Great allies in a grand adventure. For every name I knew there have been thousands of unnamed others who have benefited from our drama.*
>
> *Our exploits had been well-compensated. I still had my sight. It had not been an uninteresting life.*
>
> *The mind was on rewind. Lots of memories were being remembered for the last time.*
>
> *What a time!*

Alive and young I personally witnessed the most important event in human history when, on a December morning in 1968, I watched a Saturn 5 rocket lift three mortals to the Moon. "To see," as Archibald MacLeish would later write, "the Earth as it truly is, small, and blue and beautiful in that eternal silence where it floats."

Alice was with me even then. In the whole of my life I had never been unloved. We had been well mated; constant and tolerant. It had been a better journey shared. A lovely life. But it was time to leave.

In a metaphorical dream I saw myself staring into a mirror framed in lights, looking intently at my reflection as I wiped the grease and paint from my face. As cold cream ripped away the mask of my illusions I was anxious to walk into the cool, dark night beyond the stage door. My play was over.

At the end of July a CAT scan revealed my pancreas—which should have been the size of a small flower— was as big as a child's football. The CAT image also revealed pits and blisters—pseudo-cysts— covering the swollen surface.

"Grim?" I asked the physician.

"Very grim," he quickly agreed. "Very grim, indeed."

I was abruptly, suddenly very old. Snow white hair above a rapidly receding frame. Reality began to melt; there were gaps here and there. Solid matter seemed little more than an interruption in the flow of photons.

A plane flew high above my bed. I heard the drone and thought, I will never fly anywhere again. No matter. I had seen much in many places.

As death approached there was less fear than fascination. The mystery of tides, a setting sun, a rising moon, a heaven pock-marked by planets and stars mesmerized my apprehensions. The circle of my life was closing as, dying, I wandered into the wonder of un-worded beginnings.

"You should report to the hospital immediately," Nurse Murray commanded over the phone.

"I want to stay home," I protested. "If it gets worse we'll head for emergency."

"If it gets worse," Nurse Murray bluntly said, "you'll be dead before you get to your car, much less emergency."

I had so wanted to die in my own bed.

Hospitalized again, I was attached to tubes. Morphine through an IV pump with a generous button for extra doses. Lots of saline. Arrangements were made so Alice could wheel me outside several times a day for marijuana breaks. We had told the clinic of our medical marijuana exploits and there was the usual fascination. I omitted the fact that I was no longer using the substance. Our trips outside were a chance to savor sunlight and smoke sweet nicotine. Sitting in my wheelchair, IV bottles swaying above my head, surrounded by a sunny circle of luminous plantings, Alice and I were saying goodbye.

Efforts to "cool" my pancreas failed. The slightest bite of food, the clearest of broths, even the smallest sips of water provoked gut-wrenching vomiting. Like a caterpillar in a chrysalis I was dissolving from the inside out.

My family visited constantly. My brother flew in from Alaska. Death was imminent. "We are," the nurses assured, "going to do everything possible to keep you comfortable."

I was between here and there. Talkative, cheery, alert but ready to leave. My bags were packed for the great beyond. No fear now. I felt homeward bound.

After a week of no food and only ice to munch there was a terrible night when a vein blew and the IV technician could no longer find an alternative site. As Alice stood outside my door, a second technician was called. For an hour they slapped my arms and legs, probing, poking, searching for a place to put the needle.

They finally succeeded and left. Alice came in to comfort me. As she left I realized my bed was immediately above the place where I was born. It was a last memory. The circle closed. I was done.

Death seemed certain. At some time in the night a pseudo-cyst erupted and Robert Carl Randall, 48, suffered a massive hemorrhagic rupture of the pancreas. A rush of blood and toxins flooded into my gut. There was an instant, searing pain as my soul was released into the care of the Ferryman who arrived to take me from myself.

It was over.

37. THE END

It wasn't over for Robert in that late summer of 1995. It seemed that he would most certainly die, perhaps before Labor Day, but what seems certain can change.

While he was still in hospital surgeons inserted a Hickman dual-line catheter—a device that accessed his veins and allowed delivery of drugs and blood draws.

The procedure was not intended to save his life, merely to make his demise more manageable. Through one line a small pump delivered a steady stream of morphine. The second line was used for blood draws and hydration. He was sent home and it was expected he would be dead within two weeks.

Instead he confounded the physicians. Robert seemed to improve and physicians ordered daily infusions of TPN (total parenteral nutrition) that he tolerated without adverse effects. His digestive system was intentionally shut down and he was not allowed to eat or drink anything for three months. Only ice shavings and an occasional banana popsicle passed his lips. This allowed the pancreas to "shut down" and heal.

The treatment worked and his long fast came to an end on Thanksgiving Day 1995. There was much to celebrate.

Robert emerged from his second brush with death into a new world of AIDS therapy. He had never taken the standard anti-viral medication, AZT. We had seen the ravages of AZT and given the precarious nature of his health in the first few weeks after his diagnosis it seemed just as well to not go down that medical route. But in early 1996, as we continued to relish the simple fact of his existence, we were told about a new drug, protease inhibitors, and a new approach to therapy—the AIDS cocktail which consisted of three drugs. He tolerated two of the three drugs rather well. The third, however, provoked another brutal bout of pancreatitis. When he was recovered from that he resumed taking AZT and protease.

Robert would later say of that year, "I spent 1996, recovering from my addiction to death." As his strength returned his T-cells multiplied and he was less prone to opportunistic infections.

Our assistant Linda continued to maintain the ACT office in Washington, answering information requests and checking messages. Robert would do the occasional radio interview but he had neither the strength nor interest to "create" any media. His illness forced detachment from the issue and as he emerged from his "addiction to death" he had little desire to re-engage medical marijuana. The issue had become cluttered with new players who were charging forward with the energy that we ourselves once enjoyed. Robert didn't always like what was happening but he had no inclination to "step in." He was happy just living, enjoying our small yard and garden, canoeing on the intracoastal waterway, sitting in the warm sun with his mother and sister. He was a changed man and he had no regrets.

In November 1996 the first state-wide ballots recognizing marijuana's medical use were passed in California and Arizona. It was also the 20th anniversary of Robert's receipt of federal marijuana. We received a call from an old media friend, Tom Snyder. He asked Robert to appear on his show. Robert readily accepted.

The television appearance would be his last but it was perfect. It was an easy interview. Snyder, eyes twinkling, played with the angles before deftly introducing AIDS into the conversation. It was the first time Robert had publicly addressed his diagnosis. All went well.

It was, in retrospect, his farewell address.

Robert would live for another five years. What a gift. During this period Robert seemed to have little interest in the medical marijuana issue. It was surprising to me but I simply accepted the gift that had been given to us and did not encourage him to re-engage the issue.

I did encourage him to write and we began sifting through journals and files from the twenty years of our work. In late 1997, I found a literary agent, Alan Kellock, who lived on Florida's east coast. With his help we were able to get a contract for our book, *Marijuana Rx: The Patients' Fight for Medicinal Pot*. I'm very grateful for that because it provides a detailed accounting of the first twenty years of the movement. Robert and I worked closely on the book, writing and rewriting chapters, re-living the incredible times and memories. It was a very affirming exercise.

Publication of the book in late 1998 re-ignited press interest and there were calls and interviews. We took one or two trips to promote the book but, for the most part, Robert had let go of medical marijuana.

In 2001 he suffered additional complications from the AIDS and by late May it was clear Robert had little time left. Hospice was brought in and I once again watched as he neared what Shakespeare called, "the undiscover'd country from whose [boundary] no traveller returns." When his final day arrived we would, almost miraculously, be "visited" by an old friend.

The night of June 1, 2001 had been very hard and the morning of June 2 was not much easier. Robert was very restless and unresponsive. I would later learn that "terminal restlessness" is not uncommon, quite the contrary. But it was uncommon to me. It was distressing enough that we called hospice and a nurse was sent to assess and help out. My sister was present and Robert's Aunt Edith was also there.

As Robert's breath became more and more shallow, I realized his death was imminent. Climbing on to the hospital bed I cradled his head in my arms. A sudden mechanical sound grated my senses as the compact disc player, loaded that morning with his favorite music, shifted to a new disc. The soothing tones of Joan Baez filled the room. How appropriate I fleetingly thought, as I continued stroking his face, telling him how I loved him, telling him to go to the light, to the loved ones waiting.

An odd calmness settled on the room and in an ultimate, breath-taking closure of a cosmic circle, the words of the folk song, 'Poor Wayfaring Stranger,' penetrated my consciousness:

> Yet there's no sickness, toil nor danger
> In that bright land to which I go.
> I'm going there to see my mother
> She said she'll meet me when I come
> I'm only going over Jordan
> I'm only going over home.

I literally gasped. "Oh Bobby! Listen to the music." I said. "Joanie has come to sing you home!"

Time shifted on the recognition of all that was happening. For a few ... moments, minutes, hours? ... it seemed as if my heart and spirit joined Robert's soul, melding with the very essence of this being whom I loved so. How many times had we "died in each others' arms"—le petite mort? And now, in his final moments, as I held him so close, I felt as though I could actually feel his soul release on those beautiful words. "I'm only going over home." Tears were streaming down my cheeks onto his chest, the breathing slowed even more and then ceased. The hospice nurse came forward quietly and checked with her stethoscope. "I'm sorry, " she said. "He's gone."

I don't know how long I lay there, stroking his cheek, feeling the warmth that would soon fade and trying to absorb the reality of it all. When I finally did sit up on the bed the hospice nurse said quietly, "That was as beautiful a death as I have ever seen."

38. THE BEGINNING AGAIN

California and Arizona were just the beginning of a new surge in the medical marijuana movement. As I write this in 2014, there are 21 state laws that authorize medical use of marijuana. This time, instead of asking the federal government for marijuana, the states have authorized legal, intra-state methods of obtaining the drug. Some allow patients to grow their own supplies or contract with a caregiver who grows the medicine for them. Others authorize the state to contract with "suppliers."

All of these laws are in conflict with federal law, which still classifies marijuana as a Schedule I, drug "with no accepted medical value." The falsehood of that classification is manifested with each passing law.

I am frequently asked, "What would Robert think about the current situation?" It is impossible to know. He did not believe the seriously ill should be forced to grow a medication that is critical to their health and well-being. For some patients this may be a preferred method but for many more it is simply too daunting a task. But I think Robert would be pleased that so many individuals are at last getting regular access to marijuana for medical use. In Michigan alone, for example, there are more than 100,000 certified patients.

I know that he would be amazed and pleased with the "off-label" research that is happening in this country. Many of the caregivers who grow marijuana for patients have indulged their intellectual curiosity about this fascinating plant and they are conducting the research that NIDA or FDA should have completed years ago. They have developed strains of the plant that have little psychoactive quality but plenty of therapeutic application. The best known is Charlotte's Web, a cannabis strain that is low in THC but high in CBD, another of the 300+ ingredients in cannabis. This particular strain has been extremely effective in treating various childhood forms of epilepsy that are simply devastating to the child and family alike.

Topical preparations, tinctures and edibles are the preferred mode of administration rather than inhalation. Many patients still smoke marijuana but there is a definite trend away from the inhalation route.

What is most amazing to me is the irony of the situation. The federal government has, through its intransigence and stubborn defense of the medical prohibition, forced these states to take action on behalf of their citizens and those actions are now threatening the very foundation of the total prohibition. For years the government and its lackeys have harped on the belief that medical marijuana is the "stalking horse" for full legalization. For the legitimate patients nothing could be further from the truth. But by failing to honestly deal with these patients the federal government has struck out and, frankly, is barely in the game.

There were three excellent opportunities for the federal government to resolve the medical marijuana issue and maintain control. The first was in the late 1970s when the states initially passed laws calling for state-wide research using federally-grown marijuana. If the feds had dealt honestly with those states the research could have been completed and marijuana could have been made available under tight federal control. Strike one.

In 1988, the DEA's administrative law judge ruled marijuana was improperly classified as a Schedule I drug and that it should be moved to Schedule II. The DEA had an opportunity at that point to accept the ruling and go to its sister agencies—FDA, NIDA and NIH—and suggest a program of research and eventual release of tightly controlled marijuana for medical purposes. DEA, instead, rejected the decision and angered the public in doing so. Strike 2.

In 1992, the Marijuana AIDS Research Service (MARS) placed a tremendous strain on federal resources by flooding FDA with Compassionate IND applications. Doctors signed all of these applications and FDA could have respected the request of these medical professionals and released as much marijuana as possible while working with other federal agencies to increase marijuana cultivation and research. Instead the Bush Administration allowed its homophobic administrator of the Public Health Service to close the Compassionate IND program entirely. Strike three.

The federal government has struck out with respect to medical marijuana and has lost all credibility. It has been hoisted on its own petard. The dishonesty and lack of compassion exhibited by the federal government allowed those pursuing a legalization agenda to jump on board the medical bandwagon and they are skillfully taking advantage of the chaos created by the federal government's closure of the Compassionate IND program. Colorado and Washington have already adopted laws allowing the recreational use of marijuana. They will not be the last states to do so.

My concern is with the patients. I do not believe medical care should be dependent on geography or botanical skills. It is time the federal government take action to standardize medical access to this remarkable herb that has an ancient and honorable reputation as a medication. It is time for us, as a nation, to ask, "Who are the real criminals in this conflict?"

GLOSSARY

ACT: Alliance for Cannabis Therapeutics.

AIDS: Acquired Immune Deficiency Syndrome.

AAO: American Academy of Ophthalmology.

BNDD: Bureau of Narcotics and Dangerous Drugs, predecessor of DEA.

CSAC: Controlled Substances Advisory Committee, a public advisory committee of the FDA.

DARAC: Drug Abuse Research Advisory Committee, a public advisory committee of the FDA.

DEA: Drug Enforcement Administration.

Delta-9 THC: delta-9 tetrahydrocannabinoid, the psychoactive ingredient in marijuana. One of more than 300 ingredients. A synthetic version of the drug is marketed as Marinol.

DHEW: Department of Health, Education and Welfare. Predecessor of DHHS.

DHHS: Department of Health and Human Services

DOJ: Department of Justice

FDA: Food and Drug Administration.

FOIA: Freedom of Information Act.

HIV: Human Immunodeficiency Virus, the precursor to AIDS.

IND: Investigational New Drug. These are drugs that are not yet approved by the FDA. In order to use federal supplies of marijuana a researcher or doctor must file an Investigational New Drug application, a very complex process. In 1978, under pressure to settle the law suit in *Randall v. U.S.*, the FDA allowed Robert Randall's doctor to file a simplified IND application which became known as a Compassionate IND.

IOP: Intra-ocular pressure.

MARS: Marijuana AIDS Research Service, a project of the Alliance for Cannabis Therapeutics.

MRP: Medical Reclassification Project, established by Alice O'Leary under the auspices of NORML.

Nabilone: A drug similar to delta-9 THC, manufactured by Eli Lilly and marked as Cesamet.

NCI: National Cancer Institute.

NEI: National Eye Institute.

NIDA: National Institute of Drug Abuse.

NIH: National Institutes of Health.

NIMH: National Institute of Mental Health.

NORML: National Organization for the Reform of Marijuana Laws.

PWAs: People With AIDS.

Schedule I: the most restrictive of the five schedules defined in the 1970 Comprehensive Drug Abuse Prevention and Control Act. Marijuana is a Schedule I drug.

ABOUT THE AUTHOR

Alice O'Leary-Randall is a retired hospice nurse who spends her time between Sarasota, Florida and Franklin, North Carolina. She speaks regularly on the history of the medical marijuana movement. For further information please visit her website at: www.medicalmarijuanapioneer.com.

She is an avid photographer and regularly posts her photographs at www.aliceswanderland.com.

Robert and Alice's archives are located at the Wisconsin Historical Society in Madison, Wisconsin. For information of access please visit: www.wisconsinhistory.org

Made in the USA
Lexington, KY
04 August 2015